THE DEVELOPMENT OF PERSONALITY AND BEHAVIOUR IN CHILDREN

Margaret E. Wood

The City University, London

HARRAP LONDON

First published in Great Britain 1981
by GEORGE G. HARRAP & CO. LTD
182 High Holborn, London WC1V 7AX

ISBN 0 245-53693-0

*Composed in Baskerville type
by Elliott Bros. & Yeoman Ltd.
Printed and bound in Great Britain
at The Pitman Press, Bath*

To the memory of my parents

Contents

Preface

In 1973 Harrap published my book *Children: the Development of Personality and Behaviour*. In 1979 I was asked to prepare a revised edition of the book. During the past ten years or so research into the psychological development of children has expanded very greatly, so that it very quickly became evident that instead of revising the existing book it would be necessary to write a new book into which, however, certain parts of the first book could be incorporated. This second book, therefore, bears certain similarities to the first book: the general approach is similar, and the lay-out and chapter titles are the same; but there are differences between the two books, in addition to the new book obviously including descriptions of up-to-date research work in the relevant areas of psychology. One major difference is that more emphasis is given in the present book than in the previous book to research work into the *processes* of development. Traditionally developmental psychologists have been concerned largely with research work which has sought to *describe* development as it occurs, and which has also attempted to relate the effects on the development of personality and on behaviour of specific *causal* experiences in childhood. We still know far too little about the actual stages of child development to jettison research work which seeks to describe development; for example, in recent years a largely neglected area of development — that is, the different kinds of friendships children form and maintain at different ages — has been the subject of observational studies; psychologists are also quite naturally still very interested in the possible relationship between, say, childhood experiences and the later adult personality, so that they have not ceased to look for such a relationship despite great methodological difficulties in carrying out research in this area of study. (These matters are further discussed in some detail in chapters 1 and 8 especially.) However, during the past ten years the emphases of research studies have moved away largely from these two kinds of investigations to the study of the actual *processes* of development: we do not only want to know, for example, *what kinds* of friendships children at different ages form with one another, but to understand *how* these friendships are formed, that is, what are the processes which underlie the forming of specific kinds of relationships among peers in childhood. Indeed, the logic of discovery seems to require that a *description* of development should be followed by analyses of the *processes* of development before the *causes* of development can be understood.

This book is about the developing personality of the child. I had three major aims in mind while writing it:

(1) A child's perception of his world, and of the people in it, differs in important respects from an adult's perception and understanding. In addition, the child's standpoint, from which he views the behaviour of others and attempts to understand the world around him, is constantly and continually changing from birth until maturity. One of my aims, therefore, has been to attempt to present this changing 'child's eye' view of the world.

(2) The material in the book is both descriptive and interpretative: I cite experimental investigations into the behaviour of children and, where relevant, of animals, and I have attempted to interpret the significance of the findings of such work as far as they concern the handling of children in our Western culture. Because experimental psychology is a relatively new science, and because work which aims at the elucidation of the springs of human behaviour is notoriously difficult to carry out, modern psychologists have been understandably reluctant to offer specific advice which can be applied 'to the concrete problems of the individual person' (Vernon, 1964, page 2). Enough knowledge, however, now exists to enable conclusions to be drawn about what is *more* rather than *less* advisable in the handling of children. William James, in *Talks to Teachers on Psychology,* as long ago as 1899 suggested that psychology should enable us to be more clear as to what we are about; the second aim of this book then is that it should enable readers to be more clear as to what they are about in regard to their relationship with children.

(3) However, despite certain broad notions which can be deduced from psychological work, and which can be applied to an understanding of *all* children, it is far more important to be able to understand the *individual* child than to have at hand ready-made ideas about child rearing in general; my third aim, therefore, has been to try to present information which will enable the reader to gain an understanding of individual children.

How children are studied

Children can be studied 'cross-sectionally' or 'longitudinally'; thus if, for example, it is intended to study children's growing ability with increasing age to make moral judgements, then the investigator may either take samples of different children of varying ages and study the kind of moral judgements children of different ages make, or he may, over a period of several years, study the *same* group of children,

observing them as they grow older. The first is a cross-sectional investigation, the second a longitudinal study. In addition, research workers have carried out studies on animals, especially primates, where it
is possible to control the environmental variables in a manner not
possible with human children. Developmental psychologists are,
however, acutely aware of the limitations of extrapolating the findings
from such studies to illumine aspects of human development.

The book itself

(1) It is hoped that the book will be useful to teachers in training,
and particularly to those specializing in pre-school and primary
school teaching, but that parents and others engaged in the care of
children, such as social workers and students of paediatrics, will
also find it helpful. It can also serve as an *introductory* text for students studying Developmental Psychology.

(2) Reference has been made to the fact that the book is intended
for use within Western society. The *processes* of development would
appear to be species specific and not very largely affected by ethnic
differences as such, though it is clear that differing adult concepts
about how children should be reared most likely affect the nature of
the development which takes place. However, there are very many
variations in the concepts about children and how they should be
treated within the different immigrant communities in Great Britain, and we are still far from understanding the effects which such
child-rearing customs have in interaction with living in a European
country on the formation of personality and behaviour in children
from immigrant communities. For this reason no specific mention
is made in the book of the development of children from immigrant
communities. However, it does seem apparent that most children
whose parents have had the benefit of what is termed a 'good' education seem to enjoy special advantages regardless of their ethnic
origin, and it is this factor which appears to differentiate normal
children from one another at school more than any other single factor.

(3) The book is divided into three sections: section 1 deals with
the history of child rearing and with the theoretical aspects of child
development. Section 2 describes the development of behaviour
and the factors which influence this development. Section 3 is concerned with the role of the adult who comes into influential contact
with children. The 'Introduction and Summary' presents a synop-
sis of the book; it is not easily comprehensible by itself. A list of
further readings is appended to each chapter.

(4) As the development of the child is very rapid in infancy and

childhood, I have concentrated on these early periods, though later periods of development are not neglected. Because the book is primarily concerned with suggesting guide-lines for the understanding of individual children, special emphasis is given, particularly in section 3, to those aspects of development which affect the adult's contact with the child.

(5) There is a certain artificiality in separating discussions of different aspects of development into sections and chapters, as if these aspects of development proceeded independently of each other. However, experimental and observational work has of necessity to limit itself to certain specific aspects of child growth and behaviour, and such work is best described in the terms in which it was carried out. There will also be the inevitable duplication of material: for example, the effects of social-class membership on psychological development cannot be separated from a study of the influence of language on development, and when the growth of language use is studied the effects of social class must be considered. To reduce unnecessary duplication a system of cross-referencing has been adopted so that only the briefest mention of a particular subject need be made if this subject is reviewed more fully elsewhere in the book.

(6) I have throughout used the personal pronoun 'he' to refer to the child, and 'she' to refer to the teacher or to the child's principal caretaker. This has avoided the constant and irritating use of 'he or she'. I have also used the word 'mother' to refer either to a child's biological mother or to his principal caretaker.

(7) Whenever reference is made to certain specific developmental periods in a child's life it must be borne in mind that this indicates a *predominance* of a particular function, behaviour or ability during that period. It must not be assumed that such function, behaviour or ability either cannot occur earlier, or ceases completely at the end of the period described.

(8) Asterisked words are defined in the glossary.

(9) Books suggested for further reading at the end of every chapter are not necessarily the most authoritative but those which I consider to be generally helpful and interesting, as well as being usually easily accessible. Thus no reference is made in the 'Further Reading' lists to articles published in learned journals.

Acknowledgements

Sections of the earlier book which have been incorporated into the present volume were read by Dr C. M. Loewenthal, Dr P. E. Vernon and Mrs D. Taylor, who all made valuable suggestions to me. Any errors or misinterpretations, however, remain entirely my own responsibility. I am also indebted to the Eugenics Society for permission to reproduce in amended form as part of chapter 1 of the present book a chapter written by myself for the book *Equalities and Inequalities in Family Life* published by the society and the Academic Press in 1977.

Finally, I wish to thank my husband who has commented on style and accuracy of writing, and whose innumerable suggestions have very greatly improved the readability of the book. He has been responsible also for producing the original diagrams.

M.E.W.
June, 1980

Introduction and summary

Cross-cultural and historical review of attitudes to child development and rearing

The present-day manner of treating children in our 'western' society is unique, both culturally and historically. The attitudes adopted by adults towards children vary from one culture to another, and have indeed varied at different periods in history within our own, western, culture.

All children require that their basic needs are met. How these needs are met; what values adults place on children; the amount of discipline administered; the timing and manner of weaning and toilet training; how responsibilities are given; and how and when the transition from childhood to adulthood is accomplished — all these aspects of rearing children are managed differently in different communities.

In western societies during the past 2,000 years there have been various ways in which children have been treated by adults, and de Mause has described the six major historical 'modes' as he perceives them. These modes are described and evaluated. For a considerable period in the west children were considered to be miniature adults, and only in historically recent times has the the child in a general sense been seen *as a child*, despite the insight into children's minds exhibited by philosophers, such as John Locke and Rousseau. To keep children alive at all was in itself a great problem until the middle of the last century; but shortly before this time changing social circumstances, at least in England, had already caused parents to take a greater interest in their children. Childhood began to be seen as a period which itself could be divided into separate time spans, each carrying with it its own expectations. In the USA Calvinistic ideas were deeply influential and affected the child-rearing advice given in the mid-nineteenth century. Childhood for the Victorian child, especially for the middle-class child, could still be an unhappy period, but it is suggested that friendship between parents and children often existed in working-class families. Available historical information about parent-child relationships and child-rearing habits is largely restricted to what was customary at the time in the middle and upper classes, and does not generally inform us about working-class families.

Nineteenth-century middle-class parents were concerned with

character training, and this concern was also dominant in the baby-books of the 1920s and 1930s, though character training was probably at this time synonymous with good mental health. It was thought that character training could be achieved through the instilling of good habits; this idea stemmed in essence from the conditioning work of Pavlov. At the same time very different, Freudian, ideas were influencing parental rearing methods. This proved highly confusing, as advice given by such Freudians as Susan Isaacs was radically different from advice given by Behaviourists, such as Watson and Truby King. Advice stemming from the psychoanalytic school was generally more understanding of the developing child, but nevertheless was not entirely beneficial. Otherwise enlightened psychoanalytic writers made dogmatic pronouncements about rearing which were unsubstantiated by adequate evidence. Probably also a misinterpretation of Freudian theory was responsible for the so-called permissive rearing cult.

Dogmatic advice given by both schools often concerned relatively unimportant aspects of child development. Today children are no longer seen from an adult viewpoint only; it is known that specific rearing methods are relatively unimportant when compared with the quality of the parent–child relationship; and it is known that the subtle factors which affect the processes of development cannot easily be related as cause and effect with reference to any one developing person. The fundamental changes which are affecting society are influencing child-rearing norms. So-called child-rearing experts are no longer able to be dogmatic when giving advice; parents are encouraged to understand each individual child, and to trust their own feelings in relation to that child. It is now appreciated also that factors other than parental handling have a strong influence upon the development of a child's personality. What these factors are is examined in this book.

The developing personality

Although it can be said that personality is behaviour, the two are differentiated in this book for the purpose of study: in this section we consider the various *reasons* which may determine how a child's personality will develop, whereas in section two we review ontogenically the *changes* in a child's behaviour which occur as he grows older, and we consider also the factors which influence these changes.

Personality has been variously defined, but it can be distinguished as 'that which characterizes an individual and determines his unique adaptation to the environment' (Harsh and Schrickel, 1950). Thus 'personality' includes social and individual factors, the latter comprising a study of the intellect, the emotions and the will.

The direction in which each of the various theories of personality has developed has depended on the interests of each theorist, so that individual theories are predominantly concerned with, *inter alia,* explaining the dynamics, the development, the determinants, the description and the measurement of personality respectively, as well as being concerned with identifying the processes which cause changes to occur with increasing age, particularly in childhood. The two basic approaches for the study of the personality are the idio-graphic* and the nomothetic, and the two basic methods used are the clinical and the experimental. In the study of development psychol-ogy we are concerned with the 'what', the 'how' and the 'why' of development. The value of developmental theories is discussed, and three major theories, the social-learning, the cognitive–developmental, and the Freudian psychoanalytic theories are described. Freud's psychoanalytic theory of personality takes into account the structure, functioning and development of the whole per-sonality from a conception of man as a biological organism with energy for functioning present in the 'id';* the 'ego'* and 'superego'* develop through the need of the human organism to interact with the real world and with other people. The human being desires release from tension, and through primary and secondary processes such release is obtained either vicariously or in actuality. How the id, ego and superego interact with one another depends partly on biological factors and partly on how the child experiences life, particularly dur-ing the psycho-sexual stages of development in early childhood.

The theory of psycho-sexual development can best be understood as a way of explaining how the sexual drive, postulated as being pres-ent from birth, but unable to express itself until maturity, seeks expression in infancy and early childhood through behaviours associ-ated with the self-preservative drives, and with those parts of the body — the oral, anal and phallic areas — which provide satisfaction (or frustration) through such behaviours. The emotions evoked at each of the psycho-sexual stages are also present in the child's developing social relationships and in the manner in which he deals with the world around him. The concept of 'critical periods', used by ethologists to describe certain early and specific experiences which are crucial to later development, can be evoked to explain in part Freudian ideas of 'fixation' during these psycho-sexual stages.

The various satisfactions which are obtained by the baby and young child at the psycho-sexual stages of development cannot con-tinue to be obtained in the same manner later in life. How the psychic energy invested in such pleasurable tension-release is displaced has, according to Freudian theory, an important bearing on personality development.

3

Another influence on the formation of the personality is the manner in which the ego deals with the various demands made upon it by the id and the superego, as well as how it externalizes aggressive feelings, though in psychoanalysis there is no unified, completely accepted theory of aggression. The kind of defence mechanisms adopted, and the strength and extent to which such mechanisms are used to deal with anxiety, with threats to the personality and with aggressive feelings, in part also determine behaviour and the formation of the personality.

According to Freud the personality is formed by the manner in which the child experiences his psycho-sexual stages; by the way displacement takes place; by the kind and strength of the defensive mechanisms adopted; and by biological determinants. Many of the powerful influences which together form the personality exert their effects at an unconscious level.

Much observational work on children has, since Freud's death, confirmed many of his ideas, though whether the personality is affected by psycho-sexual experiences as powerfully and irreversibly as Freud suggested is doubted by many students of child development. Writers such as Erikson and White and other Neo-Freudians have reformulated a number of Freud's ideas in a manner more acceptable to modern thought. Sears and Farrell and others have also discussed the clinical validation and experimental testing (where appropriate) of psychoanalytic theories. Freud's influence on child rearing and on the thought and culture of our age has been immense.

The foundation for social-learning theory was laid by J. B. Watson, who considered that all behaviour could be explained by invoking principles of conditioning, that is, of learning by association. Modern learning theorists who interest themselves in child development are not concerned with the total development of the child, but investigate specific areas of development which can be the subject of controlled experiment and observation. Through 'classical' and 'instrumental' conditioning paradigms and the concept of 'drives', including secondary drives, they seek to explain the formation of complex human behaviour patterns.

Social-learning theory accounts for the development of dependency, anxiety, aggression and conscience formation by learning (conditioning) principles. Through satisfaction of his basic needs the child becomes dependent on his parents' presence, and anxiety is evoked by their absence, or threat of absence. Parental disapproval is felt by him as a threat to their presence, and so disapproval becomes anxiety-provoking. Thus the parents, by capitalizing on their child's dependency on them, and on his related anxiety, and by selectively reinforcing the child's behaviour, restrain and encourage his behaviour appropriately.

It is suggested that aggressive behaviour is caused by the baby's angry 'signalling' behaviour, arising from frustration or distress, bringing relief as well as disapproval from his mother. Consequently the conflict situation which thus arises for the baby implies that he obtains relief from distress through the pained or angry responses of another person, so that, through secondary reinforcement, his aggressive behaviour will in due course come to have a rewarding value.

A small child will usually inhibit a disapproved act in his parents' presence, but conscience formation rests on such inhibition becoming internalized. Social-learning theorists suggest that this occurs because the temptation to act in a disapproved manner brings anxiety through dependency. In time even the thought of behaving in a disapproved manner brings feelings of guilt. Social-learning theory explains how it is that parental disapproval shown before a child is about to commit a 'naughty' act is a more powerful way of helping internalization than punishment following a committing of the act. It is doubtful, however, whether the various aspects of moral growth, such as conscience development, feelings of guilt, and other related concepts, develop in the same manner in every person.

Social-learning theory has been established through short-term experimental work with children, and by relating what is known about learning to child development. There have been too few long-term studies to enable one to feel confident that the hypothesized causes always operate in the development of social learning in the manner suggested. However, social-learning theorists have undoubtedly made a valuable contribution to our understanding of child development.

Other aspects of learning, such as imitation and identification, and learning in the context of school achievement, are considered in chapter 4. The cognitive–developmental theory sees the child as a thinker, who selects the stimuli to which he will respond, and who structures and restructures the world within himself. Piaget was the first person systematically to investigate the developing thought processes of the child. His own interpretations of the meanings of his findings have in recent years been subject to extensive criticism. Piaget has concerned himself primarily, though not exclusively, with the child's cognitive development, seeking to clarify how the child's perception and understanding of the world changes with advancing age. His work is not easy to understand, and in this chapter his theories only will be discussed. (The ontogenetic* process of cognitive growth is discussed in chapter 4 and Piaget's work on the child's moral growth and on the importance of play are considered in chapters 5 and 6 respectively.)

Piaget is concerned with such problems as how 'logical necessity' emerges in the child. It is of supreme interest to know how children acquire knowledge of the world. Hamlyn has suggested three alternative views as to how this acquisition comes about, and he relates these to Piaget's biological view of man, whereby he considers that the human mind develops in relation to the environment in which it is placed; an equilibrium is maintained between the developing (changing) organism and its external contacts. In addition new knowledge has to be *structured*, which presupposes understanding. Such understanding can be elicited by experience, but has a basis other than experience. The child is an active participator in interaction with his environment.

What are the processes involved in taking in new experiences (assimilation), in adapting the existing mental structure or schema to such experiences (accommodation), and in gradually lessening the conflict which exists between perceptual information and increasing, but unstable, knowledge about the world? Mental development is, for Piaget, 'an ever more precise adaptation to reality'.

At the baby stage thinking is, for Piaget, wordless, internalized action, and Piaget attempts to account for the developmental process by which this early form of thinking is transformed by the time adolescence is reached into stable thought processes which are capable of dealing with all manner of abstractions, and mathematical and related problems.

In Piaget's theory development takes place due to

(1) maturation,
(2) learning and experiences of life and
(3) 'organization'.

The child has to organize his thoughts in relation to his experiences and activities, and this organization is called 'equilibration'. Young children are more advanced in action than they are in language or thought; their explanations of causality are in terms of 'intuitions' because they still lack the ability to co-ordinate percepts and actions into a logical structure. The young child is percept-centred and egocentric; his is unable to practise reversibility of thought, but by about seven years of age when he enters the 'concrete operational' stage his thought processes are better structured and less rigid. He is able to carry out an act in the imagination (an 'operation') but usually only in the presence of 'concrete' objects. He has to await a further maturing process before he is able to indulge in abstract and entirely logical thought. The small child *acts* on objects; the older child can *think about objects and act on them in their presence*; the child over twelve can *reflect* about objects and actions. At this stage equilibrium is near to being achieved and the schema is a stable mental structure.

The criticisms directed at Piaget's work have come both from philosophers and from psychologists. Philosphers have criticized, for example, the vagueness of the notion of 'mental structure'; also Piaget does not appear adequately to explain how objectivity is brought about, and he seems to make insufficient allowance for social–emotional effects on the development of understanding. Many experimental psychologists maintain that young children are able to think much more effectively than Piaget would allow in situations which have meaning for them. Children do not normally *reflect* on how they think, nor are young children always able to use the abilities they have, under their own direction only. By helping them to reflect on their mental powers the display of their cognitive capacities can be greatly increased, though the several difficulties exhibited by young children indicates that qualitative changes in cognitive growth do occur with changing age. Piaget's work has generated the research which is beginning to clarify these changes in detail.

Chapter 2 ends with a comparison and assessment of the theories described.

Influences affecting the formation of personality characteristics and the development of intelligence

The problems which a discussion of the origins of human behaviour presents are reviewed in relation to the 'nature–nurture' debate, and an analysis is made of the factors contributing to personality formation. Because of the 'plastic' nature of both the environment and the organism we are studying a transactional model, through which to attempt to understand the effects of the forces which act on the developing child, is more helpful and realistic than using a 'main effects' model. However, the various factors which are probably influentially effective on the developing personality are discussed. The methods which are used to study the human personality and the problems which exist in their study are examined, particularly the difficulty of isolating core personality characteristics, and also the likely effects of any one particular situation on the behaving personality.

In considering the factors which affect personality development, the nature of intelligence and of other human abilities is examined in an historical context. Although 'intelligence' is difficult to define there is no doubt that it shows itself most clearly when a human being is engaged in relational thinking. Various views regarding the nature of intelligence are discussed and an attempt is made to console the reader in his possible dismay that there is no easy way in which this ability can be understood. A present-day hierarchical view of intelligence is discussed in some detail; the nature of the general, underlying 'g' factor is described, as well as the 'group' and 'specific' factors. 'g' accounts for the biggest source of variance between people, and it is suggested that despite popular views to the contrary, a good intelligence test testing for 'g' is still the best *single* instrument for predicting a person's suitability to engage in intellectual or educational pursuits. The IQ is a measure of a child's intelligence in relation to his age, and is a sample of his intelligence obtained at a particular period in his life; it is not to be confused with intelligence itself. A number of different group and individual intelligence tests are described in this chapter. The nature of creativity is examined in relation to intelligence.

The findings of various studies, including twin, consanguinity and sibling studies, as well as studies of adopted children, indicate that there is a considerable genetic element in determining intelligence. This innate contribution to measurable intelligence cannot, however, be assessed in any one individual person, and the degree of variance of the genetic factor when comparing individuals in different cultural and social groups with one another will depend on the homogeneity of the groups concerned.

In discussing the genetic influence on other personality characteristics the possible relationship of body build and temperament is reviewed. The results of twin studies which have examined the heritability of two major personality types, extraversion and neuroticism (anxiety), appear to indicate a genetic contribution to the development of such types. A longitudinal study purports to have discovered nine 'primary reaction patterns' of behaviour which appear in infancy and remain during childhood. The investigators who carried out this work conclude from their follow-up studies that there is an appreciable but by no means exclusive genetic role in the determination of temperamental individuality in the young infant.

In considering the effects of the environment on the development of the personality, the highly diverse nature of the environment is stressed, and the effects of social disadvantage on scholastic achievement described. The contribution of perinatal experiences, family size and birth order to intelligence is assessed in relation to a persistently poor environment, and the quality of early mother–infant interaction, and the type of language spoken in the home, are viewed in relation to later scholastic achievement.

The relationship between the rate of brain development in the first two years and life experiences is discussed. We discuss the view of several writers that the nature of a child's early life, which is mostly heavily dependent on the social class of his parents, affects later cognitive development. The environment acts as a threshold variable, and for this reason it is the responsibility of society to behave *as if* the environment were of crucial importance in the development of intelligence. The efficacy of various compensatory schemes, both in Great Britain and in the USA, which have attempted to remedy the cognitive disadvantages which are suffered by many children, are assessed. It is clear that early intervention is better than later compensation. The improvement on academic achievement which later experiences in school can bring about are also discussed.

As far as the influence of the environment on personality characteristics other than intelligence is concerned, the reader is reminded that the problem of studying what characteristics a person actually 'possesses' is very great, so that actually to trace their origin is a much more complex task than was envisaged by earlier investigators. A child is, however, obviously affected by the various factors which impinge on him, some involving him more deeply than others. The possible effects of gender, cultural and social-class influences are described, including the effects of social-class differences in the use of the spoken language. Parental child-rearing methods and their effects on the development of a balanced personality are discussed, though these are reviewed further and more fully in chapters 5 and 8.

The possible importance of the early mother–child relationship is considered, particularly as it is clear that the whole period during which development takes place is important, not just the very early period. Many previous studies are critically examined; it is concluded that largely because the baby is a social being who requires this propensity to be developed, and because a loving relationship experienced early in life probably acts as a prototype for similar, later experiences, such experiences are of importance to the infant. It is difficult to say, however, to what extent inadequate mothering *by itself* affects the developing personality. Extreme experiences usually lead to extreme consequences, but a linear relationship between less extreme causes and their effects cannot easily be shown to exist. However, for reasons already discussed, for example, the speed at which in infancy the brain is developing, comforting, pleasurable and need-reducing experiences encountered mostly through the mediation of one or two adults who have become well known to the infant are likely to leave their beneficial mark on the growing child's personality.

Growth of the intellect

The reader is reminded that though the development of the personality is, for the sake of convenience, studied as if specific aspects of the personality develop separately, the interaction of aspects of the personality such as motivational and emotional forces with, for example, the development of the intellect is inevitable.

Piaget's theory in relation to child development is considered in chapter 2. In this chapter the ontogenic, cognitive development as described by Piaget is reviewed. At the beginning of the 'sensorimotor'* stage — that is, while the child is under twenty-one months of age — much motor activity is of the reflex kind, and the child's perceptual and motor apparatuses operate simultaneously. By the time he is a year old he can form intentions and behave purposively. By the end of the sensori-motor stage the baby's thinking can take the form of internalized, wordless action; he can now 'represent' things and actions to himself, which, says Piaget, is what thinking is about. He also now has an *anticipatory* knowledge of causality, but no real understanding of causality as such.

A child has, according to Piaget, to learn progressively to free himself from two influences which are dominant in his early childhood: his percept-centred and his egocentric views of the world. In early childhood his thinking is confined largely to the information produced by his perceptual faculties, and while proceeding beyond this limited appreciation, he also has to learn about the objectivity of things, and about their existence apart from himself. This learning takes place between about two and seven years of age, when he is at the 'pre-operational' stage of development.

Until the child is about five or six years of age, therefore, he will make judgements about quantity or number based on what he sees and not on what is logically right. A child under seven years of age does not usually appear to understand about the conservation of number and quantity, but at that age, when he reaches the 'concrete operational' stage, he is much more free from the dominance of the senses, though these are still influential in guiding his thinking and behaviour. During the next period, between seven and eleven or twelve, his thinking becomes more systematized, and he learns about the truth and value of measurement. The ability to use and understand language greatly helps the process of 'de-centring', though verbal reasoning remains a limited capability throughout the concrete operational period. Before early adolescence children have difficulty according to Piaget in understanding verbal puzzles or proverbs.

Ideas of causality change from 'animism' in early childhood, by which life is ascribed to everything that moves, to a logical deduction of cause in adolescence. This occurs in various intervening stages, described by Piaget, in which effects are progressively ascribed to more and more realistic causes.

After twelve years of age new intellectual processes become available to the child, according to Piaget, and he enters the 'formal operational' period; he can manipulate verbal propositions, entertain hypotheses, build concepts, consider abstract ideas, understand proverbs, etc. Because of these new abilities many other kinds of comprehension become available, though the extent to which such abilities and comprehensions can be developed and used will depend in part on cultural and social factors; some adults never reach the formal operational stage of growth.

Criticisms of Piaget's interpretations of his findings are discussed in chapter 2. What is of pedagogic interest, and has arisen from a critical examination of Piaget's work, is the importance of teaching children how to think about thinking, and of encouraging early reading ability, as well as teaching reading in a manner which bears in mind a child's conceptions of his world, which conceptions are appropriate to his age.

The study of language development involves considering the role of language in human affairs from a number of viewpoints: *what* happens when a child learns language, *how* this happens, and what the *functions* of language are.

Psycholinguists have found children's ability to speak grammatically from a relatively early age of infinite fascination, and this study has, until recently, caused psycholinguists to neglect the study of what meaning language has for the child, and how language relates to his development generally. Chomsky's differentiation between 'surface' and 'deep' language structure was an attempt to account for the early understanding of the rules of language. It is evident, however, that from birth the infant is a social-conversational being, and his conversational abilities are enhanced in many ways by responsive caretaking. The particular manner in which mothers 'naturally' communicate with their babies is discussed, as well as the pre-verbal means which the baby employs in order to communicate. The non-verbal stages between early communication and later verbal exchanges are described in some detail, and it is emphasized that it is in the interpersonal relationship with other humans that babies learn to understand about the functions of language; these relationships aid social development and increase the baby's understanding and vocabulary. In addition his ability to make himself understood, through the use of his idiosyncratic preverbal cues, aids his self-confidence. Indeed, it is this attempt by the mother to understand her infant's early communications, and the infant's own ability to understand her words before he himself can speak, which, *inter alia,* contribute to his eventual sentence-formation ability. It seems that there is a subtle relationship between parental understanding of a child's early vocalizations and his later stages of speech behaviour.

It is also suggested that possibly the ability to form sentences, because of its close association with thinking, is, in its process and age-stage limitations, related to general, cognitive growth, and is not a special and separate (language) ability. However, it nevertheless remains true that the ability by about three years of age to speak grammatically is a remarkable ability learnt with amazing speed.

Using language as a social tool also means understanding about the quality of objects and their relationships. Piaget and Vygotsky have both studied the development of speech, and have expressed views on the function of egocentric and social speech in children of different ages. The speech of younger children appears to be more egocentric, and this may in part be due to the fact that the child has not yet fully learned to differentiate between himself and others. A child's vocabulary normally increases tenfold between two and six years of age; by the time he goes to school his speech is usually grammatically correct, and the kind of words he uses indicates the stage of social development he has reached. At this time he is beginning to be able to exchange his thoughts with others. After seven years of age or so his use of language is much influenced by the peer group to which he belongs, and his individuality emerges in part through the verbal reactions of others to his behaviour.

In recent years it has been realized that small children, despite their fluent use of language, often do not understand simple, but in their life not very frequently used, words, such as, for example, the word 'less' when contrasted with 'more'; indeed, they do not understand the diametrically opposed meanings.

In order to be able to think, a child must be able to make a mental representation of objects in their physical absence. Piaget has termed this internalization an 'operation'. (His theory of cognitive development is described in chapter 4.) He suggests that early thinking is independent of language, but to what extent even later thinking abilities are helped by, or are merely reflected by, the use of language is not yet fully understood.

Bruner considers that children must be able to internalize 'techniques', such as language, if they are to progress to the 'symbolic' stage of thinking, though not all psycholinguists agree with this view. Bruner holds that language, particularly in children between four and twelve years of age, becomes a tool for the translation of experience. He describes four stages of the development of language and of thinking, ranging from, in early childhood, the use of words in speech which the child is unable to use in thinking, to, in adolescence, powers of organization in thought which exceed the child's organizational speech powers. Vernon has written that the achieving of higher-order thinking is totally dependent on the quality of speech models to which the child is exposed. Despite these views Herriot considers that there is great confusion at present in the field of language and thinking, because there is no *absolute* proof which indicates that the quality of language affects thinking processes, though it is difficult to believe that a child's awareness of the many cognitive uses of language would not be an advantage in helping him to use it for appropriate cognitive tasks.

The development of moral, social and emotional behaviour and the child's growing perception of his social world

The preamble to this chapter outlines the various aspects of development which come together under the above heading, and the reader is then reminded that environmental factors alone do not determine the social, emotional and moral behaviour exhibited by children, and that socialization influences also are not uni-directional. A definition is given of the morally, socially and emotionally mature person, and the learning which has to take place, and the skills which have to be developed, before such maturity is attained are described. Regarding moral development, it is clear that as a society we are not really clear what we mean by 'moral' behaviour, although what we think of as morally praiseworthy behaviour seems to arise from a consideration of other people's feelings and needs, and from an informed conscience. In the study of the development of moral behaviour one must differentiate between moral knowledge, moral feeling and actual moral behaviour. It is suggested that moral behaviour need not necessarily arise from fixed, inner traits which are always displayed, regardless of the situation, but will depend on a number of factors relating both to the aspect of a person's personality which happens to predominate at any moment and to the particular situation in which behaviour is taking place.

The major theories of moral development stemming from Freud, Piaget, Kohlberg and the social-learning theorists are examined. Freudian theory attempts to account for both conscience formation and the adoption of the positive values of parents and society through the resolution of the Oedipus complex and through identification with the 'aggressor'. Piaget has studied the child's acquisition of moral knowledge, both through investigating how children's understanding of the rules of behaviour change with age, and also how their ability to make moral judgements develops. Kohlberg has been particularly concerned with the nature of the moral judgements made by adolescents, and also with the problem of how children of this age resolve moral dilemmas. Kohlberg suggests that his cross-cultural work shows that there is a natural sense of justice intuitively known by children. Kohlberg, like Piaget, outlines maturational stages of moral development. These various theories are evaluated for their contribution to our understanding of the nature of a child's developing moral sense.

Other empirical work examines the antecedents of 'pro-social' behaviour, though there appears to be no single determinant which is of overriding importance as an antecedent. However, a number of parental ways of behaving, coupled with certain characteristics exhibited by a child, can serve as predictors of the kind of child who will behave altruistically. It is suggested that as aids to the development of such behaviour adults should, *inter alia,* help children to reflect on their own feelings and other people's possible feelings. The development of empathy for others is probably complex in origin, resting in part on the biological necessity for a social organism to be able to interpret the expressive behaviour of other members of the species, and in part also on the internalization of other, loved persons' norms and values, so that the feelings experienced by these others are also experienced vicariously by the onlooker. By making children aware of the emotions experienced by others, and of the consequences of their own behaviour to others, feelings of empathy are developed.

The many and various skills which have to be acquired as part of the social-learning process are discussed, and the role of the development of the self in relation to the development of social relationships is referred to in some detail. The various cognitive and affective aspects of understanding the uniqueness of other people's personalities are examined developmentally. Coupled with this developing ability is a growing skill in making reasonably accurate assessments of other people's personalities. The development of social competence in relation to understanding the thoughts, motives, traits and characteristics of others is reviewed with most reference to recent empirical work; the beginnings of these social skills can be seen in the social–verbal interactions of mother and infant in early life, which result in a two-way bond being formed. This relationship, further discussed in chapter 3, can be seen as the prototype of later social and personal relationships.

Children's friendships change in style and mutual expectations with changing age, and these changes, as well as the sex differences which exist in relation to friendships, are reviewed. Childhood friendships also have their value as socializing agents, though it does appear that differences between children in being liked by others are already evident in infancy. Children's awareness of sex differences and how these relate to role expectancies are present early in life and are, no doubt, reinforced by social norms.

Children's knowledge of the adult social world is still inadequately understood, but it does seem that few children even of eight to ten years of age seem to understand how, for example, personal qualities and the demands of society interact. Nor do they seem to understand what is entailed in the occupation of a role, or, *inter alia*, precisely what shops are for! The social world of the child has also to be structured, as has his cognitive world, though children receive less help from adults to do this than they receive with the structuring of their cognitive world.

The development of a child's emotions is strongly tied to his growing social abilities and awareness. A child's self-awareness must come about through his awareness of his own feelings, and the specific emotions which become available to him with increasing age are discussed in relation to the experiences which come his way. Children seldom discuss their feelings, and they are not usually encouraged to reflect on them. It is suggested that Erikson's theory provides a helpful framework for the study of the development of emotions in relation to psycho-social and physical development, and the development of emotions is described within this context. The several anxieties which children feel, their need to give, as well as to receive, love, and the frustrations and unhappinesses, as well as the satisfactions which personal relationships bring in different ways at different ages, are discussed.

Play

Play is a curious activity, being neither real nor unreal, fulfilling many purposes and changing in style and function with changing age. It is freely entered into and is an end in itself, and requires a special attitude of mind. It has therapeutic value.

Play has to do with the development of skills, whether these are physical, social, cognitive, linguistic or manipulative; it is also concerned with the child's inner and fantasy life, and with the linking of this life to external reality. Bühler and Piaget have been largely concerned with the development of various kinds of skills through play as described above, whereas the psychoanalytic school has described the function of the fantasy aspects of play.

Bühler and Piaget have observed that a baby's first efforts at play help him to learn about the nature of the objects around him; that at eighteen months to two years of age his play helps him to deal imaginatively with objects and with people, and that after about four years of age he needs play in order to cope constructively with the real world. Piaget considers play during this period to be used predominantly to aid social and moral development, enabling the child to recognize the importance of rules in play and in games, and consequently how rules relate to social play. Play for Piaget is an 'assimilatory' process. Recent observational work on play is described in relation to these theories.

Such writers as Piaget, Freud and Isaacs consider imagination and symbolism to be important in a child's play, and although Piaget thinks that in infancy such play is devoid of fantasy, psychoanalytical writers stress the importance of fantasy life for the development of the child's personality. It is possible that the importance of fantasy life to the manner in which life experiences are interpreted has not received sufficient attention by non-psychoanalytic observers. Psychoanalytic writers and Piaget agree that imaginative play is of great importance in enabling the child (as opposed to the infant) to express and deal with reality. Such play can link the child's inner world to the real world, and can enable him to reconstruct reality to suit his ego, and so deal with experiences which he might otherwise find painful; this also enables him to indulge vicariously in forbidden desires. As children grow up imaginative play, as in role-taking play, more and more *reproduces* reality instead of being symbolic of reality. The advantages also to cognitive development of fantasy play are discussed.

The manner in which babies and children interact with one another in social play is described, and the value of mother–infant 'non-literal' interaction, both for the development of language ability and for linking the child's inner world to the inner and outer worlds of another person, is discussed. Three stages of social play, as they relate to the use of objects by and between children, are considered in relation to various aspects of interactions between children. The extent to which a child can play with other children is closely related to his ability to communicate with another, and also see another's point of view.

Freud considered that play, while apparently unrelated to reality, has a purpose, and that in play 'children repeat . . . everthing that has made a great impression on them in their actual life . . . and so-to-speak make themselves masters of the situation'. Thus Freud thought of play as a repetition–compulsion mechanism, which enables the child to work out his anxieties. Isaacs, from her observation of children, developed Freud's ideas, specifying the variety of anxieties experienced by children, and explaining how these are dealt with in play. According to Isaacs there is a constant interaction between fantasy life and reality which is of great importance to a child's development. Imaginative play also enables a child to test new experiences in safety.

Psychoanalytic writers consider that role-taking has a deeper significance in personality development than merely linking the world of imagination to the world of reality. It is considered to aid identification and to help the child through the Oedipal* situation (chapter 2).

With regard to the function of play in relation to social growth, a certain degree of sophistication in the use of language and an appreciation of other children as individual personalities are necessary in order to be able to play co-operatively, and hence such play is not usually possible for children under five years of age. Although at times younger children appear to be playing together, closer observation will show that usually one dominant child is using the others for his own purposes. However, children who are well acquainted with each other often seem to be able to play together at an earlier age.

In early childhood play involving movement helps the development of bodily expertise and skills; play with objects of various shapes, sizes, colours and textures stimulates most of the child's senses as he plays with them, and is one of the most influential factors aiding cognitive growth. A plentiful provision of play objects and materials in infancy and childhood will also enable the child to contend more competently with reality.

Individual, gender, familial and cultural differences in play are considered briefly. Boys usually prefer noisier games in larger groups. Cultural norms and expectancies appear to influence the kinds of toys bought and the sort of games adults encourage boys and girls respectively to play; boys seem on the whole to play more imaginatively than girls. As far as individual differences are concerned, the children who engage more in fantasy play appear to differ in certain personality characteristics from those who use less fantasy play. Also children who come from deprived backgrounds (chapter 3) engage in fantasy play less than other children. The greatest cultural differences in relation to play are noted between children who are expected to share in the work of the community, who engage less in make-believe play than children who live in communities which do not have these expectations of children.

Observing and understanding children

Because of the unique individuality of each child it is desirable that, if this is at all possible, a teacher should understand every child in her care. The several means by which teachers can learn to assess a child's individual characteristics are discussed in this chapter.

It is not possible to review *in detail* all the disadvantages, difficulties and varying family circumstances from which many children suffer, as well as to review the needs of the highly gifted child. The reader is referred to the many helpful publications of the National Children's Bureau.

The teacher should constantly bear in mind that a child's behaviour is often an expression of inner drives and needs which he cannot easily change, and that these drives largely constitute his temperament. Various studies show that when the demands of home or school conflict with a child's temperamental characteristics he is placed under strain. Situations can arise which cause acute distress to some children, while being quite tolerable to others.

Temperamental characteristics, which make one child lovable and another hard to tolerate, can also affect children's learning abilities. Easy distractibility and a short attention span, for example, adversely affect the learning abilities of otherwise gifted children. Various personality characteristics other than intelligence can also influence academic and scholastic achievement.

The effects of sex differences on the development of aspects of behaviour is discussed in other chapters in this book. In this chapter the greater involvement of boys in detected delinquent behaviour, and the greater incidence of behavioural disturbance in boys are referred to.

17

Concerning children's use of language, the reader is reminded that young children do not necessarily themselves understand all they are able to say, and there is also the problem of the disadvantage suffered by the child from a working-class home for whom school is the first experience of middle-class 'elaborated' language. Such disadvantages are not confined to scholastic pursuits, but can also cause behavioural problems, for it is probable that the different manner in which language is used by the two major social classes affects the development of conscience in the child, and it also has an influence on the relationship between the teacher and her children.

It is only by appreciating a child's egocentric and percept-centred view of the world, his different understanding (when compared with adults) of the motives and behaviour of other people, and his changing concepts of moral behaviour with advancing age, that adults are able to understand children at different stages of their development.

It is important for a teacher, if at all possible, to know the parents of children in her charge, since by this acquaintance the teacher is enabled the better to understand the child. Certain children may present problems where parent–teacher contact is essential, and these are discussed later in this chapter.

A child's body-build may also be related to the behaviour he exhibits. Types of children who are *markedly* 'linear', 'round' and 'muscular' in body-build have been found in one study to differ from one another in a number of characteristics, including scholastic achievement, social behaviour and certain personality traits. Although assessment by physical appearance is only one of many ways of making evaluations of a child's characteristics, physical appearance is the most immediately obvious factor about a child. By knowing the likely strengths and weaknesses of children who are particularly extreme in body-build the teacher can form an approximate expectation of such children's performance; for example, the thin child is more likely to be anxious and the muscular child will find sitting still for long rather difficult.

Even children who enjoy the experience of a normal childhood not infrequently suffer distress and anxieties. Most adults and children have to suffer stress at some time in life, and small children learn something about human behaviour by noting the reactions of other people to stressful situations. It is not yet fully understood in what way stressful experiences are either damaging to the personality or, alternatively, may help to establish a suitable resilience, yet in spite of such ignorance decisions are often made about the future of children with insufficient consideration of the possible consequences of such decisions. Eighty per cent of all children appear to suffer some form of difficulty in the infant school, nearly half of these being of moderate or marked severity. The teacher of infants should be particularly sensitive to, and understanding of, such difficulties.

Difficulties which children of all ages meet in their lives are described as falling under the three headings of (1) what the child may be suffering, (2) the known adverse family conditions which exist and (3) the anti-social or otherwise disturbed behaviour which the child may be exhibiting. In the handling of so-called 'problem' children, the teacher should recognize that the difficulties of most children have more than one cause, and that each child's unique situation must be studied individually before an explanation is attempted. Also to *describe* problem behaviour is not to explain it. The teacher has a unique opportunity to notice when something has gone wrong in a child's life.

Some children have to live in residential institutions from birth or from very early in infancy, and the possible effects of such an experience are reviewed. It is suggested from much evidence that following such an experience which has lasted, say, three or four years from infancy onwards the forming of normal, happy, unselfish relationships may not easily be possible. A recent study of a limited number of children who were removed for caring adoption after the mean age of three years appears to show that certain relationships can be formed, but that the early experience nevertheless leaves a differentiating mark on the child's personality.

As far as temporary separation is concerned, the effects of the child's age at the time of separation, the quality of the alternative arrangements made, the child's experience during separation, and other, related factors are discussed in relation to the noted consequences on the child. It is conceded that psychologists still know too little in detail about the many factors which affect the dynamics of human relationships and their interruption, though it is suggested that for optimal development children need continuity of care by familiar people. However, other factors apart from separation from a loved person in early childhood can cause distress and affect personality formation, and these are discussed in some detail. Drawing on the work of Rutter *et al.*, the conclusions of these workers are cited: when more than one adverse factor is present in a child's life the risk to the child is four times as great as when only one such factor is present. These various factors, such as separation or divorce of parents, family discord, and bereavement are discussed, as well as the kinds of help which can be given to children suffering under one of these adverse conditions.

The various circumstances relating to non-accidental injuries inflicted annually on 5,000 children in Great Britain are described, and both the causes for such violence and the effects on the child, as well as the ability to, and the need for, predicting abusing parents, are discussed. It is stressed how important it is to treat both the children and the parents in order to prevent a vicious cycle of abuse continuing from generation to generation.

There are great individual differences in the ability to withstand the stresses of life. Some of these differences are due to temperamental factors, others due to the quality of early life experiences. It is stressed that adults must gauge what any one *individual* child can withstand without being overwhelmed by anxiety. A teacher can be particularly helpful in comforting children who are suffering distress.

The personality disorders, anti-social behaviour or psychiatric symptoms from which children can suffer can be a particular problem to a teacher. It is difficult to know in most cases when such disorders are manifestations with the likelihood of serious later consequences, or are only of temporary duration. The various factors which should be taken into account when considering whether a child should be referred for professional help are enumerated. The child of nursery school age who is 'troublesome' or does not easily play with others can be helped by the regular, daily, individual attention of an adult, and it is better for children of all ages wherever it is possible to divert and reward rather than punish or reprimand.

Thieving in the classroom can present a very worrying situation for any teacher, often creating acute tensions. Small children may have difficulty in understanding the difference between communal, private and loaned property, in addition to their often tenuous hold on moral concepts. The reader will find in this chapter also a detailed discussion of the problems presented by aggressive, over-anxious, withdrawn, rigid and attention-seeking children. Also the variety of causes which may result in a child's non-attendance at school are examined.

The teacher is often the first person to notice that certain children suffer from minor, although debilitating, physical defects, and can be viewed as 'bridge' children between those suffering acute physical disability and those with emotional problems but no obvious physical disabilities. Such defects, including poor visual and auditory discrimination, may cause spelling and reading problems, and a combination of these and/or similar symptoms in a child should cause the teacher to observe him closely.

A section on reading and its difficulties discusses the problem from a number of points of view, including stating the estimated number of illiterate or semi-illiterate adults, the relationship between social-class membership and backwardness in reading, the great advantage scholastically to the child who learns to read relatively early in life, and the possible means of distinguishing between backward and retarded readers and so-called dyslexic children. In addition, the work of a number of recent investigations into children's reading abilities is discussed. These seem to show that the most significant factor relating to level of attainment in literacy at seven years of age is the child's knowledge 'about the activities of reading and writing'. The factors in the child's home which contribute to his achieving this knowledge are discussed, and the quality and type of written material to be used in the infant school is described. It is stressed that adults have, until recently, probably spent too little time trying to discover what precise difficulties *individual* children experience. It seems very necessary for adults to 'decentre' in order to understand how individual children see the total classroom situation and their own learning process within that situation.

The child who is especially gifted also needs special care if his gifts are to mature. Such children are often unusually sensitive and have a need to express their gifts; special educational facilities exist for them.

The ways in which the child defined as 'dull' or 'ESN' can be helped are discussed. With these children also it is important for the adult to attempt to see the child's viewpoint.

Formal group intelligence tests, administered from time to time by teachers, prove most useful in discovering the intelligent child who is underfunctioning in his work. Such tests, however, cannot yield as much information as individually administered tests given by an educational psychologist. Also the psychologist, if called in when a particularly acute problem cannot be dealt with by the school alone, can often also enlist parental co-operation when this has not been possible earlier.

The adult in interaction with the child

Loevinger has suggested that whatever child-rearing methods parents use, children will always seek to circumvent these in order to gratify their own needs and desires. Whether parents basically use reward and punishment, or teach through insight-learning, or rely on the identification process, children cannot be expected to appreciate their parents' intentions upon which the rearing method employed has been based! This somewhat frivolous approach to a serious problem emphasizes the real difficulty facing the experts when they are asked how children should be reared. This chapter examines a number of reasons why there seems to be no direct relationship between parental actions and child behaviour, which reasons include the fact that far too little is known as yet in detail about the many possible influential factors which go to form the human personality. In addition, as far as the normal ranges of behaviour are concerned, the hope of finding main causes for the development of certain personality characteristics, as mentioned earlier, seems unrealistic. There are also acute methodological difficulties involved in attempting to trace the relationship between rearing habits and personality development. Such problems and difficulties are discussed in some detail in order to inculcate in the reader a certain wariness regarding the acceptance of dogmatic statements about child rearing and its attendant effects. Nevertheless, research work has established some principles.

The advantages for the development of a balanced personality of good social-emotional experiences, particularly during the early childhood period, are again stressed. Children who are pro-social in behaviour come from parents who exhibit certain desirable and example-setting personality characteristics, and who discipline by reasoning. Certain characteristics relating to a child's temperament in connection with the likelihood of his engaging in pro-social behaviour are discussed; it is also questioned whether the several influential environmental factors examined only affect a child's *behaviour* or influence his *disposition* also.

The role of rewards and punishments in, respectively, encouraging approved behaviour and discouraging disapproved behaviour is reviewed in some detail, for society by and large uses punishment frequently but for the most part ineffectually in attempting to correct the behaviour of miscreants.

The terms 'punishment and reward' cover complex happenings in widely varying situations, and the 'common-sense' viewpoint that, for effective control, approved behaviour is to be rewarded and disapproved to be punished is too simple a view. Several investigators have established that the use of physical punishment and physical control is associated generally with the development of a number of undesirable characteristics in children. At the same time the giving of 'unconditional love' in all circumstances does not help the child to discriminate between approved and disapproved behaviour. Psychological punishment, more usually employed by middle-class parents, is more effective in producing a child with a strong superego,* though recent work stresses the 'informative effect' of occasional physical punishment for specific acts. It is important, however, to differentiate between the occasional act of physical punishment and a generally punitive atmosphere, which is not very effective in controlling behaviour.

The use of the 'inductive' method, whereby adults explain to children the consequences to others of their behaviour, was associated in one study with strong conscience formation when this method was used by middle-class mothers. It is suggested by the workers engaged on this study that the bases for internalizing authority and values may well be different for children from the two major social classes, and this finding would seem to be of importance to teachers who have to handle children from both social classes. One worker in this field achieved success in correcting nursery children's behaviour by immediately rewarding approved, and ignoring disapproved, behaviour. Summarizing these findings, one can say that habitual physical coercion produces, among other undesirable characteristics, fear of detection; that expressions of warmth towards the child help him to identify with his parents; that explanations about behaviour can help in the formation of a strong superego; and that the rewarding of desirable, and the ignoring of undesirable, behaviour encourages the former and discourages the latter.

A number of current studies of the respective effects of permissive rearing on the one hand, and firm but non-authoritarian discipline on the other, in producing desirable qualities in children, suggest that these considerations are less important than whether the adults concerned are loving, understanding, value the child as a respected person, and are generally rewarding and non-punitive. It is also possible that a firm regime suits one child, and a permissive one another. However, not only is the child influenced by his parents' behaviour, but he is also influenced by his, the child's, own interpretation of this behaviour, and by his fantasies in relation to important people in his life. One must also realize that not only do parents affect child behaviour, but children also affect parental behaviour.

Some adults, because of their own personality problems, appear to have special difficulties when dealing with children; they are apt to belittle children, or to use physical force unnecessarily, or in other ways to use their relationship with children to satisfy their own needs. It is tragic when a young teacher is accepted for training whose own problems create such attitudes and behaviour towards the children in her care.

Children themselves at various ages have expressed their views about desirable characteristics in teachers. In the main children consider that a teacher should be helpful, should enable them to learn, should be able to keep control, and should have respect for each child as an individual. Understanding the child is particularly important in the primary school, because unhappiness occasioned by the first experience of school can adversely affect a child's learning capabilities.

Reference is made to a recent study (also referred to in chapters 3 and 8) which indicates that certain 'common-sense' variables present or absent in a secondary school can make a decisive difference both to the behaviour and to the academic performance of secondary school pupils, whereas other 'common-sense' variables make no such difference.

Retrospect

It will be clear to the reader that many traditional ideas about child-rearing have rested on inadequate foundations. Although the influence of the environment on personality development has not been decried in this book, we understand better today how difficult it is to define a 'good' environment, and we also know that possibly children vary as much in innate psychological characteristics as they do in physical characteristics. We have noted that children born into homes belonging to the lowest social classes — a high proportion of children in the community — are handicapped in very many ways, and that in order to minimize such handicaps it is important to involve parents in the education of their children from an early age.

The problem of a young child's limited ideas about moral behaviour is considered in connection with adult aims relating to the moral training of children; it is suggested that parents and teachers can capitalize on the desire most children have to please other people most of the time.

Universally applicable advice on child rearing which disregards the individuality of children is not known to be of little value, but it is suggested that probably most parents would like their children to be able to get on well with other people, and also to develop in such a way that their innate abilities can be used to the full. In order to fulfil these aims children's four basic needs, as defined by Kellmer Pringle, must be met: the need for love and security, for praise and recognition, for responsibility, and for new experiences. It is suggested by Kellmer Pringle that not only parents but the whole of society are responsible for meeting these needs.

SECTION ONE

Background to behaviour

CHAPTER ONE

Cross-cultural and historical review of attitudes to child development and rearing

Cultural variations

The present-day attitude of Western societies to children is unique, both culturally and historically. The concept of childhood, of children's position and role in society, and how children should consequently be treated by adults, has varied from one period of history to another and from one culture to another. The factors which at any time and in any one society determine the attitude of adult persons to children depend on the norms and values of that society, and on the society's state of development. Thus that which is important to one culture will have little relevance in a neighbouring society; and the particular views held about children at one period in time may be of little account in the same society in later years.

Child-rearing practices, and the place of children in relatively primitive societies, are related to the habits, needs, expectations and values of each society, but, as Margaret Mead (1955) has pointed out, if one wishes to study the personality differences seemingly produced by different child-rearing patterns, one must start by considering what it is that all human children have in common. All children must have their bodily needs satisfied, they are all helpless for a relatively long time and they must all learn the behaviour which is relevant to the culture of their society. A child, wherever he is born, must learn to eat on his own, to walk, talk, identify with his own sex, behave appropriately for his sex and age and eventually take on the adult roles assigned to him or chosen by him. It is because of these basic similarities that comparisons can be made between childhood rearing patterns, and also between the varying attitudes adults hold and have held about children in different cultures and at different times.

Problems of discipline and restriction, for example, are handled differently in different communities. The Samoans think of the process of socialization as one of unfolding development: children do not have to be taught to behave properly, but if left to develop naturally they will eventually conform to society's norms. However, they are not permitted to be a nuisance to the group (Mead, 1955). Weaning times and methods also differ greatly from culture to culture: Whiting and Child (1953) compared a great many societies from whom reports about weaning ages are available. In most societies, weaning is begun between two and three years of age, although in one Indian tribe weaning does not start until the child is five or six years old. The American children, with whom children from other societies were compared, are normally weaned between birth and seven months. Time of weaning has been of interest as a cross-cultural study, because of the emphasis placed on oral* experiences in relating to personality development in psychoanalytic literature (chapter 2).

If survival depends, as Benedict (1955) found it did for the Canadian Ojibwa family, in trapping alone during the winter months on frozen hunting grounds, then self-reliance is of supreme importance, and the boy is taught by the age of twelve to set his own traps and bring the meat to his sister, who has learned to skin it for him, as his mother skins his father's catches. If, as is believed in Bali, life is seen as a circular stage which includes the returning dead, then the child is viewed as a small human being who, like old members of society, is nearer the spiritual life than the middle-aged members of the community, who are closest in time to the secular life. There is no distinction as such between child and adult, and people do not increase in stature and respect merely because of their position in society (Mead, 1955). Indeed, in many communities the extreme distinction which Western societies make between child and adult is not made. Benedict (1955) quotes Underhill as telling her how a Papago grandfather in Arizona asked his three-year-old granddaughter to close a door. The door was heavy, but she was considered equal to the task and no one helped her. In our own society we think of children as wanting to play and adults as having to work, but in societies where no such distinctions are made children accompany their parents, or other members of the group, to their work, and are given tasks graded to suit their age and strength. The transition from childhood to adult life is thus one of degree and not of kind, though often elaborate initiation ceremonies, mostly at puberty, do mark the child's entry into adult life and adult responsibilities. Thus the gradual adoption of more complex or more responsible tasks, added to a clear conception of his own status in the society, means that the adolescent in the more primitive groups does not have to suffer many of the difficulties which in sophisticated communities afflict both him and his elders as a result of his ambiguous status. (Many descriptions of cultural patterns no longer hold, but were part of the culture in the days before the Second World War.)

However, these differences between cultures in particular child-rearing habits are not in themselves very important, nor do they alone account for the personality differences which can be observed in members of different societies. It is the dissimilar manner in which the many habits and practices of dissimilar cultures are patterned and made to fit together which account for some of the differences. Weaning habits, toilet training, parent–child relationships, the use of disciplinary methods, the assignment of responsibilities and many other aspects of child rearing, when combined together, provide a background of learning which enables the adult eventually to fulfil his roles in his society. Children in most cultural groups also have to learn, in relation to roles, what has been termed 'continuity–discontinuity' in cultural conditioning (Benedict, 1955). The boy is obedient: the father authoritarian. The son, first sexless, then seeks sex outside the family: the father is always potent and confines his sexual relationships to within the family. The boy, particularly in our society, has little or no responsibility: the father has full adult responsibilities. As the child becomes the adult one kind of behaviour has to be discontinued and other kinds of behaviour begun; but in addition many habits and ways of behaving remain continuously relevant, regardless of age. Where, for example, the kind of 'age grading' occurs in relation to responsibilities, to which reference has already been made, particularly where ceremonies accompany the transition from one grade to another, children and adults seem able to move from role to role without apparently suffering psychological harm. Often quite different types of behaviour are exhibited by the same person at different stages of life, such as when members of the Arapaho tribe exhibit aggressive behaviour during the head-hunting period, followed by calmness in later life, by which time the role of the elder is to uphold the society's rituals, and it is also proper for him to exhibit peaceable virtues (Benedict, 1955).

Cultural conditioning is not, however, the only determinant of personality. Emphasis has been laid above on child-rearing patterns in order to stress the variety of habits which exist in relation to upbringing, and to indicate that the customs from which these habits are derived are at least in part related to the needs of the society. The more primitive a society and the nearer to subsistence level are its living standards, then the more role-related are its child-rearing customs likely to be. Sophisticated industrialized communities have complex and diverse needs, and there is therefore not the relatively close relationship which exists between the group's need to survive in the face of natural hazards and its consequent child-rearing customs which seek to ensure survival by training the potential adult to act appropriately.

This might be taken to mean that sophisticated communities were homogeneous in their attitude to children. Unlike most primitive groups, however, Western societies are formed from groupings of classes and sub-classes, so that one cannot state with certainty that particular customs are applicable universally within a specific geographical area of the society, or that such customs are universal in all classes of the society. In addition, the vast social changes which have occurred in the west during the past hundred years have brought about successive and sporadically adopted changes in the way children have been regarded by adults in the community.

Historical variations within European and North American societies

There are a number of factors to be borne in mind when considering from an historical viewpoint the changing social attitudes to children of adults living in European and North American societies. The first is that, as mentioned above, even within a society which has certain shared cultural and social values, there have been, and still are, at least marginally different attitudes to children in different countries within so-called Western society.

Then, nearly everything that has been written and pictorially illustrated about childhood, about child rearing, and about the family has been written by, written for and written about people belonging to the middle and upper social classes. Even the baby books published in the 1920s and 1930s assumed that their readers were at least middle class. We have knowledge of the conditions under which working-class children have lived, but this knowledge is meagre when compared to our knowledge of the attitude of upper-class adults towards children. It is only relatively recently that specific differences have been noted between customs of child rearing, which vary not only according to social-class membership in one country, but also according to different geographical areas within that same country (Newson and Newson, 1963).

Another point to remember is that most of what has been written about childhood and about attitudes to children before the nineteenth century appears to have taken it for granted that by 'child' one in fact means 'boy'! It is common knowledge that in England certain privileged girls, such as Elizabeth I and the daughters of Sir Thomas More, received an education equal to that of their brothers, but it was not until the eighteenth and nineteenth centuries that girls went to school, though a few girls' schools did exist earlier; but generally we do not know very much about society's attitude in the past specifically to girls, though we do know that the birth of a girl was nearly always unwelcome. Finally, although it is possible to trace a pattern of a more-or-less consistent change of attitudes towards children from medieval times to the present day, there are, nevertheless, not infrequently different viewpoints discernible within any one historical period, and there have also been some remarkable 'swings of the pendulum' from one period to another.

According to de Mause (1974) this pattern of consistent change can be seen in six 'modes', as he calls them, which, he considers, 'represent a continuous sequence of closer approaches between parent and child as generation after generation of parents slowly overcame their anxieties and began to develop the capacity to identify and satisfy the needs of their children' (page 51). It is necessary to stress that de Mause's views regarding the particular emphasis which each historical period carries in relation to parental attitudes to children is a highly personal one. These modes were, first, the mode of 'infanticide', which prevailed until approximately the fourth century, though the practice of exposing children, nearly always girls, and leaving them to die, seems to have been carried out well into the nineteenth century. The mode of infanticide was, according to de Mause, followed by the mode of 'abandonment', practised until the thirteenth century. Children were handed over to others to be brought up. The third mode, which lasted until the eighteenth century, he has termed the mode of 'ambivalence'. Children now began to enter into their parents' emotional life. This mode was succeeded by the 'intrusive' mode, which was characterized by the parents' attempt to conquer their child's mind and will. In the nineteenth century and the first half of the twentieth century the need to raise a socially acceptable human being seemed to parents of first importance, and de Mause has termed this mode of upbringing the 'socialization' mode. The final mode, the 'helping' mode, which de Mause says is now current, signifies an awareness of the child's actual needs, and an attempt by parents to meet these needs. However, the manner in which the parental activities and attitudes associated with this mode is described by de Mause implies that 'helping' is seen as being almost synonymous with what has been termed 'permissive rearing'; but whereas most child psychologists will agree that it is wholly admirable to be aware of children's needs and to attempt to meet these at various stages of development, this does not necessarily mean applying permissive rearing methods. We shall return to this theme later. So we have a pattern of attitudes which ranges from the unsentimental disposal of unwanted children to the devotion of much time, energy and loving thought to their upbringing.

It is difficult to separate the changing concept of childhood from the evolution of the family. The historically modern family is a unique institution. Medieval families of all classes sent their children at quite an early age to other families for service, for training, or for education; children from seven or eight years of age thus shared in both the domestic and the professional life of adults, but of adults who were not their parents. Since children left their home early in life they did not have much contact with their own parents or with their siblings, and so the pattern of relationships between family members was clearly different from that of the often somewhat introverted and emotionally close families of later times. This early removal from home strongly reminds one of the fashion still current among certain classes of sending boys away to preparatory school at a very tender age.

However, during the later middle ages parents generally preferred to keep their children nearer to them, to remove them from the exclusive influence of other adults, and to allow them to obtain their education while living at home. Thus it is clear that as schooling became a more usual experience for many children, the family, as a child-centred institution, came into being.

It is surprising to realize that in most paintings of medieval art children are shown as if they were miniature adults — for example, in Piero della Francesca's 'Virgin and Child with Two Angels' — though it seems that artists were able to depict children realistically and not infrequently did so, even in early medieval paintings (Lasareff, 1938); but one feels that those paintings which showed children as small adults, with the same head–body ratio as adults, more accurately reflected the prevailing feeling that after seven years of age, or so, children were merely smaller and less experienced adults, but in no important way different from grown-up people. During the seventeenth century three concepts of childhood seemed to have been held more or less simultaneously: that children were unimportant and should be ignored; that they were playthings, to be petted and fondled for the pleasure they gave; and that childhood was a time of ignorance, irrationality and levity, and that adults had to learn to understand this period of life in order to correct children's behaviour (Ariès, 1962). Attitudes about how this 'correction' should be carried out varied. Lord David Cecil reports that during the reign of Elizabeth I in the sixteenth century Lord Burghley, who 'kept a school for young noblemen', believed that pupils were more easily led by kindness than by severity; he also took a great interest in his own children, they 'occupied much of his attention', and he took pains about their education (Cecil, 1973). Others, however, believed in a sterner discipline. It is interesting to note that the difference in viewpoint between those persons who advocate a 'hard' method of bringing up children, and those who advocate a 'soft' method, is not something which exists only in the twentieth century!

There have, of course, always been enlightened people, such as John Locke and Rousseau, who viewed the period of childhood in an understanding way. John Locke especially was remarkably modern in his view of children, and his book *Some thoughts concerning education*, published in 1693, was well known in other countries of Europe too. He was perceptive enough to realize that for the young child work and play were synonymous, and that much could be taught through play; but it seems certain that his appreciation of the important differences between children's minds and adult minds was exceptional. Locke also disagreed with flogging and beating (Plumb, 1975). But beatings were the generally accepted rule from the earliest times as an aid to child rearing, and de Mause mentions that the earliest record he could find of children who were not beaten at all dates from 1960.

Speaking generally, the period before the eighteenth century at least was grim for most children; indeed, only a relatively small proportion of those born survived to endure life for long. The child mortality rate prior to the civil registration of births is variously estimated for the seventeenth century as being 25 per cent before one year of age, with 50 per cent of all children dying before they reached teenage, to, as late as the mid-eighteenth century, 75 per cent of all children dying before they reached five years of age (Newson, 1967). In a recent biography (Gerin, 1976), of Mrs Gaskell, who was born in 1810, mention is made of the fact that she was the youngest of eight children, six of whom had died before she was born! Although such a death rate in one family was probably not common, it may well not have been very abnormal. Elizabeth Newson (1967) considers that the early death of children inevitably influenced attitudes to child rearing, and that only when infant mortality had been very considerably reduced in the mid-nineteenth century did a major change of attitude towards children occur. Plumb (1975), however, suggests that a fundamental change occurred in parental interest in children in the eighteenth century. His findings are that people then generally began to feel differently about their children, and that this change of attitude was not only due to children living longer than previously, but came about because they were more healthy and their parents also were better off. He has described how, while prior to the 1740s there were very few books available specially produced for children apart from grammars, by the end of the century a mass of titles, spanning a wide range of subjects, appeared each year. He writes that by 1780 'there was no subject, scientific, or literary, that had not its specialized literature designed for children' (page 83). It is interesting to note that the less affluent working-class parents also bought these books. The number of provincial theatres which were built at this time in England also meant that children could be, and, indeed, were, taken to the theatre and to concerts; drawing masters were engaged, and a number of educational entertainments could be enjoyed (Plumb, 1975). Because of the many books which were now available, the family outings and entertainments which were possible, and the variety of educational pursuits which could be followed, it is clear, as Plumb writes, that life for the middle-class child of the 1780s was very different from that lived by the child a century earlier. No doubt the founding of the Royal Society in 1660, and the excitement engendered by the various scientific discoveries made during the following decades, contributed in the ensuing century both to an interest in education and an appreciation of its advantages.

The period of childhood was also by now much more clearly specified, so that a person was no longer merely an infant or a child before becoming adult. During the medieval period people had been much concerned with the importance of age and its relation to man's changing position throughout life, but as far as the early period of life was concerned even Shakespeare's seven ages of man allowed only for 'infancy', 'the whining schoolboy', and then 'the lover'. The meaning of the word 'child' related then as much to the dependence of a person on others as to his chronological age. However, Ariès (1962) tells how Pascal's pupils in the eighteenth century were described as being either 'little ones', 'middle ones', or 'big ones', and it is noteworthy that as we move from the eighteenth century to the nineteenth century childhood begins to be seen as an experience which is different not only between infancy on the one hand and adulthood on the other, but different also between one period within childhood and another. Yet just at this time children were once more sent away to school, and their child life separated from their adult life. This period saw the development of the boarding school in England; and despite a greater interest in children and in their education, much more physical punishment was meted out than in previous decades, particularly in schools.

This separation of all the childhood years from those of the rest of a person's life still shows its effect today in society's attitude to adolescence. Margaret Mead (1928) suggested that in some primitive societies, at least as she observed them in pre-war days, children were given tasks of increasing complexity and responsibility suited to their increasing age, and adulthood was achieved gradually as childhood was equally gradually relinquished. The state of 'adolescence', she suggested, did not exist as it exists in western societies. In our society, adolescents seem to live in a kind of temporal no-man's land, where adults, according to their whim or the situation, alternately accuse young people of being irresponsible for their age, or tell them they are too young to do something they may wish to do; and while they are physically mature, they are economically still dependent.

By the mid-nineteenth century infant mortality in Great Britain was down to 15.4 per cent. By now a large body of literature on child-rearing problems had appeared in the USA. Sunley, in Mead and Wolfenstein (1955), has outlined the reasons which led to the particular kind of child-rearing advice which was given to parents during this period. Already by the end of the eighteenth century parents had a clear idea of the kind of adult they sought to raise, but in the nineteenth century parents appear to have had a greater confidence in being able to achieve their aim. It is interesting to note not only how the values of society, then as now, are inevitably reflected in what parents and educators seek to achieve when bringing up children, but also how at this particular time — the mid-nineteenth century — the optimism which sprang from a strong feeling that man could control his environment and influence his future also gave him the belief that he could 'shape' — to use a later, 'Skinnerian', term — the character of the children in his care. Such confidence, later reinforced by Pavlovian ideas of conditioning, lasted well into the next century.

In the mid-nineteenth century, however, as Sunley further points out, Calvinistic religious ideas were particularly influential in the United States in determining the kind of adult person parents wanted their children to become. Such a person should be 'a moral, honest, religious, independent individual, who could take his proper place in society' (page 51). Dwight, quoted in Mead and Wolfenstein (1834), said that 'no child has ever been known, since the earliest period of the world, destitute of an evil disposition — however sweet it appears' (page 159). Because the likelihood of a child dying in 1850 was still seven times as great as it would be a hundred years later, it was important that the child should be trained from earliest infancy to learn to overcome its 'evil disposition', and to earn grace and avoid eternal damnation. The child's will had thus to become pliant to parental and religious demands. Both Plumb (1975), writing about the development of schools in the eighteenth century, and Sunley (1955), concerned with the new child-rearing advice given to American parents in the nineteenth century, make the point that a scholastically successful child and a well-mannered child enhanced parental standing in society. A modern parallel consists in the great importance which until only recently was placed by many parents on their children passing the 'eleven plus' examination, often as much for considerations of family prestige as for academic reasons.

Judith Temple (writing in Temple, 1970) refers to the fact that in Victorian England 'duty was the foundation of all family relationship' and that 'childhood seems to have been a condition to grow out of and master'. The middle-class child who appeared in Victorian fiction for children 'could never escape from the clutches of his parents or his conscience' (page 14). Green's Nursery Album of 1848, quoted by Nigel Temple, contains poems ostensibly written by children, which are almost unbelievable in the kind of eulogy expressed for both parents, and the admission of follies of various kinds by the children. For the Victorian child, parents must have appeared only slightly lower in the hierarchical structure of their society than God himself. No wonder Freud wrote (1916) that the major task which every individual had to accomplish in life was to free himself from his parents! It has been suggested that friendship between parents and children in such an authoritarian atmosphere in middle-class families was not possible, but Thompson, in a study he began in 1969, put forward the view that the distant relationship which was in vogue even later in the nineteenth century between parents and children in the middle classes did not exist to the same extent in working-class families; and Thompson also remarks on the relative absence of physical punishment of children in working-class families of the period.

The idea that children could be trained to exhibit the character and personality determined by adults was reinforced by Pavlov's work once it became known in the English-speaking world in about 1912. Watson, who did so much to popularize Pavlovian ideas, is famous for his remark that he could condition a child to become whatever he, Watson, desired it to become; and the ideal end product of child training in the early part of the twentieth century was not dissimilar to the mid-nineteenth century ideal. Character training was still the important aim, and Sir Truby King used the ideas inherent in conditioning to evolve a system of child rearing which was based on the establishing of a regular regime of eating, sleeping and defaecating. If good bodily habits could be established in the child it was assumed that good mental habits could also be formed, and among these 'good mental habits' was to be the realization by the young baby that adults were in charge of his life, and that his desires would not be indulged. The notion that a child's 'desires' might be dictated by his needs does not seem to have been appreciated. One aspect of children's spontaneous activity which troubled parents at the turn of the century, and later, was their auto-erotic behaviour. This was considered dangerous, and, as is well known, masturbation in particular was thought to have quite dreadful consequences. Even as recently as the late 1940s the author saw a mother sew up the sleeves of her baby's garment so that the child could not touch his own body! It is interesting that, as Plumb (1975) suggests, though little is known historically about attitudes to sex, already in the eighteenth century 'the world of sex was to become a world of terror for children' (page 92).

Although character training was still considered important, the baby books of the 1920s and 1930s, especially those written by psychoanalytically orientated writers, began to be more concerned with bringing up children who became mentally healthy, although probably mental health was by now more-or-less synonymous with having a 'good' character; but whether mental health was best produced by inculcating good habits, as advocated by Truby King, or by being effectively conscious of the child's psycho-sexual development, was a question of dispute. In 1929, only shortly before the publication of Truby King's manual, Susan Isaacs, a Freudian child specialist, published her *Nursery Years*; the only point of agreement between these two books, however, seems to have been the importance of early childhood experience to later development. The difficulty for middle-class parents from about 1930 onwards was that, able to read about child-rearing practices from both points of view, they received no help in deciding which was more likely to be the true point of view! Families were now smaller, so that parents could give much more attention to their children, and having themselves been brought up in a tradition which laid great emphasis on parental responsibility for their child's character, they were deeply concerned to do the right thing. While the psychoanalytic writers, in part at least, were concerned with the effects of repression, Truby King later wrote that 'obedience in infancy is the foundation of all late powers of self-control' (1937).

This statement is remarkable for a number of reasons: it indicates how overridingly important a particularly Victorian aspect of child behaviour — obedience — was still thought to be as late as 1937; then, by stressing infant obedience, it shows how very little was understood at this time, less than forty years ago, of the infant mind; and it showed too how important was the notion of self-control — an eighteenth century ideal — as an eventual major characteristic of the mature person. The idea that the child was a miniature and potential adult, but not a person in his own right, was still extraordinarily current. Indeed Watson, who in 1928 himself wrote on the psychological care of the infant and child, said that the child should be treated as if he were a young adult! He advocated no hugging or kissing, or any other kind of sentimental interaction with children. At the same time Susan Isaacs was writing that 'if we can really get into our bones . . . the sense of the slow growth of the infant's mind through various bodily experiences and the knowledge that each phase has its own importance in development, we are more likely to give him the gentle and patient friendliness which he most needs' (Isaacs, 1929, page 31). This is a very different approach from that of Watson and King, yet for two decades at least middle-class parents were subject simultaneously to the influence of both the Behaviourist and the Freudian viewpoints. Newson (1967) quotes reports given by mothers of the time who longed to respond to their babies in a 'natural' way, but, possibly because it demanded self-sacrifice and self-control for them not to do this, they considered that they ought, for the child's sake, to be unselfish and adopt the rigorous 'Truby King' regime. Freud himself wrote very little about child rearing, except to stress the need for patience, so that his own influence was an indirect one; but one can say that possibly one of his great contributions to beneficial changes in social attitudes has lain in the effect of his discoveries concerning the processes of development of the infant and child on the concept of childhood. His work, coupled with that of such later writers as, for example, Erikson and Piaget, each concerned with different aspects of child development, now make it impossible for us to see childhood merely as a period of preparation for adult life, but enables us to view it as a unique stage in human life, existing in its own right.

However, even the effect of Freudian writers such as Susan Isaacs was not entirely for good, although she displayed a wisdom and understanding when writing about the infant and young child which was sadly lacking in the writings of the Behaviourists. For example, Isaacs remarked that the only child will be unable to tolerate the least denial of his demands. For this statement and others like it, there was no experimental and, one suspects, little if any clinical evidence. Further, a misunderstanding of the nature of repression would appear to have been the cause of the cult of permissive rearing, so dominant at one time, particularly in the United States. It is likely that Freud himself would not have approved of this!

What is, on reflection, so depressing about much of the advice given at this time by writers of both schools is that so often dogmatic answers were given to what seem to us now to have been quite irrelevant questions and worries. Of course parents, being anxious to be good parents, have always worried about a child who, for example, is unkind to other children, but many of the worries of parents thirty or forty years ago concerned behaviour of children far too young to understand what was required of them, or the parental anxieties were focused on what we now know to be really non-issues, such as on the apparent importance of early toilet training, or the correct weaning time, or the prevention of thumb sucking (Wood, 1975). On reviewing the history of adult attitudes to children, the most interesting aspect lies in observing the move away from seeing children through adult eyes and from the standpoint of adult values, and in place of this notion a move towards understanding the individual child at various phases of his particular childhood. To this end we are at last learning not to ask irrelevant questions: for example, we no longer ask when to wean and toilet-train, for we know that it is the mother's attitude while handling her baby which really matters. Similarly, child psychologists cannot really advise in a general way whether it is better to discipline firmly or to be permissive: again, the importance lies in the quality of the relationship which exists between parent and child. We now know that the socialization process is not uni-directional, as Bell (1968) and others have pointed out, but that children affect our behaviour as much as we affect theirs; indeed, it is rather charming to reflect on the fact that most mothers probably imitate their babies more than babies imitate their mothers! We also know that the influence we exert on our children is subtle and difficult to identify and to measure.

Now we are no longer concerned to train children primarily to 'take their proper place in society', nor, in early childhood at least, to form good habits. However, most adults think it important that the children in their care should grow up being able to live happily with other people, respecting their rights and wishes, and also, when mature, to be able to use their gifts and abilities fully. We now realize that it is by meeting children's needs at various phases of their development that these aims can best be fulfilled. Pringle (1975) has written that children have four basic needs which are: for love and security, for praise and recognition, for responsibility and for new experiences. And she suggests that it is the ultimate responsibility not only of parents, but of the whole society, through its health, housing and social and educational institutions, to meet these needs.

However, although Pringle writes about what we now think we know children need, and how these needs may be met, does this knowledge represent the present-day attitude to children? However much social agencies may try to meet children's needs, the prime responsibility for doing this must in all normal circumstances remain with the parents. During the past two decades fundamental changes have taken place in society, the long-term effects of which we have hardly begun to understand. These major changes all involve a great increase

(1) in the divorce rate,
(2) in mothers going out to work and
(3) in television viewing, which disrupts family life.

Family life, at least as the middle-class family has experienced it for some decades, hardly seems to exist any more; and it is doubtful if it is possible for many parents, under present conditions, to exercise the 'helping mode', as de Mause suggests is the current child-rearing fashion. Indeed it is possible that a large proportion of our children have seldom been given *less* help of the kind which is of real importance to them than at the present time.

However, very many parents are still anxious to be good parents; they look to the expert for help, but now the experts will not help; they are themselves only too well aware of the complexities of the problems of child rearing and aware, too, of their own lack of reliable knowledge. They know of the many strands which form the human personality, and that no magic panacea exists for ensuring that one's child will grow up with the kind of balanced, responsible, happy personality one would wish him to have (chapter 8). Today's experts seem also to understand better than previous writers on child development that each child has unique qualities which make it impossible for any textbook to give hard-and-fast rules about rearing. In a way this attitude is comforting, for inexperienced parents can feel that, if there is no simple solution, then they cannot be blamed for not applying it; but it does seem to leave parents in a quandary.

Nevertheless, the encouragement given to thoughtful parents to trust their own feelings and do whatever appears right for any one individual child is now restoring to parents at least a measure of confidence in their own actions, which confidence had been so undermined for the previous generation of parents by the so-called experts in child rearing. Parents can also be assured that, among other things, they should retain some authority; that the occasional losses of temper will not do irreparable harm; and that they need not feel their floundering actions alone will determine a child's future personality. There is a notion abroad that 'we are all in this together'; that most parents seek to do the best for their children, but that everyone is fallible; and that in the last resort other factors influence personality apart from parental handling. What these other factors are we will examine in this book.

Further reading

MEAD, M. and M. WOLFENSTEIN, (eds.): *Childhood in contemporary cultures* (University of Chicago Press, 1955)
ARIES, P.: *Centuries of childhood* (Penguin Books, 1973)

CHAPTER TWO

The developing personality

What is personality?

This book is entitled *The Development of Personality and Behaviour in Children*. We are concerned to understand how human beings come to possess the personalities they have, and how this determines their behaviour. Personality and behaviour are difficult to differentiate: Eysenck (1952) indeed suggests that personality *is* behaviour. We can, however, differentiate between the *reasons* which determine, as far as we understand them, the kind of personality a child may develop, and *how* his behaviour changes as he gets older, reviewing the factors which influence this change.

The section on the development of behaviour deals ontogenically* with the way in which children, as they grow older, become normally more able to cope with the social, emotional and intellectual aspects of their lives. In this present section on personality we are concerned with what we mean by the term 'personality', with the way personality is studied by psychologists, with outlining methods of study, and with three theories of personality which have been particularly influential in child guidance and education.

When we talk about 'personality' we know that we generally mean by this how another person impinges on us. Is he pleasant or unpleasant? Does it make us happy and comfortable to be with him? Is he sincere or two-faced? And so on. We think basically of his *qualities* as a person, and of the peculiarly individual combinations of such qualities which makes each person unique. Although such qualities are highly personal they are also social, in that they manifest themselves in interaction with other people. Indeed, it has been suggested that personality is primarily a person's way of interacting with other people. Possibly Harsh and Schrickel's definition (1950) combines the personal and social aspects of personality in that they consider personality to be 'that which characterizes an individual and determines his unique adaptation to the environment'.

Philosophers have interested themselves for a very long time in the human personality. Plato, in his *Republic*, distinguished three aspects of the 'soul', which we might term today the intellect, the emotion and the will. Plato likened these three parts of the personality to the horses driven by a charioteer: the charioteer himself, who directs the horses, represents the intellect, and the horses represent the emotions and the

41

will, thus supplying the energy for personality functioning. Although by the term 'personality' we mean all the attributes of the integrated person in whom these three aspects are joined, man's intellectual qualities have been the subject of investigations independent of the remainder of the personality. It was because Binet (chapter 3) was so successful in empirically studying and quantifying the intelligence of children that psychologists were encouraged to study, and some to attempt to quantify, other personality characteristics.

The study of personality and theories of personality

The study of the human personality can take a number of forms, depending on the particular overriding interest of the investigator: one might study how the personality functions, that is, the *dynamics* of the personality; or one might be concerned with isolating and *describing* traits and characteristics which are universal to all humans and from which the structure of the human personality can be inferred and the constituents of this structure *measured* in individual people; or one might seek to elucidate the forces which *determine* the personality, that is, what factors — genetic or environmental — influence its development; again, one might be interested in finding how the human personality *develops* from birth to maturity, seeking to understand the changes which take place with increasing age and the *processes* which cause these changes to occur. Dynamics, description, measurement, determinants and development are all aspects of the study of the human personality. In this book we are primarily concerned with the development and the determinants of the personality, but if we are to understand these adequately we cannot separate them from description and dynamics.

There are two basic approaches to the study of the human personality, the idiographic and the nomothetic. The aim of the idiographic approach is to *understand* the unique qualities of one individual person; and studies carried out within the idiographic approach are focused on the individual. The aim of the nomothetic approach is to arrive at *universally applicable* laws which have relevance to the study of all personalities. This approach seeks to explain and predict human behaviour, and studies carried out within the nomothetic approach are focused on suitably selected statistical samples of the population. These two approaches to the study of the human personality have developed largely for historical and practical reasons. It is clear that whereas all men are unique, all men also have characteristics which they share with others; therefore, the study of any one individual person in depth and the study of common human characteristics are relevant to each other.

Usually researchers interested in this idiographic approach have used the *clinical* method whereby one researcher in a (normally) one-to-one relationship with a subject or client has been concerned to discover something about that one subject's behaviour. Researchers using the nomothetic approach have more usually employed the *experimental* method, where sample subjects of the required statistical population have been investigated on some specific aspect of functioning in a controlled situation.

In the study of developmental psychology we are primarily interested in four questions about child growth: *what* actually happens when a child grows physically and psychologically; *how* changes came about; *why* they occur and *when* they occur. We seek to describe the *changes*; we then try to understand the *processes* involved in the changes, then we seek to understand the *influences* which affect the changes and finally we try to fix the *period* when changes occur.

The value of developing psychological *theories*, and of paying such close attention to established theories, has in recent years been questioned. The reader interested in the philosophical problems involved in the formulation of psychological theories is recommended to consult Westland (1978) where the various crises which psychology at present faces are discussed. However, Bannister and Fransella (1971) make the point that a theory is 'a working tool and not a sacrosant creed — it is to be used, developed and ultimately replaced. It should provoke us to ask new questions while providing an orderly framework within which to seek new answers. It should enable us to transcend the obvious' (page 9). A theory, therefore, has heuristic value, and a good theory is fruitful, generating much research, even if such research eventually destroys the theory from which it sprang.

In this chapter three theories of personality will be discussed: the Freudian psychoanalytic theory; the cognitive–developmental theory, with particular reference to Piaget's theory of child development; and the social-learning theory. Freud's theory is considered in some detail, for his theory has probably had the biggest impact on child guidance work.

The other two theories have also had important influences, but they will be described in somewhat less detail than Freudian theory, for their influence on specific areas of development will be covered more fully in later chapters. As Piaget's interests lie mainly, though by no means exclusively, in describing the child's cognitive growth, his description of cognitive development is given in chapter 4. Mention of his work is also made in chapters 5 and 6, when the child's moral growth and the importance of play are discussed. Similarly, various forms of learning are considered in the chapter on learning (chapter 4). Freud's contribution to the development of moral feeling and his ideas regarding play are also described in the relevant chapters.

Freudian psychoanalytic theory of personality development

Freud, who lived from 1856 until 1939, was a medical doctor who specialized in the treatment of nervous diseases. He worked for a time in France, under Charcot, where he was introduced to the use of hypnosis as a possible method of curing hysterical symptoms which manifested themselves as apparent physical illnesses. On return to Vienna he at first collaborated with his friend Breuer and together they began to use the 'talking cure', in which patients talked quite freely, as if talking to themselves; but how this method helped in their cure is not relevant. What concerns us here are the apparent discoveries Freud made about the dynamics, development and structure of the normal personality through his association with many patients over a period of over fifty years.

The structure of the personality

Freud's view was that man was a biological, psychological, and social or moral being. As a biological being he has a body, like other animals, whose needs and drives require satisfying; as a psychological being he is self-conscious, he has to maintain a balance between the needs of his body and the demands of society, and he has to learn also to cope realistically with objects and other people in the world; as a social and moral being he has to develop a conscience and to adopt the ideals of his society. Freud named these three aspects of the personality the 'id', the 'ego' and the 'superego'* respectively. These are, of course, 'hypothetical constructs', that is, they are not actual physical properties of the brain or of the nervous system, as some people have erroneously interpreted them to be, but names given to observed functionings of the personality, and there is no sharp division between them, as there would be if they were separate entities.

Freud suggested that only the id is present at birth, containing all the energy for the functioning of the personality, and that during the child's first years of life the ego and superego develop. The id and the superego influence behaviour entirely on an unconscious level — that is, the energy invested in them affects behaviour and the way the personality develops, but one is unaware of the forces which prompt one's behaviour. Only behaviour motivated by the ego is consciously directed, and then not always entirely so.

Freud thought of man as a biological organism, whose social and psychological self develops from the way physiological needs are met, or fail to be met, by the environment. Freud considered it probable that a young infant is conscious of little other than his bodily needs, and that he is also not very easily able to differentiate between himself and the rest of the world around him. He thought of the personality as a homeostatic* organism which seeks constantly, through the operation of drives, to return to a state of satisfaction, a state of non-tension. Thus, if an infant is hungry or thirsty, he desires food or liquid to relieve the tension. However, the infant has no means of obtaining what he needs; he has no conception of a 'world out there' from which objects are brought which will reduce bodily tensions. Freud, therefore, postulated that the child's first use of mental processes is to produce, in fantasy, imaginings of the tension release he seeks, and that this to an extent, though by no means adequately, at least temporarily reduces the tension experienced. The 'primary process', which is the name given to the use of fantasy for tension reduction, serves the 'pleasure principle', which is the overriding need of the organism to experience 'pleasure', or, in this context, non-tension; but the primary process has in time to give way to the 'secondary process'. The secondary process represents the thinking and problem-solving ability of the personality. As the human personality develops it must learn to obtain *true* satisfaction, not the vicarious and inadequate satisfactions obtained through fantasy. Thus the secondary process serves the 'reality principle'. In order that the child can give up, at least to an extent, the use of the primary process the ego must develop; that is, a part of the energy of the id must split off and must become conscious, and must be in touch with reality, the actual world with which all normal humans have to interact. This is, however, a gradual process and is never fully completed, for fantasy and dreams remain as part of the life of all human beings.

The superego is formed from the ego and it represents the social and moral part of the personality. How it is formed we will consider later; it is made up of the conscience*, which is aware of the kinds of acts which are disapproved, and of the ego-ideal*, which knows what is approved by parents and society.

The id, having no contact with reality and influencing the personality on an unconscious level, seeks immediate gratification of needs. The small child and the immature adult are governed more by the demands of the id than by the realistic ego, or the controlling superego. The ego is able to postpone action which will bring tension release if such a postponement is in the long-term interest of the personality as a whole. The superego is seen as an internalized authority which punishes through inducing feelings of guilt, and which produces such feeling even at the mere prospect of behaving in a disapproved manner (chapter 5).

The inevitable interaction of these three aspects of the personality is dependent on personal constitutional factors, and also on the way in which a child experiences life in reality and in fantasy, and particularly on how psycho-sexual development in the first five years of life takes place.

Psycho-sexual development

The account given here of psycho-sexual development is somewhat broader than a straightforward Freudian view would permit; it is influenced by Erikson's theories (1950). Psycho-sexual development is viewed by many neo-Freudians*, especially Erikson, as more than a mere account of how the sexual drive expresses itself before maturity; it is seen as part of a total, interacting process, which includes the child's developing sensori-motor* apparatus, and his enlarging social experiences.

Freud suggested that the development of the personality can best be understood if one thinks of the human person as motivated by drives which seek satisfaction through expression in the external world; and of the external world in its turn making demands upon the individual. Man is, according to Freud, born with a drive both to preserve his own life and to propagate the human species. These are the life 'instincts', as the term has been translated from the German, or more accurately, the life 'drives'. Freud's dual instinct theory holds that two drives motivate the psyche*: the life drive (or 'libido', as it is called) and the aggressive drive.

Though there is no unified, completely accepted theory of aggression in psychoanalysis (Rosen, 1969), the idea that there is an innate aggressive drive which seeks expression seems to be accepted by most psychoanalytic writers. Freud postulated that although the sexual aspect of the life drives is not able to express itself directly until maturity is reached, it is nevertheless present at birth. All other bodily functions, such as breathing, excreting, eating, although affected by learning, can be expressed directly from birth. Only the sexual drive has to await maturation for consummatory activity, but meanwhile it seeks expression through other drives, through their functioning, and through the bodily parts by the use of which they express themselves.

By the term 'sexual' Freud did not mean only genital sexuality, but pleasurable experiences and feelings which are aroused through stimulation of various bodily parts or 'erogenous zones', as they are called; and Freud connected the experiences which the child has in this way through his body with the child's social, emotional and even his cognitive experiences. Thus for the very small baby his mouth, or 'oral zone', is of outstanding importance.

Not only is food one of the child's primary concerns in early infancy, but because his various perceptual and motor mechanisms are not yet very well developed, his mouth seems to be the most important part of his body for the purposes of interacting with the world. Recent work has indicated that the newborn baby has a much more highly developed perceptual mechanism than had previously been recognized, but this does not necessarily invalidate the importance of the oral region in early infancy. The small infant will investigate objects by putting them in his mouth, and he also *takes in* much experience visually and by touch at this stage, just as he takes in food. His contact with his mother is through nearness to her and, very frequently, through a simultaneous feeding experience. The pleasurable or frustrating sensations which he experiences orally are an outlet for, or a damming of, his sexual drive, and they link him emotionally to the people who most frequently give him these experiences. His aggressive drive is expressed at this stage through biting and chewing. He also begins to be aware of himself as a being which is separate from other people and objects. De Monchaux (1957) has suggested that the child's first experience of his own drive processes as externalized in behaviour is when he has contact with his own body; thus sucking his thumb is a substitute activity for sucking at the teat or nipple, but it is also one step removed from, and nearer to reality than, a fantasy image of the teat or nipple. De Monchaux says that the child transfers to his relationships with other people the experience he has, and the fantasies which are evoked, through interaction with his own body. This concept of the influence on development *of the self* through interaction *with itself* has been evoked to contribute to an understanding of neuro-biological development (Roberts and Matthysse, 1970).

When later the baby is able to control his bowel movements he not only experiences satisfactions or frustrations related to these functions, according to how he is being trained, but he can use his new power to please, trouble, or annoy other people. Now he is much more aware of his relationship with other people and how he can influence these relationships. At this time — between about eighteen months and three-and-a-half years — his musculature is getting stronger, he is getting better at manipulating objects, just as he is learning to manipulate people; he is easily roused to pleasure or anger, is quickly aggressive, and is both possessive and generous in turn. An example of these developments is shown in his withholding or expelling his bowel motions at will. The fusion of aggressive and libidinal drives can be seen clearly at this stage.

By the time a child reaches the next psycho-sexual stage at about three-and-a-half years of age he is deeply involved emotionally with those close to him. Now the phallic region of his body is the erogenous zone and the boy, according to Freud, experiences jealousy of his father, because the child's love for his mother has taken on a possessive and sexual nature, though these feelings are not, Freud said, consciously understood. Again the aggressive drive can be seen in the child's dominant and assertive behaviour at this age. This is the time too when, in addition to these intense emotions of love, rivalry and jealousy, he is intrusively curious. Freud considered that such feelings of love and jealousy were a normal part of growing up in ordinary families, and he named these experiences the 'Oedipal situation' (or Oedipus complex*). In Greek mythology, Oedipus, who did not know his natural parents, was destined to kill his father and, later, unknowingly to marry his mother.

At this stage the child's awareness of his relationship with others emotionally close to him is fused to his phallic state* of development to lead to intensely emotional feelings, which, however, have to be repressed, for all societies frown on incestuous acts and feelings. It is suggested by Freud that the superego develops not only from learning about approved and disapproved behaviour (chapter 5), but through the repression of the Oedipus complex. The child, unconsciously aware of the impossibility in normal circumstances of having his feelings reciprocated, gives up the struggle and identifies* with the parent of the same sex. In this way he becomes like the envied parent, and so, vicariously, receives what he desires. Through identification he assumes the values and norms of the same-sexed parent, and this results in a boy becoming manlike and at the same time accepting the standards and ideals which are considered right for the men in his society. When this occurs at about five years of age the Oedipus complex is repressed and the child enters the 'latency'* period, during which the expression of his sexual drive, according to Freud, remains latent until adolescence.

The ethologists (students of animal behaviour) have observed that there are 'critical' periods* (chapters 3 and 4) during which animals must have certain experiences in early life, in order that they develop appropriate behaviour patterns later in life, and similarly Freud's psycho-sexual periods are considered to be 'critical'. He suggested that there is an optimum period of time for each child at each of the psycho-sexual stages, and that if this period is unnaturally shortened or prolonged, then this interferes with experiences at the next stages of development. The term 'fixation' is used to indicate when a child either has had too satisfying an experience, or, alternatively, a frustrating experience at one of the psycho-sexual stages. Whiting and Child (1953) have termed these fixation periods positive and negative respectively. If the experiences at a particular period have been very satisfying there is a reluctance on the part of the child to move on to the next stage; if the experience has been frustrating then a change to the next stage is anxiety-provoking. Such fixations express themselves in later, often even in adult, behaviour, indicating either the unsatisfied needs of early childhood, or a desire to recapture a very satisfying experience.

Because the sexual drive expresses itself through the activities of the other, life-preserving drives, satisfactions other than the release from tensions which arise from immediate bodily needs are obtained. Thus, for the baby, sucking brings relief from hunger, but it also brings pleasurable sensations through the stimulation of the lips. Freud suggested that the development of the personality depends to a large extent on how the psychic energy invested in such pleasurable activity is 'displaced'* from the original 'object'*, in this example the nipple, to other substitute objects. Thumbsucking is often the baby's first displacement activity. Two influences govern how such displacement takes place as the infant grows into a child: one is that tension release through the original object only cannot always be achieved just when it is needed, and the other is that society expects behaviour to change as children grow up, so that displacement activities which were suitable for the infant are unsuitable both for the child and for the adult. Thus these two pressures on the developing personality to find suitable displacement objects result in the resemblance which successive displacement objects have to the original becoming less and less. In the final analysis the ego has to make its selection from those displacement objects which are available, and the use of which is also a compromise between the demands of the id, the superego and reality. Because displacement is a substitute activity and not, therefore, wholly satisfying, Freud suggested that there is always a residue of undischarged tension in the personality. This energy is used for many activities in which man is engaged, and which have little or nothing directly to do either with the maintenance of homeostatic* physiological functioning, or with the expression of the sexual drive. Indeed, it is through displacement that, according to Freud, the development of human civilization has been made possible; he gave the name 'sublimation' to displacement when it takes the form of artistic, intellectual, humanitarian or other activities of a cultural kind.

In normal development the aggressive and libidinal drives act together, and for normal growth to take place the aggressive drive must be externalized, although the prohibitions which are placed by parents and society on aggressive behaviour require that these externalized expressions be limited or displaced. However, in addition to having to deal with aggressive feelings, the ego has constantly to keep a balance between the demands of the id, the superego and reality. Indeed, Freud considered that internal pressures of this kind were more difficult to overcome than frustrations provided by the environment. One means of externalizing aggression and coping with internal frustrations is through the use of one of the defence mechanisms. Excessive or extreme use of mechanisms of defence is abnormal and their use distorts reality. However, all persons have at times to cope with anxieties, and most normal people employ such defences from time to time to alleviate anxiety.

We may, for example, ease the pressures on the ego by repressing sexual promptings from the id; or project the cause of some anxiety on to an external factor; or disguise unsuitable or unbearable feelings by behaving as if, in fact, we had opposite feelings — substituting, for example, love for hate. Whichever of the mechanisms of defence we use, they are all means of dealing with anxiety and threats to the personality, and are means too of externalizing the aggressive drive in a (usually) acceptable manner. According to the defences which we quite unconsciously adopt, so our behaviour is determined and our personality expressed.

Freud, then, suggested that how the personality is formed is in part due to how the child experiences life at the various psycho-sexual stages; how he deals in fantasy with the emotions which are, so Freud suggested, experienced so intensely during the first five years of life; how displacement takes place, and what mechanisms of defence are used. All the operations of the infantile sexual stages are, of course, experienced at an unconscious id level, but they influence personality and behaviour nevertheless. So much of what is experienced in life is not consciously recollected, but has its influence on emotional reactions, which show themselves in behaviour which cannot be explained at a conscious level. One has to remember, however, that according to Freud the formation of the personality is only in part due to such experiences, for he recognized biological differences between people which influence their development; thus one person's personality will develop normally following experiences which might cause a breakdown in another person.

Freudian theory of the development of the personality is much fuller and more detailed than this brief account can indicate; the main features, however, in relation to personality development are: a recognition of the basic biological nature of man, and a description of how the human infant, which a non-Christian view can credit at birth with little more than the basic drive to ensure continuity of life, becomes a civilized adult. Freud's analysis of the processes by which a small baby is changed from a 'polymorphous pervert' to a (not infrequently) rational, moral, controlled, creative, loving adult person was the first attempt to account for this process, and in many respects it is a very brilliant account. He showed understanding of the emotions which are experienced by small children as they develop within the family circle, and the feelings which are evoked by their bodily needs expressed within a framework of social relationships. How tensions are created and how they are eased, and the manner in which the personality is shaped, are all fully described in his *Two Short Accounts of Psycho-Analysis* (1910).

Although Freud himself wrote comparatively little about how children should be reared, some of his followers have made deductions from his theories, particularly in relation to 'permissive' rearing, with which he himself would most likely not have been in agreement. The 'permissive cult' seemed to spring from the idea that repressions are harmful, but Freud specifically said (1910) that 'disagreements . . . between reality and the id are unavoidable'. It seems from his writings that he might have advocated that children should not be expected to exhibit self-controlled behaviour which is inappropriate for their age, or, to put it in psychoanalytic terms, when the ego is undeveloped and powerless. That is why so much emphasis has been laid by psychoanalytic writers of baby books on a gentle and gradual weaning and toilet-training process, as opposed to the firm, habit-training regime advocated by followers of Truby King (chapter 1). However, allowing the baby to progress at his own pace in relation to these matters is different from allowing the older child unbridled licence. We discuss in chapter 8 the relationship between parental handling, parental personality, and the development of behaviour in children.

Freud's theories about child development were derived from his analysis of adult patients, but since his death much observational work with children has confirmed many of his ideas. Observation of children leaves little doubt that the idea that sexuality is present in infancy and childhood is a correct one, though some psychologists dispute the conclusions about personality development which Freud drew from this observation. Neo-Freudians, too, suggest that possibly he placed too little emphasis on the influence of conscious drives. Erikson has placed stress on the growth of the ego; and within the eight stages of ego development which he outlines he gives due weight to the latency period, which held such little interest for Freud. He also carries his 'eight stages of man' on from adolescence to maturity. His scheme relates critical periods, in which the first five years correspond to Freud's psycho-sexual stages, with ego qualities 'by which the individual demonstrates that his ego at a given stage is strong enough to integrate the timetable of the organism with the structure of the social institutions' (1950). Thus he relates the oral, anal and phallic stages with the predominant development of 'basic trust', 'autonomy' and 'initiative' respectively; and during the latency period and in adolescence, young adulthood, adulthood and maturity the 'ego qualities' of 'industry', 'identity', 'intimacy', 'generativity' and 'ego integrity' should develop respectively. ('Generativity' means the 'establishing and guiding (of) the next generation'.)

White (1960) considers that Freud's explanations of development are inadequate, and that an adequate developmental theory must account for a child's developing social manipulative skills, and his growing cognitive and linguistic abilities. White argues for motivating forces which are *not* biological drives, and which energize the *persistence* with which children seek to master their environment in a number of ways. He terms this 'effectance motivation': the child's efficiencies and inefficiencies form his general competence to deal with the world, and it is this strong desire to be able to deal competently with his environment that, says White, motivates the child's many activities.

Attempts have been made with varying success to verify some psychoanalytic ideas experimentally, both with children and with animals, though it is by no means easy to test clinically derived ideas in an experimental setting. Work in this field has been reviewed both by Sears (1944) and Farrell (1951). Kline (1972) has produced the most exhaustive review to date of the testing of Freudian theory, and his evaluations have in their turn been criticized by Eysenck (1972) and Eysenck and Wilson (1976) and answered by Kline (1973).

It is easy to criticize many aspects of Freud's work, but the fact remains that even if some of his theories have, in the light of further experience, to be modified, even if others have to be radically recast, and some even abandoned, he has nevertheless provided a rich insight into the functioning of the human psyche*. His influence on many aspects of human life — literature, art, education, child rearing, child guidance, psychiatry and penology — has been immense. It seems important, therefore, that persons who are going to be in close touch with the developing child should have some acquaintance with his theories, and this is the reason for the outline of his work given in this chapter.

Social-learning theory: general consideration

J. B. Watson (1925), who can be said to have founded the Behaviourist school of psychology, laid the foundation for learning theory, though its philosophical basis can be found with the eighteenth-century associationist philosophers, and its experimental groundwork rests on Pavlov's work on conditioning (chapter 4).

Watson held the view that:

(1) human behaviour could be explained by associationist principles — i.e. learning by conditioning;

(2) genetic factors as determinants of behaviour counted for very little (though this was not Pavlov's view); and

(3) only observable behaviour was suitable for psychological study, so that no account must be taken of such concepts as conscious-

ness, will, desire, goals, etc., in explaining behaviour and the development of personality.

Modern learning theorists who interest themselves in child development neglect rather than discount genetic factors in their preoccupation with discovering how man learns, and they are Behaviourist in a methodological rather than in a philosophical sense. Like Watson they pay little attention to such factors as fantasy and the influence of unconscious drives and memories on the functioning and on the development of the personality. Unlike Piaget and Freud they are not concerned with the *total* development of the child, but rather aim at elucidating specific areas of development and behaviour which can be made the subject of controlled experimentation and observation. They are interested in the extent to which the child's development into an adult acceptable to his culture is dependent on learning; in how this learning occurs; and in the terms in which this learning procedure might be explained (Hindley, 1957).

Learning theorists have made, and are still making, the following major contributions in the field of child development: they attempt to account for

(1) how the child's sensori-motor apparatus develops;

(2) how perceptual learning takes place; and

(3) how motivated behaviour occurs.

Through the social-learning theories they show

(4) how the development of such traits as dependency and aggression, and the development of conscience and anxiety, can be understood; and

(5) they give an account of such learning processes as imitation and identification.

The importance to human learning of the two forms of conditioning, so-called 'classical' and 'instrumental' conditioning, are described in chapter 4. In that chapter too imitation and identification are discussed in some detail. In the present chapter we consider the theoretical aspects of the two forms of conditioning, and their relevance to the social-learning theory of personality development.

'Classical' conditioning takes place whenever a natural (unconditioned) stimulus, such as the sight or smell of food, is paired in suitable conditions, including appropriate timing, with a neutral stimulus. Pavlov, the discoverer of classical conditioning procedures, caused a bell to be rung about the same time as he presented food powder to his experimental dogs. In due course the neutral stimulus (the bell), called the conditioned stimulus, or CS, by itself evoked more or less the same response from the experimental animal as the original, the unconditioned stimulus, the UCS. The dog's response to the UCS, in Pavlov's experiments, was to salivate, and once he had been thus conditioned he salivated *for some time at least* whenever the bell was rung by itself — that is, without it being further paired with the presentation of food powder.

It is usually difficult to condition animals unless the UCS, the natural stimulus, meets some need. The animal learns to associate the need-reducing stimulus with the neutral (conditioned) stimulus, and to respond to the latter as if it were the former. For this reason 'classical' conditioning has been called stimulus-substitution learning.

The simultaneous appearance on many occasions of the mother's face and the baby's feeding bottle (the CS and UCS respectively) causes the baby after a time to respond in the same way to the appearance of the mother's face only as he previously responded to the appearance of the bottle: he will make excited and pleased movements and noises.

In an 'instrumental' conditioning set-up an action performed by an animal in a particular situation will be at once rewarded (or 'reinforced' as learning theorists prefer to say) by the experimenter if the particular action is one the experimenter wishes to encourage the animal to repeat. The animal thus learns that his particular response in a particular situation will bring a 'satisfying consequence', and will be more likely to make that kind of response in the same situation another time than to perform other kinds of action. Thus by a process of reinforcing approved actions, and ignoring unnecessary or disapproved actions, the experimenter is able to train animals to perform complex behavioural patterns. (The relevance of instrumental conditioning to a child's learning is discussed in chapter 4.)

When in the presence of his mother the baby makes sounds which approximate to 'Mamma', and when he learns that this causes her to be pleased with him, which is the 'satisfying consequence', he is more likely frequently to repeat 'Mamma' than to make other sounds in her presence (at least for a period of time). The 'satisfying consequence' is normally termed 'positive reinforcement', which is approximately synonymous with 'reward'. 'Negative reinforcement' is punishment for an act.

Learning theorists have sought to clarify the motives for the activity of all organisms, including man. They have postulated 'drives', at least some of which are internal states, such as hunger or some hormonal condition, which lead to behaviour which reduces physical need and is of survival value. Although there are differences of view among experimenters and theorists, many learning theorists hold the view that such drives are innate; that they energize behaviour (that is, they supply the *power* to act); but that the *goal* towards which the energy is directed is learned. However, observation of babies does indicate that drives appear also to have an element of 'goal-directedness' (Vernon, M. D., 1969).

When carrying out conditioning experiments with an animal it is found that a hungry animal will usually pay more attention to food stimuli than to other stimuli. In such a state of deprivation positive reinforcement will be more effective for learning than in circumstances where there is no need for food, and, therefore, no drive to satisfy that need. However, once a *response habit* has been established an animal is usually not very selective; a rat which has been taught to run a maze while hungry will still run the maze, even though it is thirsty and not hungry; that is, it will respond to the stimulus offered by the presence of the maze.

This ability to adapt a habit is particularly useful to humans, who must be able to change their ways of responding to the many and various demands made by their environment, and such adaptation is facilitated by the use of language. According to learning theory, simple habits which are formed through conditioning are built up into ever more complex behaviour patterns.

However, one may ask how such theories can explain the many human activities involving *inter alia* cultural, educational and humanitarian types of behaviour which are neither need-reducing in the physiological sense nor of survival value. The principle of learning by association is again invoked as an explanatory concept, though this is not too happy an explanation since in due course, without further association with the 'primary' (need-reducing) drive, the associated 'secondary' drive is likely to cease to be active (to 'extinguish'); but this does not always happen in real life, such secondary drives continuing to motivate behaviour after the pairing of the two stimuli has long ceased. One must postulate, therefore, that the secondary drive itself seeks satisfaction through the achieving of *its own* goal. Thus drives are not merely goal-directing energizers, but are themselves subject to learning. In other words, *we learn to have fresh needs*, which probably arise through association with primary needs, but which, as it were, take on a life of their own.

Learning theory is immensely complex and involves many concepts which have been tested experimentally, mostly with animal subjects; only the barest outline of the relevant theoretical and experimental aspects of learning have been given here. (In chapter 4 learning is discussed in greater detail from the practical point of view.)

Social-learning theory applied to child development

A group of American students of child development, including Mowrer, Sears, Miller, Dollard and Bandura, has attempted to show how the socialization process, the social learning of the child, can be explained in terms of learning theory. Fundamentally they state that the child's dependency on those who succour him in infancy can be shown to be the basis of all social learning. By a process of association the presence of those who minister to the baby's needs brings him a sense of comfort, and hence he becomes dependent on them and their absence will make him anxious. This production of anxiety is, according to the theory, an essential part of social learning, for the child learns by experiencing anxiety what is approved behaviour and what is disapproved behaviour; he learns to associate the satisfying of his needs with the presence of those who look after him, and their disapproval threatens that presence and makes him anxious. In due course, and in addition to his mother's mere presence, other more subtle signs, such as her facial expression, her tone of voice, or her handling of him, and other stimuli, will be interpreted by the baby to indicate approval or disapproval, and so produce corresponding feelings of happiness or anxiety in him.

The mother's approval is positively reinforcing for acts which she wishes to encourage, and through her disapproval (negative reinforcement) undesirable acts can be 'stamped out'. This dependency on the parents makes children susceptible to taking their parents as models for behaviour. The effect of children modelling themselves on the behaviour of their parents 'generalizes' to other adults, such as teachers and persons with power.

It is difficult to account for aggressive behaviour, although the kinds of circumstances in which it is likely to occur are established (chapter 7). Often it arises as a result of frustration, but this is not an inevitable cause. Social-learning theory suggests that aggression springs from certain kinds of 'signal' behaviour displayed by the baby — for example, the asking for relief from distress of some kind — this signal being answered by maternal attention. The particular signal which is the precursor of aggressive behaviour, however, is an expression of anger by the baby, possibly arising from frustration or some other kind of distress. When the mother relieves the frustration her attentions reinforce the baby's angry behaviour, and so it is likely to be repeated. There are two further consequences of this happening: the first is that the mother's manner, because of the angry behaviour through which the baby obtained her attention, is likely to be hostile or irritable or pained, and if this happens her behaviour will be associated by the baby with release from his own distress and/or frustration. Thus he will indirectly obtain pleasure from another person's pain or discomfort, and hence, even without his being frustrated, through a process of association (secondary reinforcement) his aggressive behaviour will in due course come to have a rewarding value in itself. The second consequence is that the baby will experience conflict. His angry behaviour will be both positively reinforced, as described above, and also punished because of his dislike of the disapproval his mother will have shown.

If the child seeks to inhibit his anger because it brings punishment as well as his mother's desired attention, he will add to his frustration, and this can produce further aggression.

The development of conscience

(In chapter 5 the nature of moral growth is discussed, and in chapter 8 we review the various parental rearing habits which influence the development of moral behaviour. Here we will discuss briefly how, according to social-learning theory, conscience is developed.)

The term 'conscience' usually includes feelings of guilt arising from an actual or contemplated disapproved act, which implies that resistance to temptation is an important component of a conscience. It is suggested by social-learning theory that when a child is reproved for an act he will inhibit that act. At first this reproval restrains him in his parents' presence. Then he restrains himself, often by first actually saying 'No' to himself. This self-restraint is considered to arise because the tempting thought, evoking recollections of parental disapproval, brings anxiety; this anxiety is due to the child's dependence on his parents, and their disapproval threatens the satisfying of his needs because these are brought about by his parents' presence (chapter 5). In this way parental disapproval is considered to be internalized, so that feelings of guilt arise even at the *thought* of behaving in a disapproved manner.

The reasons why parental disapproval, particularly when manifested just as a child is *about to commit* a 'naughty' act, is better internalized than when the child is physically punished can be summarized as follows:

(1) The inhibiting of actions in the parents' presence is associated with the tempting thought and also with the anxiety evoked by the temptation, so that the anxiety is likely to be evoked by tempting thoughts on some similar occasion later, even when the parents are not present; this, being associated with the previous inhibition of action, will probably result in the child desisting from doing what is disapproved.

(2) If the child is punished *after* he has given way to temptation, then he will associate the satisfied feeling which follows the disapproved but tempting act with the performing of such an act, and it will thus be reinforced. This punishment, coming after the immediate feelings of pleasure experienced by doing something enjoyable but forbidden, is thus not as effective as it might otherwise be. The child will still feel *anxiety* as he gives way to temptation, but inhibition to act will take longer to establish because the initial reinforcing of the disapproved act through the

immediate satisfaction experienced by doing it has first to be overcome.

Much experimental work with children has been carried out in an attempt to elucidate different aspects of moral growth (chapter 5). It is clear from much of this work that, for example, conscience development, guilt feelings, dependency needs, achievement need, etc., are in part at least independent concepts, and that the way they combine together varies from person to person.

Although social-learning theory is constantly being revised in the light of new experimental evidence, much of the theory is not based on experimental work *with children*, but is hypothetical, in that deductions about causes of child behaviour are made from what has been established about learning without it really being known whether such hypothetical deductions operate in actually forming the described behaviour. Learning theorists are concerned to be rigorous in their experimental and observational work, and a great deal of their short-term work on imitation is highly relevant to child rearing; yet there have been few long-term studies which directly relate actual child-rearing practices to social-learning theory. In a paradoxical way short-term social-learning research has certainly contributed to our knowledge of what kind of rearing methods are effective, but it has not enhanced the theory itself very much.

Nevertheless, social-learning theorists always attempt to base their theories of child development on empirical foundations, and they aim at the objective study of the child. Undoubtedly they have contributed, and are still contributing, very greatly to our knowledge of how children become social beings.

Cognitive–developmental theory, particularly the theory of Jean Piaget

The events of the world occur, and people and objects exist, but the human organism has only indirect access to events and people/objects through its perceptual mechanism. In order, therefore, for the world to be understood an *interpretation* has to be made of what is perceived. Although all humans at times *respond* to stimuli in their environment, the cognitive–developmental theorists stress that the child largely *constructs* his own inner reality from the objective external reality mediated by his senses. Thus, according to this theory, the child's main characteristic is that he is a *thinker* (hence the name of the theory) who, to a large extent, *selects* the stimuli to which he will respond. *How* he responds will be influenced by mediating mental structures which process the information which his senses give him. The drive to make an inner construction of the world, which is another way of talking about learning or understanding, does not, according to cognitive–developmental theory, require any kind of reinforcement, because interest is activated by the mere 'newness' of an experience, and it is only necessary for an infant or child to be introduced (exposed) to a new stimulus to enable him to attend to this stimulus, and make an inner construction of it. In addition, as is described more fully on pages 60f, cognitive–developmental theorists consider that it is necessary for students of any developing organism to understand the relationship between the environment which provides perceptual data and the developing organism. One aspect of this relationship is that the developing organism, as it matures, continually changes its manner of structuring the world. Thus one of the major aims of these theorists is to study the *processes* whereby this restructuring occurs.

Piaget was the first person systematically to investigate children's thought processes and to chart their development in detail from infancy to early adolescence. In doing this he produced a most valuable body of knowledge, not only about child thought processes, but also about children's moral development, their language learning, their ideas about causality, and other related matters. During the past ten years, however, many of the interpretations which Piaget himself gave to his findings have been revised by other psychologists, but this does not mean that Piaget's findings themselves are completely in dispute. It is for this reason, and because his influence has been so great, that his basic discoveries are presented in this chapter. At the end of this section, a reinterpretation will be given which many psychologists feel must now be made regarding the significance of his work.

Piaget's ideas about child development will be considered in the present chapter from a theoretical viewpoint only, because in chapter 4 we discuss in detail the actual developmental processes which take place in relation to the child's cognitive growth according to Piaget's theory. His findings about the importance of play, about the child's moral development and the child's ability to use language are considered in chapters 6, 5 and 4 respectively.

Jean Piaget, who was born in 1896, has concerned himself primarily with investigating the development of the child's cognitive growth, and with his perceptual development, though Piaget has found that these cannot be studied in isolation; the manner in which the child's mental powers develop influences his changing ideas about the world, his notions of morality and causality, and his use of language. Piaget is interested in changes which take place during development in the child's perception and understanding of the world around him. It is not a question of a small child merely *knowing less* than an adult, but rather that his perception and understanding of the world are, according to Piaget, *qualitatively* different from that of older children and of adults.

Whereas Freud used the clinical method to make discoveries about the nature of personality development and functioning, and the learning theorists use experimental techniques, Piaget varies his methods according to the particular aspect of development which he is studying. Normally he gives children a task to do and then asks them questions about the task; according to the responses he obtains he frames the next task and the next question, and so on.

Piaget, in addition to being a psychologist, is also a biologist, and he has interests in mathematics, logic, physics and philosophy; terms from these disciplines are used extensively in his descriptions of child development. However, his work has primarily a biological and philosophical, as well as a psychological, basis, in that he is concerned with the way a child comes to obtain knowledge of the real world. How man acquires, structures and interprets knowledge about the world has been a problem of philosophical speculation for a considerable time. Piaget has aimed to discover the processes which enable a child to develop ideas about time, space, mathematics and logic. How does 'logical necessity' emerge in the child's mind? How do concepts about the permanence of objects and the conservation of quantities develop? Piaget himself (1968a) gives an example of the kind of problem which has to be explained: if A equals B, and B equals C, the small child cannot be sure that A equals C, whereas the older child of seven or so is in little doubt, and for the child of eleven and over it is a self-evident truth. Yet how does this ability to understand come about? 'Genetic epistemology' is the term Piaget uses to denote his basic investigation into how the knowledge of what is real and logical about the world develops.

Since Chomsky in 1957 first discussed his ideas about the possibly innate nature of human language ability, the question of how one is to account for the *acquisition* of knowledge by human beings has again become of particular interest. How do children obtain a knowledge and understanding of the world? This question was first discussed by Plato, and has been much debated by philosophers since, but Chomsky's ideas in relation to a child's acquisition of language (chapter 4) and Piaget's theories regarding intellectual development (chapters 3 and 4) have brought about a reconsideration of man's acquisition of knowledge about the world which can now take into consideration experimental and observational work done with children. Hamlyn (1978) puts forward three alternative views about this:

(1) that all knowledge is derived from experience only — what Piaget has called 'genesis without structure';

(2) that experience is the catalyst for an automatic unfolding of what is already innately there — a kind of Platonic idea that

through experience we are reminded of what we already
know — 'structure without genesis'; and

(3) the Chomskyan view that 'there must be something that is capable of structuring the "information" that the child receives, a set of "hypotheses" which the child can apply to the data so as to construct for himself the rules that he must follow (in language use)' (Hamlyn, page 24 — 'genesis with structure').

Though this latter interpretation of Chomsky's ideas relates to language use, Hamlyn suggests that these ideas clearly can also relate to the acquisition of other forms of knowledge. The philosopher Kant has written (Hamlyn, page 37) that 'while all knowledge may come *through* experience it does not necessarily come *from* experience' (my italics). What this means is that whereas experience is mostly the occasion for our *coming* to know the world it does not follow that the knowledge we have has come *entirely* from experience. It is as if experience in life provides a vehicle through which knowledge is acquired, but experiences have to be made sense of, have to be structured. It is, of course, difficult to be explicit about the nature of what it is, within each developing child, that is capable of structuring experience so that the child can make sense of the world. It would be out of place here to enter into a complex philosophical argument about the nature of this 'something', but it is clear that in interpreting experiences in life, the biological nature of man must stand in relationship to the environment in which he functions, and that both of these must interact with one another in a specific manner to allow for the constant changes which take place during man's long childhood period. By the 'biological nature of man' I mean *in this context* that he is an organism with a very high capability of processing complex information. This ability must be related to the environment from which the information emanates; and because of man's long period of maturation one must assume that there are changes during his development which enable the processing of information to take place with ever-increasing efficiency as development takes place.

When one tries to relate all this to the child's intellectual development one can bring in the notion of homeorhesis*. Just as homeostasis refers to the internal regulation of a system, whether natural or mechanical, by which a necessary balance is maintained with the organism for efficient functioning (e.g. thirst will normally indicate to a living organism that it is necessary to take in more water, and when this has been done the feeling of thirst will disappear), so homeorhesis* is the system by which, within a dynamic organism, a steady *progressive development* is preserved while the organism is interacting with its environment. The assumption is that a maturing organism which is in interaction with the environment must be in equilibrium with this environment, but this can only be so if there is a system which regulates the interaction between this internally changing organism and its external contacts.

Piaget has borrowed the term homeorhesis, originally used to describe the interactive effect of a *biological* organism and its environment, and it would seem that he sees the mind as developing in relation to its environment in terms very similar to the development of a purely biological organism; but the mind's relationship to the environment requires not just the acquisition of knowledge but its *structuring*, by which one means that the child has to acquire an *understanding* also, which is much more than just absorbing knowledge. Piaget's idea is that intellectual development is governed by mental structures which become ever more complex as the child matures, and it is this development of complex structures which brings about progressive understanding.

In this context Hamlyn is again helpful, in that he suggests that this progressive understanding is akin to the Kantian '*a priori* principle'. Russell (1946) interprets this principle as 'a proposition . . . which, though it may be elicited by experience is seen, when known, to have a basis other than experience' (page 733), and the example Russell gives is that once a child has had the experience of two marbles and another two marbles making four marbles he needs no further instance to understand that two and two always make four.

A child is not, however, a passive 'structurer' of experiences: Piaget's view is that the child has to be active in relation to his environment. In addition, however, to physical activity, we shall see as we study the child's total development that socio-emotional factors, such as an increasing self-awareness, the need to communicate, and the development of close interpersonal relationships, all importantly relate to intellectual development.

Piaget has also borrowed the terms 'adaptation'*, 'assimilation'* and 'accommodation'* from biology in order to explain how this knowledge of the world is arrived at. The term 'arrived at' is used deliberately in place of the word 'learned' because for Piaget the process is more than a learning process. By 'assimilation' the child takes some new action or thought process into his existing internal mental structure, and by 'accommodation' he adjusts his mental structure to accept the new action or thought process. Thus the child achieves 'adaptation' to his constantly changing environment.

A child has to learn to perform many acts, and he has to learn to think many new thoughts. The improvement in the skill of performing any one of these acts, or in thinking new thoughts, is the 'accommodatory process', but once this has been accomplished, then one can say that the child has 'assimilated' the act or thought. Piaget suggests that a child is motivated to carry out tasks which are partly assimilated already. Once a task is fully assimilated then it ceases to be motivating, but the new skill or thought process is available to be used at a later time. Piaget himself considers mental development 'to be an ever more precise adaptation to reality' (1968b).

The 'internal mental structure' into which new experiences are assimilated, and which has to accommodate to change in order to take in new skills and new thinking abilities, is called a 'schema'. A schema can be simple or it can be complex. A simple schema is just a response to a stimulus; a complex schema could, for example, be *all* the processes involved in the infant sucking at the teat or nipple, starting with the head-turning movement and continuing with mouth-opening, sucking and swallowing.

A schema is either sensori-motor — that is, it is an action — or it is cognitive, it takes place in thought. Because for Piaget thinking at the baby stage is wordless, internalized action, the use of the term 'schema' to denote both a skill and a thought structure is not inconsistent. Also the use of such a comprehensive term is justified because Piaget attempts to account for the total cognitive developmental process from the infant's first acts, through the growing complexities of actions and thoughts in childhood to the adolescent's ability to engage in logical, abstract thought.

Although a schema is defined as an 'internal mental *structure*' it is nevertheless a flexible structure, otherwise it could not accommodate new experiences of various kinds. A schema is also 'mobile' in that once a skill or thought process has been mastered the skill can be applied in a variety of ways and the thought process applied to related problems.

Piaget's theory of child development is an age–stage theory. He suggests that all children must pass through certain stages of development, and that with every child the earlier stage must precede the later stages. His theory of how mental development takes place is not an easy theory to appreciate. It is not a learning theory nor is it merely a maturational theory, but a third kind of developmental theory. The child *organizes* his thoughts in relation to his experiences and in relation to his activities. Piaget has termed this organization of experiences 'equilibration'.

Through social learning, through being taught about the properties of the world, such as weights, measures, etc., and the conservation of quantities, and through experiences with his environment generally, through all these means a child builds up a set of beliefs about the physical world. These beliefs, however, come into conflict with one another. For instance, a young child can see that water poured from a tall, slender glass into a short, squat glass will look less, and he may indeed think that it is less than it was in the tall, slender glass; but at about six years of age he will also have acquired a belief, at least in relation to some materials which can be quantified, that quantities do not become less unless something is taken away from them; thus to such a child the perceptual evidence, and what has been learned about the conservation of quantities, conflict with one another. This conflict, which is seen by adults as illogical behaviour or as the holding of illogical views, has to be resolved; the child's ideas have to be brought into agreement with one another. In order to do this he must reach a certain stage of maturity, he must also have experience of the world, but over and above this he has to be able to organize his thoughts into a system which is self-regulating. How does it become possible for the small child gradually to organize his thoughts into a logical system?

Mention has been made of Piaget's assertion that a child's thinking before he is two years of age or so is internalized action, but after that age the child has to learn to represent to himself in thought what he has already mastered in action. He is able to be more advanced in action than he is in language or in thought. Consequently what children aged about seven say, or how they apparently think, is far less logical than how they behave. The child under this age is indeed pre-logical. Instead of logical thought he indulges in what Piaget calls 'the mechanisms of intuition'. The child has internalized actions and percepts, but he is without the power to co-ordinate these into a logical structure. His answers to questions which require logical thought are often of an intuitive kind. 'Why does the moon move when you walk?' 'Because it follows me.' 'Why does it follow you?' 'Because I walk', or 'Because it wants to.'

In chapter 4 reference is made to the child's inability at four or five years of age to detach himself from information presented by the senses in order logically to evaluate a situation. If a child of this age is given eight red discs and a handful of blue ones and asked to make a row of blue discs of the same *number* as the red ones, he will make the row of blue discs the same *length* as the red row without bothering about whether the *number* of blue discs coincides. Piaget says that at this stage the child is midway between *actual* experience and *mental* experience. These intuitive actions lack what he calls 'mobility' and 'reversibility'. Action habits, such as performing a task which has a goal, are *irreversible*, because one can only work *towards* a goal, not away from it; but thought processes must be reversible. Thus 4 plus 2 is 6, but equally 6 minus 2 is 4. Because, for the very young child, all thought is internalized action, the thought process at this age is irreversible, as well as being rigid and yet also unstable. However, by four or five years of age some of the rigidity has been lost, and at this 'intuitive thought stage' the child is able to move his thoughts towards reversibility. He is preparing to enter at seven or eight the 'concrete operational' stage of development (chapter 4).

An 'operation' has been variously defined as an action which takes place in the imagination (Beard, 1969); an act which is an integral part of an organized network of related acts (Flavell, 1963); and an internalized action which has become reversible (Piaget, 1968b). One may best think of an 'operation' as an internalized action which has become organized into a coherent and reversible thought system.

When a child moves from the intuitive thought stage to the first operational stage, the 'concrete' operational stage, it has been found that he is able to manipulate his thoughts, although at seven or eight years of age this manipulation is still very much linked to actual action. For example, if a child under four years of age is asked to put a number of sticks in order from the shortest to the longest, he normally only manages to arrange them in pairs, without comparing the pairs with one another. Only when he is about six or so will he have a sufficiently organized thought system to enable him to look for the shortest first and then move on to put the others in order in the same manner. This ability presupposes an understanding of reversibility, because it must be possible for him to see each stick as both shorter than the next one and longer than the one before. Such understanding of seriation is just one of many kinds of understanding which become available after six or seven years of age. However, operations at this age are still very 'concrete', for the child cannot carry out this kind of thought process without the aid of perception — in this example he is ordering actual sticks. He is still very dominated by perceptions and has no thinking powers at his command which enable him to use words, symbols or other abstractions in the same logical manner in which he handles physical things. The child between seven and eleven years of age has to move from this largely *percept-centred* view of the world to a view which is based on logical deductions; and similarly he has to move from an *egocentric* stand to a more objective viewpoint.

When the child enters the 'formal operational' stages at about eleven or twelve years of age his thought processes are largely released from the influence of perception, and he is much more free to think logically and mathematically. He is now operating on a plane of reasoning where he can think without the support of perception and with the use of language, whether there is a language of words or of symbols. The small child *acts* on objects; the older child is able to *think* about *objects in their presence* and then act on the results of his thinking, but the child of twelve and over should be able to *reflect* about objects in their absence in a propositional sense. Piaget says that at this stage 'thinking takes wings' (1968b).

It is clear that by the formal operational stage the mental conflict between perception and logical structures has been *largely* resolved. The child now has at his command mental abilities of various kinds, but linking them all is the ability to think logically. His cognitive structures are now more stable, capable of being highly complex and organized. Equilibrium has been achieved, and thinking becomes freed from concrete reality. (The actual developmental process from the sensori-motor stage to the formal operational stage is described in some detail in chapter 4.)

Criticism of Piaget's work

Piaget's ideas first aroused interest in the 1930s in the USA, but only since about 1955 or so has his work been considered to be of genuine importance and significance, although it has not survived without criticism. Philosophical critics of Piaget's work have included Hamlyn (1978), who has suggested that Piaget's notion of a 'mental structure' is too vague to be helpful as an explanatory concept. For example, referring to the conservation experiments (chapter 4) he asks what, if a child pours liquid from a wide, shallow glass to a tall, narrow one, and then says there is more liquid in the narrow glass, is the child *not* understanding? Does the child understand what a liquid is, what 'volume' means, the principle of identity of a liquid, or what? Or has he a partial understanding of these matters? These problems, writes Hamlyn, make it hard to know what kind of 'structure' Piaget has in mind, and 'what kind of rationale for the theory of stages is provided in speaking of structures' (page 47). Hamlyn also comments on Piaget's notion that 'objectivity comes through activity' (page 53). The child, according to Piaget, has to be *active* in relation to his environment and his experience, in order to develop; even perception is not a passive process. This view is very different from that of the empiricists who see the child as a passive recipient of, as it were, 'overflowing' experiences. Piaget's view seems the more appropriate view, but nevertheless Hamlyn criticizes Piaget for not, for example, allowing for *how* the notion of objectivity is brought about. Decentration indicates a turning away from the self, but Piaget implies that decentration and the reversibility of thought together lead to objectivity; Hamlyn's comment here is that although reversibility indicates that the thought process is sophisticated, it does no more than give this indication. One can add to Hamlyn's criticism that it is one thing to say that cognitive development progresses somewhat like biological development, that is, that an 'unfolding' occurs of a pre-determined arrangement; and that for humans this unfolding occurs in relation to experiences in the environment; but how does the acquiring of knowledge and the development of understanding fit into this scheme? Knowledge and understanding are things which are shared with others, they are social concepts; and it is here that cognitive development overlaps with emotional growth. The child's feelings have, as Hamlyn puts it, to be educated. What he experiences he is taught to structure, very often through the emotional relationships he has with other people, notably with his mother; 'feelings, wants and attitudes play a large part' in the development of understanding, and so emotion is 'an essential component in intellectual development' (Hamlyn, 1978, page 102). J. and E. Newson (1975) also, although they have no quarrel with Piaget's notion that objective knowledge is acquired through interaction between an organism and objects in its environment, emphasize that 'the object with which the human infant interacts, most often and most effectively, particularly in the earliest stages of development, is almost invariably another human being' (page 437).

Apart from such criticisms, experimental psychologists criticize Piaget because he has worked more as a naturalist than as an experimentalist, which implies that much of his work lacks precision and control, and it is difficult precisely to repeat some of his research. He seldom gives statistical analyses, and he has usually used only small samples. Several researchers have also in recent years examined the experimental settings, and the type of language used by both Piaget and his co-workers and by others who have attempted to replicate his studies when they are speaking to children. Donaldson (1978) has described much of this research. By examining the extensive work with young children produced by developmental psychologists, including herself, she concludes that small children are able to think very effectively indeed, as long as their thinking is directed to *real life situations which have a meaning for them*. She makes the point that because young children do not reflect on *how* they think, they are not able to use their thinking abilities in an objective manner to tackle what are for them often quite unreal problems. Flavell (1974) describes something similar when he shows that young children exhibit what he calls 'production deficiency', that is, they often have abilities without even being aware of these abilities; and, at a somewhat later stage when they are aware of a particular ability they do not see the need to bring this ability into play in a relevant situation. So what one is saying here is not that the findings of Piaget as here described are entirely wrong, but that these and other findings which were generated by Piaget's work, when reinterpreted, have indeed even greater significance for the understanding of children and for our educational practice than one had previously thought.

In what ways, then, will Piaget's findings have to be reinterpreted, and what might be the significance of these reinterpretations?

Piaget concluded that young children's thinking is *qualitatively* different from that of older children and adults; Flavell's notion of 'production deficiency', which can be shown to exist in relation to, for example, child speech, memory, understanding other persons and problem solving, indicates that children often possess abilities before they can exhibit them in the appropriate situation. However, the school situation and psychological testing situations are situations where adults structure what is required of children according to an adult view of life, and these are situations where, as Donaldson puts it, a child is expected 'to call the powers of his mind into service *at will*' (pages 121 and 122). Donaldson discusses this in terms of what she calls the child's growth of consciousness, by which is meant self-consciousness, which, she says, cannot be isolated from the development of the intellect. Piaget himself (1977) and his co-workers, such as Inhelder (1978), are also obviously aware of this relationship between intellectual development and the development of a self-conscious awareness. Inhelder writes that 'surprise and interest [by the child] when confronted with unexpected phenomena is only a beginning: the next step implies reflection on one's own thinking and a capacity of drawing inferences from what has been observed' (page 127). When children cannot do this at an early age we think they cannot understand *at all* the particular problems we present to them. What we have learnt from Flavell's observations, from recent research work attempting to replicate Piaget's works, but using different experimental settings and instructions, and from Donaldson's interpretation of the significance of recent findings, is that young children can indeed solve many problems we had previously thought they would not solve if

(1) we structure the presentation of problems so that the presentation has 'real life' meaning for children according to their age and

(2) we help them to reflect in an objective manner on their own thought processes. Of course, there will still be an age barrier below which complex problems cannot be understood by small children, however well presented; this goes without saying; but it is now clear that this age barrier is probably a good deal lower in the age range than Piaget's findings seemed to indicate.

However, young children's difficulties in understanding certain conceptual problems do exist. The fact that they, and not older children, are confused by the adult *use* of language, even when simple words are used; that they cannot call on their mental powers at will; that they do not objectively recognise what they do know, and so cannot make use of this knowledge except in certain settings; all this means in the writer's view that there are qualitative differences between the cognitive abilities of children of different ages, as Piaget asserts. Despite philosophical problems relating to Piaget's epistemology it would be foolish to jettison Piaget's theory of age-related stages in cognitive development. What is required now is a much more detailed analysis of the development of thought processes, including how these relate to social and emotional development; and empirical work by psychologists could benefit from a philosophical examination of epistemology set in the broad context of the development of social, moral and emotional capacities.

Comparison and assessment

The three theories which have been discussed in this chapter differ one from another in a number of important respects.

(1) *Freudian psychoanalytic theory* concerns itself with *emotional* and *motivational* aspects of the personality, and seeks to elucidate the unconscious aspects of behaviour, whereas

(2) *social-learning theory* views man primarily as a *learning* organism, and the

(3) *cognitive–developmental theory* as exemplified largely, but not wholly, by Piaget's work, is concerned with the *qualitative changes* which take place in the child's *perception and understanding* of the world around him as he grows from infancy to adolescence.

We have seen that psychoanalytic theory stresses the importance of unconscious processes which affect behaviour and the development of the personality, but social-learning theory places no emphasis at all on such processes, and views the developing child as an organism whose behaviour is primarily a response to external and internal stimuli; in Piaget's theory neither unconscious processes nor the responsive nature of behaviour is of supreme importance. The student of child development, viewing these theories objectively, can be forgiven for asking

(1) whether it is at all possible to integrate the theories and formulate a unified theory of child development and

(2) if this is not possible, whether one can, or indeed should, make an assessment of the relative value of each of the three theories.

Most child psychologists would be of the opinion that we cannot yet expect to be able to formulate a comprehensive theory of child development. Such a theory would have to be descriptive and explanatory, and would therefore have to account for the development of, and change in, all aspects of observable and measurable behaviour, as well as non-observable 'behaviour', such as fantasy, thoughts and feelings, all within a unified theoretical framework. The theory would have to be one of individual personality growth as well as one of social interaction. It is doubtful whether research has progressed sufficiently far to enable such a unified concept to be formulated.

Nevertheless, it is possible to see some similarities in such apparently divergent views of man as those described by Freud, the social-learning theorists and Piaget. For example, both psychoanalytic theory and learning theory see man to a greater or lesser extent as a reactive being. Freud considered man to be motivated at least in part by drives which seek satisfaction through interaction with the external world, and he also thought of man as being subject to pressures from the world; social-learning theory offers a not entirely dissimilar view of man as seeking to satisfy internal needs by reacting appropriately to those external stimuli which promise to satisfy such needs. Although Piaget's theory of adaptation does not specifically view the child as a reactive being, he says that mental development is an 'ever more precise adaptation to reality', and he describes how this adaptation occurs. It is also not unreasonable to suppose that a child's development occurs both through the working out of psycho-sexual drives *and* through processes of reinforcement, while at the same time the cognitive apparatus is changing qualitatively along the lines suggested by Piaget.

However, the differences of approach to the *study* of child development, and the *contribution* to knowledge made by each of the three theories is so fundamentally different from that of the other two that comparisons are not easily possible. The theorists themselves are, indeed, critical of one another, the Freudians, for example, considering that most other theories, particularly learning theory, are too superficial to take sufficiently into account the deeper-lying influences which shape the personality; learning theorists are sceptical of the interpretations made by Freudians of clinical material, and also critical of Piaget for his manner of sampling and the methods he employs to analyze his data; and Piaget appears to consider that learning theory views the child *too much* as a reactive, rather than a maturing and participating, being.

The fact that several aspects of all these theories must, in the light of recent experimental and observational work, be considered inadequate does not detract from their heuristic value. All have generated new ideas, and useful research, and they remain as a foundation to our knowledge of how the human organism develops and functions. Taken together they provide a rich insight into the processes affecting the development of the child's personality. They are complementary to one another, and each theory enables students of child behaviour better to understand the psychological development of children.

Further reading

PECK, D. and D. WHITLOW: *Approaches to personality theory* (Methuen, 1975)

FREUD, S.: *Two short accounts of psycho-analysis* (Penguin Books, 1962)

STAFFORD-CLARK, D.: *What Freud really said* (Penguin Books, 1965)

CIOFF, F.: *Freud: modern judgements* (Macmillan, 1973)

BANDURA, A. and R. H. WALTERS: *Social learning and personality development* (Holt, Rinehart and Winston, New York, 1973)

PIAGET, J.: *Six psychological studies* (University of London Press, 1969)

BALDWIN, A. L.: *Theories of child development* (John Wiley and Sons, 1967)

TURNER, J.: *Cognitive development* (Methuen, 1975)

DONALDSON, M.: *Children's minds* (Fontana, 1978)

CHAPTER THREE

Influences affecting the formation of personality characteristics and the development of intelligence

General considerations: the 'nature–nurture' controversy

A discussion of the origins of behaviour, and of the factors influencing the development of the personality, inevitably includes a discussion of the 'nature–nurture' question. Man is naturally interested in whether his dispositions are brought about more by his genetic inheritance than by the influences to which he is subject during life, particularly in childhood. These discussions are themselves affected by historical, political, philosophical and humanitarian considerations. During certain historical periods when man felt himself to be in growing command of his destiny — for example, during the middle and later parts of the nineteenth century (chapter 1) and under political regimes which assumed that changes in the environment would produce greater equality and opportunities for many persons in all aspects of life — during such periods and under such regimes the role of the environment was, and still is being, stressed.

Philosophically also the notion that man's intellectual capacities and personality characteristics may be predetermined from birth by his genetic inheritance appears unacceptable to believers in human free will; most sects of the Christian Church hold that man has capabilities which enable him to change aspects of his behaviour, particularly when these are anti-social or injurious to his fellow men. Similarly all attempts to change the existing social order, whether in the field of penal reform, the treatment of the mentally ill, or the education of children, have relied on the belief that improving environmental conditions would also improve man.

For a considerable time, then, despite the writings of Galton in the nineteenth century (1869), it has been fashionable to stress the importance of the environment to man's behaviour, and it is only in relatively recent years that psychologists have conceded that there may be a sizeable genetic component in testable intelligence. Even here recent discussions of this problem have produced more heat than light.

The nature–nurture problem is one which touches deeply man's concept of himself, and as such produces strongly held opinions, which often prevent objective assessment of the evidence. Psychologists in the past have been interested in the extent to which behaviour and personality are each affected by genetic and environmental factors. Without the inherited foundation there could be nothing on which the environment could operate, and without the environmental framework there would be no way in which the inherited factors could express themselves. In recent years it has become clear that what are termed 'main effect models', that is, seeing the major influences on the formation of a trait or a piece of behaviour as due to genetic *or* environmental factors, are too simple as models by which to explain the form a particular aspect of human development has taken; many writers (e.g. Clarke, 1978) have advocated the replacing of such models by a 'transactional model' which, as Sameroff (1975) writes, 'stresses the plastic character of both environment and the organism as it actively participates in its own growth' (page 282). And, as is discussed in chapter 2, the notion of the child simply as a passive receiver of stimuli from the environment to which he makes responses has now been superseded by the model of the child as an active *selector* of the particular stimuli to which he chooses to pay attention. We are also aware that different children will respond to the *same* situation in different ways. Furthermore, the 'environment' does not 'consist of discrete variables external to the individual' (Urbach, 1974, page 237); nor do different aspects of the environment normally have their effect on the developing child in isolation of one another. It is likely, for example, that the social class of the family (page 96), the kind of language spoken in the home (page 130), the number of children in the family (page 95) and the income of the family are environmental factors which, in interaction with one another, all have their effect on the developing child (Wedge and Prosser, 1973). Other factors which clearly influence personality and behaviour are the chemical and nutritive factors which affect him before and after birth; the culture and society into which he is born; the school he attends; his own position in the family; the personality characteristics of his parents; and the peculiarly individual and possibly even traumatic experiences which he himself has undergone, particularly in childhood, including the products of his own fantasy.

When we consider the meaning of the word 'genetic' we find that the way this word is used often tends to confuse innate, constitutional, pre-natal and truly hereditary influences with one another. Cattell (1965) has shown clearly and interestingly how several terms, which are often loosely and interchangeably used, should be differentiated (diagram 1). Thus the term 'innate' includes not only what is inherited, but mutations which may have occurred in the genes between parent and child; 'congenital' need not mean innate only, for it can include changes which occur in the womb before birth; and 'constitutional' can include changes which occur after birth due to possible physiological changes.

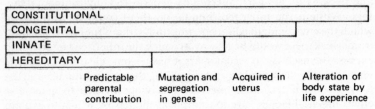

CONSTITUTIONAL			
CONGENITAL			
INNATE			
HEREDITARY			
Predictable parental contribution	Mutation and segregation in genes	Acquired in uterus	Alteration of body state by life experience

Diagram 1: *Definitions of contributions to personality commonly considered 'non-environmental'*[1]

It is important to separate those factors which are definitely due to inheritance from those which are acquired after conception. Such a separation also stresses the fact that the influence of the environment does not commence at birth but at conception. Only in relatively recent years has the importance of the uterine environment been acknowledged.

When we consider the influence of the total environment we must also keep in mind the differential effect which it can have on different human characteristics. Thus eye colour, blood grouping and finger-ridge counts cannot be affected by the environment at all, but other characteristics, for instance, intelligence, are undoubtedly affected by the kind of experiences the child undergoes; it is most probable, however, that genetic factors set a limit to the kind of intellectual achievement which is possible. In such cases the environment probably acts as a 'threshold variable' (page 97), making it possible for the genetically determined potential to be reached. However, the environment cannot, as Watson in 1925 thought it could, enable a child to become a specialist in any field in which he might be trained, regardless of his innate potential. Other aspects of human behaviour and personality, particularly social behaviour, are likely to be much more affected by various environmental conditions than by genetic influences.

Consideration has also to be given to the periods in a person's life when he is subject to specific environmental influences. There is some evidence to show that the effects of experiences early in life, particularly during the first two or three years, may have a more profound and lasting influence than later experiences, though the evidence about this is somewhat ambiguous. For example, an individual's IQ does not necessarily remain constant throughout childhood, as we discuss in chapter 4, though it does not, for at least half the population, change a great deal from early childhood onwards; and it is

[1]Reproduced from Cattell, R. B.: *The scientific analysis of personality* (Penguin Books, 1965) by kind permission of the publishers

uncertain to what extent other personality characteristics are affected by early experiences. As Clarke (1978) states, 'within *limits* [my italics] human development may be regarded as somewhat open-ended, at least potentially so' (page 255). This question is further considered later in this chapter, and in chapters 5 and 7, where the effects of depriving experiences, especially in early childhood, are discussed.

Lastly, it must not be forgotten that although a factor may be genetic in origin it may nevertheless be possible to change its possible effects. For example, the congenital metabolic disturbance called phenylketonuria, which is caused by the body's inability to convert phenylalanine to tyrosine, will, if left untreated, cause mental retardation. This condition can now be identified immediately after birth and is treatable by adherence to a suitable diet.

Methods of studying the factors which influence the development of the human personality

Although it has been stressed that development is due to a *transaction* between the genotype* and the environment which impinges on it from the moment of conception, psychologists are still concerned to study all the factors which may influence development, and some of these are undoubtedly innately determined. It is important, therefore, to look at the *methods* which have been used to study these factors, though psychologists are much more aware now than they were in the past of the great complexities inherent in attempting to arrive at a valid analysis of the relative importance of the many influential factors. Not only is the establishment of the factors which may affect a child's personality development in itself a most difficult matter, but the study of how to assess accurately *what* particular characteristics any one adult or child actually possesses has in recent years been seen to be a very difficult matter in itself. (Vernon, 1964, has suggested that perhaps we should not think of personality traits as actually being *in* people, though most people do tend to think of others as *having* certain characteristics.) A discussion of this complex matter is not appropriate here (see Mischel, 1974). It is, however, relevant to mention briefly just a few of the problems with which psychologists have concerned themselves in recent years, such as: what human characteristics may be said to be 'core' characteristics, and thus fundamentally unchangeable with increasing age and with other life changes? Does a trait always affect a person's behaviour in the same way regardless of the situation? In other words, am I always honest or does my honesty, or degree of honesty, depend on the situation? (Hartshorne and May, 1928, conducted a classic study in relation to children's honesty which raised many similar questions.) To what extent do human personality characteristics *actually influence the situation* in which they express themselves, thus making a study of these characteristics even more difficult? How accurately do the various methods used to discover personality traits actually measure these traits?

However, having made these points it is still not impossible, particularly in relation to the study of intelligence, to study the factors which may affect the development of personality characteristics. One major problem in studying the *relative* influence of genetic and environmental factors in the formation of personality traits springs from the fact that usually the environment in which a child is reared seems to support the child's genetic endowment: for example, a child from an advantaged environment usually comes from parents who have also supplied him with a favourable inheritance. For this reason much use has been made in this study of identical twins, called 'monozygotes'* (MZ twins), who have been separately brought up. The assumption behind their experimental use is that since they are genetically identical, each being developed from one half of a divided ovum fertilized by one sperm, any differences in personality and behaviour can only be due to the effects of the environment. One criticism of such studies is that twins are an unusual sample, not representative of the general population, and that any discoveries made about such twins are applicable only to other twins and not to the general population. Another criticism about the use of separated MZ twins is that whenever such separation occurs the circumstances under which the children live subsequently are unusual, particularly for the child who has been fostered or adopted. However, we cannot accurately define what a usual or 'normal' family is; and some disadvantages suffered by the adopted twin may be offset by compensating advantages he may experience. A criticism made by Mittler (1971) of such studies is that since many of the sample twin pairs who were studied were obtained by means of appeals on the mass communication media they may have been a biased sample, because presumably only certain kinds of persons will respond to appeals of this kind. It is obviously desirable that the selection of twins for future studies should be carried out by methods which ensure as far as possible a random sample from the twin population.† However, since the findings from twin studies have by and large been supported by consanguinity* studies and other studies of various kinds, the evidence about similarities and differences between twins cannot be dismissed as valueless. Indeed, since the pre-natal environment of MZ twins is *not* at all identical, one twin, most frequently the younger, being at a disad-

†The twins studied by the National Child Development Study (Adams, Ghodsian and Richardson, 1976) were part of the 1958 NCD Study cohort and so not a self-selected sample.

vantage through obtaining a poorer share of the maternal blood supply and for other reasons, the similarities which have been found between separated MZ twins are somewhat surprising.

Longitudinal studies, some commencing very shortly after birth, have aimed at the elucidation of human characteristics which appear to persist from early childhood to adult life, although the assumption is not necessarily made that such persistence indicates that the characteristics in question are genetically determined.

Another possible source of information about the influence of genetic endowment and environment respectively comes from animal studies. It is possible when studying animals to control genetic and experimental variables in a way that is ethically impossible with human children. Although it is admitted that extreme care is necessary in the extrapolation of findings from animal studies to provide an elucidation of human problems, it is possible to make such extrapolations, particularly when such findings can be supported by observations on humans.

Attempts have also been made to study the possible relationship between temperament* and body build. If it were to be found that, regardless of life experience, persons of similar body build were also of similar temperament, then one could reasonably assume that a relationship existed between body build and temperament; and, as the final adult human morphological* structure is, except in very extreme circumstances, only marginally affected by the environment, one might surmise that temperamental characteristics too are only marginally affected by the environment.

In addition, many cross-sectional studies have been carried out on practically all aspects of child development. Such studies are not usually concerned with elucidating the contribution of genetic and environmental influences, but to clarify aspects of the environment which have their effect on the development of behaviour. These influences are discussed on pages 93–101 Clarke (1978) has recently quoted Bronfenbrenner (1977), who wrote 'if you want to understand something, try to change it' (page 255). By this is meant that rather than study what has happened to, say, disadvantaged children and attempt to relate this to their present behaviour or performance, psychologists should, where appropriate, actively intervene in the lives of such children, comparing the outcome not only with their previous behaviour or performance but also with those of a control group of children with whom such intervention did not occur. In this way the effects of such an intervention can be studied as an on-going activity rather than as a retrospective study.

The formation of the personality

Since Plato's time it has been helpful to think of the human personality as having three aspects: the intellect, the will and the emotions; what we mean by the term 'temperament' is composed of the will and the emotions; the cognitive aspect of the personality relates to intelligence and to other associated abilities which human beings display. It has become customary for psychologists to study separately those aspects of the personality which broadly can be termed the temperament, and those parts which are cognitive in nature. Before proceeding to look in some detail at the various influential factors which affect the development of the total personality it will be necessary to discuss the nature of intelligence.

Intelligence and abilities: general considerations

The study of human intelligence, its nature, development and measurement, has occupied psychologists for a longer period than that of any other human trait. Galton (1822–1911) first interested himself in the origin of intellectual ability and Binet (1857–1914) empirically laid the foundation for the measurement of intelligence. The discussion concerning the nature of intelligence, and also whether it is developed primarily by environmental conditions rather than being determined innately, has continued from the time when Galton first suggested that innate factors were the prime influences. During the past ten years the controversy has been reawakened since Jensen (1969) brought together evidence which seems to him and others largely to support Galton's view (pages 85–87).

There are a number of reasons why 'intelligence', its nature and the means of its assessment, should be discussed in this book. The measurement of children's intelligence and the assessment of their abilities were fundamental in selecting children for secondary education under the 1944 Education Act, in order that they could be placed in schools which suited their particular intellectual level and their specific abilities. Though this scheme of secondary education is now largely obsolete in Great Britain, children are still streamed or grouped in various ways according to their intelligence and abilities within many comprehensive schools. For this reason teachers are from time to time called upon to administer group intelligence tests. Many parents, particularly from the middle classes, are deeply interested in their children's IQ level (see pages 81–84) and in their scholastic achievement; indeed, they often seem more concerned with this aspect of their children's personality than in whether they are, for example, able to achieve happy human relationships!

It is certainly difficult to state exactly what one means when one attempts to define any human characteristic including intelligence. But Jensen (1978) has stated that 'a wide range of individual differences in ability to perform mental tasks of many kinds is obvious and undisputed' (page 9) and it should not, therefore, be impossible to describe the nature of this particular ability which underlies the differences we observe in people. Spearman (1923) thought of intelligence as being that capacity which enables man to indulge in relational, constructive thinking. Jensen (1969) suggests that we best think of intelligence as 'a capacity for abstract reasoning and problem solving' (page 19). Vernon (1979) has written of intelligence as referring 'to the more generalized skills, strategies of thinking, and overall conceptual level, which apply in a wide range of cognitive activities or in new learning' (page 51). We have, therefore, a trait which involves intellectual functioning; which seems to enter to a greater or lesser extent into every mental activity; and which shows itself most clearly when humans are engaged in relational and conceptual kinds of thinking.

The nature of intelligence

There are two aspects of the nature of intelligence which have been the subject of much experimental and statistical work, and also of much controversy. The one aspect concerns the 'general' quality of intelligence. The other aspect concerns the relative weighting that should be given to the genetic factor, and this is discussed later in this chapter.

Spearman, a British psychologist working in the first four decades of this century, considered that the performance of every intellectual task involved two 'factors'; one such factor was *specific* to the task which was being carried out, and the other factor was one of *general* intelligence. His statistical work seemed to suggest that the relative influence of the general factor to that of the specific factor varied according to the task, so that, for example, the ability to do mathematics depends more on a higher level of general intelligence than does the ability to do music, which requires a higher level of specific ability. Spearman called the specific factor 's' and the general, underlying, cognitive factor 'g'. Though he did not equate 'g' by itself with 'intelligence', nevertheless he thought of 'g' as being of prime importance, for it was in his view the one common factor that entered into all intellectual activities to a greater or lesser extent.

Thurstone, working largely from 1935 to 1955, carried out similar analyses of mental abilities in the United States. He postulated seven 'primary' abilities, but he found later that there appeared to be an underlying relationship between such abilities, and he agreed that one could extract a second-order factor which might be called 'general intelligence' from the primary abilities. This left other factors, which Spearman had originally called 's' factors, special factors, such as spatial, numerical, verbal and mechanical abilities.

Vernon (1961) and others formulated an hierarchical model of intelligence which allowed for the 'g' factor and for these other group factors. Other models of intelligence which have been proposed are those of Guildford (1967), whose original model implied that there might be 120 separate factors which are inherent within intellectual ability. Cattell (1971) has approached the analyses of intelligence by supposing there to be four *levels*, which he categorized as

 (1) *powers*, which relate to such abilities as vision, hearing and motor abilities;

 (2) *proficiencies*, that is, skills of various sorts;

 (3) *agencies*, that is, mostly culturally acquired 'tools' such as language and strategies of thinking and

 (4) *general capacities*, such as spatial abilities, memory, speed of thinking, and so on.

The reader unfamiliar with the complexities of psychological models, their underlying hypotheses and mathematical analyses can be forgiven for wondering why such a variety of notions about a human characteristic can exist, and how one can know the 'truth' about the nature of such a characteristic. Whenever we try to understand something about the nature of a human personality trait, such as intelligence, we are dealing with a highly complex factor whose expression in daily life can take many forms. In the many years that this characteristic has been studied many different intelligence tests have been used by different experimenters, on different kinds of populations, and on populations of different ages, so that it is not surprising that different ideas about the nature of intelligence have emerged. It is clear, for example, that young children display their intelligence in a much less differentiated form than older children and adults; again, a homogeneously selected sample of persons, such as college students, will show in the analysis of their test scores much more clearly discernible factors than will the analysis of the test scores of a sample of persons coming from a wide variety of backgrounds of varying ages.

However, it does seem that we can think of the trait called 'intelligence' as being made up of an underlying characteristic which comes into operation, as it were, whenever an intellectual activity of some kind has to be carried out, but which is itself made up of several other underlying discernible characteristics; and the extent to which these underlying characteristics, which we can continue to call collectively the 'g' factor, are required, will depend on the cognitive *complexity* of the intellectual task being undertaken. This means that the extent to which one or more of the other characteristics are required in the execution of an intellectual task will depend on the *nature* of the task. For example, the degree of *general* intelligence which is required for success at mathematics will be relatively higher than the degree of intelligence required for success at an artistic activity, where a relatively higher degree of *specific* ability is required. Thus a good and well-tried intelligence test (page 83) will, as psychometricians put it, be 'highly loaded on "g"'.

Thus, when we take the measure of a child's intelligence we are not measuring separate abilities, but that quality of intellectual power which enters into all mental activities. For this reason modern psychologists do not claim that an intelligence test is a complete indicator of a child's range of abilities, but that a good test is the best *single* predictor of a child's capability for engaging in intellectual pursuits as far as his general intellectual capacity is concerned. It is a better predictive instrument than school reports or school tests. What it does not necessarily measure are a child's ability to concentrate, his need to achieve, or other motivational factors usually considered necessary to make use of a good intelligence in an academic setting.

The 'IQ' and intelligence tests

When an intelligence test is taken by a child, the score which is arrived at through such testing is called the IQ, the 'intelligence quotient' of that child. It is important not to confuse 'intelligence' with 'IQ'. The IQ is a *sample* of a person's intellectual performance, taken at a particular period in such a person's life.

Binet first investigated the possibility of measuring children's intelligence when, in 1904, he sat on a committee which had been asked to find means whereby those children in French schools who were in need of special tuition could be discovered. He worked empirically, evolving tests which children of particular ages could do, and he decided that when between 50 and 75 per cent of a large sample of children of a particular age could do his tests, then these tests must be suitable for normal children of that particular age. Thus he arrived at the notion of 'mental age' as a means of assessing a child's retardation or advancement in intelligence compared with that of other children of the same chronological age.

What is the 'quotient' referred to when we speak of the 'intelligence quotient'? It is the relationship between a child's mental age and his chronological age multiplied by one hundred. Thus

$$(\text{mental age})/(\text{chronological age}) \times 100 = IQ$$

Thus a child with a mental age of twelve whose chronological age is ten would have an IQ of 120. The multiplier of one hundred was cho-

sen arbitrarily by Stern, the originator of the IQ, so that the average or mean intelligence quotient could be represented by the figure 100. Obviously a child of ten years of age whose mental age was also ten would have an IQ of 100. By using such a method of evaluating intelligence the IQ does not increase as the child gets older. Obviously, a child's intellectual abilities increase with age, but this is an increase relative to the child's age, and is what one would expect. The intelligence of adults cannot be arrived at by assessing a mental age, but the scores obtained from adult tests can be transformed into IQ scores.

Vernon (1979) in summarizing the findings to date on the stability of IQ, reports that 'a typical repeat reliability figure of 0.70 over 5 to 10 years implies that five-sixths of retested children obtain the same IQ within plus-or-minus 15 points, though some of the remaining one-sixth may fluctuate much more widely' (page 82). And, he adds, group tests give a much less valid forecast than do individual tests (see page 83). Hindley and Owen (1978), in a longitudinal study, found that between the ages of 3 and 17 years the scores of 50 per cent of their subjects changed by 10 IQ points or more.

The stability of the IQ measure when taken early in a child's life is not so good, largely, it would seem, because the abilities being measured in infancy and early childhood do not correspond to the abilities being measured in later childhood. However, these findings do indicate that, during the major period of a child's life at school, for at least half the children in our schools the IQ measure changes relatively little. The reasons for any marked changes which may occur can be many, and will depend on the specific life circumstances of the individual child who has been tested. The nature and possible effects of such life circumstances are discussed later in this chapter. Certainly, if there were to be found an apparently large increase or decrease in any particular child's IQ score then this would be something which the educational psychologist would wish further to investigate.

Intelligence is more or less normally distributed. This means that, as in the case with most measurements which can be made on man, such as height, weight, shoe size, etc., most people fall within the middle range of the scores, with relatively few people at the extreme ends. Diagram 2 shows this normal distribution of intelligence, and one can see that approximately 68 per cent of all people have scores of between 85 and 115 IQ points, and only about 2¼ per cent of the population has a score of over 130 points. The curve is somewhat skewed, as statisticians put it, towards the lower end, and this indicates that there are, due to brain injury and/or pathological and genetic reasons, more people of lower intelligence, but there are also a very few more people of higher intelligence than would be expected if intelligence were actually distributed completely normally.

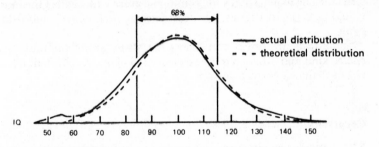

Diagram 2: *Theoretical and actual distribution of IQ in a British population*

Intelligence tests are constantly being revised and new tests developed, and this work is undertaken with the greatest care. Only when a test is both valid and reliable can it be used to measure intelligence. By 'valid' is meant that the test really measures what it is intended to measure: that is, it measures what we mean by 'intelligence'; it does not measure, for example, slickness or knowledge. By 'reliable' is meant that the test will give the same result when administered at different times to the same child, allowing, of course, for test familiarity.

Tests of various kinds have been constructed both for administration to individuals and for administration to groups. Some of these are pencil and paper tests; others, such as the Wechsler–Bellevue, involve verbal and performance tests. As an example of the latter, children are required to complete and arrange pictures and carry out other tasks, such as trace a path through a maze without entering blind alleys (the Porteus Maze test). The best known individual tests for children are the Stanford–Binet and the WISC (Wechsler Intelligence Scale for Children). Both these tests seem to be able to predict scholastic achievement fairly well, though one must remember that the human characteristic measured by IQ tests is only one factor, although a very important factor, which is required if a child is to be successful scholastically. However, both the Stanford–Binet and the WISC can also give the tester some insight into a child's specific difficulties which group tests cannot give. These tests take both more time and more skill to administer than group tests.

Group tests can be primarily verbal or non-verbal, and among the former the Moray House Tests and those produced by the NFER (National Foundation for Educational Research) are most widely used. The best-known non-verbal tests are the 'progressive matrices', which are made up of sets of patterns, each pattern in a set being different from the others in the series but all having a common feature. The testee is asked to select from a number of additional random patterns the one which shares the common feature with each of the individual patterns in a series. The tests become progressively more difficult.

Some tests are timed and others not, some are of the multiple-choice kind and others require the insertion of one recollected, inferred or deduced correct answer.

Creativity

The particular qualities and needs of the so-called gifted child are discussed in chapter 7. The term 'gifted' is usually used to include those persons who are of exceptional intelligence, or have a specific ability not normally possessed, or to a degree not usually possessed, by other people, or who are highly creative. Because of the way intelligence tests are constructed, the high scorer is thought more likely to be a convergent thinker rather than a divergent thinker, and so such tests have been criticized for failing to pick out the creative child.

It is important to understand that a high intelligence does not mean that a person has creative abilities, and that being highly creative does not necessarily imply a high intelligence; research work which has attempted to establish a connection between intelligence and creativity suggests that the very highly creative people, whom we might describe as being geniuses, are nearly always superior in intelligence; but below this level of creativity one could not predict a person's IQ score except within certain reasonable margins, by knowing his level of creative ability.

For some time tests called 'divergent thinking' tests were used in an attempt to differentiate the creative person who is also scientifically minded but, who, so it was said, was seldom identified by conventional IQ tests as being especially able. Divergent thinking tests, rather than having one correct answer as intelligence tests have, encourage the use of the imagination, and the answers are scored for their unusualness and for the number of ideas they contain; however, these tests have proved to be disappointing. Vernon, Adamson and Vernon (1977) suggest that the variety of abilities which are inherent within the creative imagination, depending on the particular area of creative endeavour involved, whether, for example, the scientific, artistic or literary, cannot easily be tapped by tests which appear to investigate the more superficial aspects of the creative process, the very aspects which are the least representative of the quality we are seeking to measure. In chapter 7 the ways in which the more generally gifted children can be identified and helped are discussed, whether these children are potential exponents of, say, one of the musical arts, or have creative abilities, or have a very high intelligence, although it is clear, of course, that the reliable and valid intelligence test will pick out the child who has an exceptionally high intelligence.

Factors influencing the development of temperament and intelligence: The inheritance of intelligence

The psychologist Hebb (1949) has suggested that one should think of intelligence as being of two kinds: one kind he termed 'intelligence A', the other kind 'intelligence B'. 'A' is the assumed, innate capacity with which men are born, and 'B' is the intelligence which is displayed by humans when they engage in intellectual activities. Thus 'B' is the *product* of 'A' *and* the effects of the experience of life, that is, the influence of the environment, on 'A'.

Since the IQ is a sample of a person's intellectual performance measured, usually, by one test, Vernon (1955) has suggested that one might term the IQ score 'intelligence C'.

Before discussing what is known about the inheritance of intelligence it is necessary to make one or two points about the study of human genetics. Unfortunately, the science of human genetics is a complicated one, and the subject is not easily understood, yet because the question of the inheritance of human characteristics touches us deeply, as discussed earlier in this chapter, many people feel able to comment on seeming findings about this difficult subject as if it were a non-technical subject.

It is important to understand two matters: one is that it is not possible to state what is *the* genetic contribution to the IQ score of any *one individual person*, since what is termed by geneticists *broad heritability* is a term which denotes the *difference* between individuals in a population. The second matter is that broad heritability is not a constant, so that one will never be able to say that a certain percentage is *the* contribution of heritability to tested intelligence. If one is examining the possible reasons for the difference in intelligence between two groups of people, then, if the environmental conditions under which these two groups live are very disparate, the greater part of the difference in their mean IQ scores is more likely to be due to the difference in their respective environments than to genetic factors; but if one is comparing two groups who live in rather similar environments, then the greater part of the difference in the IQ scores is more likely to be due to genetic factors.

It does not follow that because heritability is not a constant one cannot make statements about the heritability factor in relation to intelligence. It is true that when one is seeking the causes of the development of human traits one cannot, as is customary when working with animals and plants, overcome the problem of the covariance of heredity and environment by selective breeding work, or by controlling the environment of the experimental organisms; but, again, this does not mean that *probabilistic* statements cannot be made based on the sort of research work that *is* possible with humans.

Twin studies have provided much of the evidence for the genetic view, though these have certain weaknesses, which are discussed on page 89. However, such evidence is also supported by other studies which do not involve the assessment of twins. As far as the study of twins is concerned, it is normally found that when MZ (monozygotic* or identical) twins, who have lived *apart* from one another since early babyhood, are tested for intelligence, the similarity of their IQ scores is greater than that of any other pair of children *whether brought up apart or together* other than MZ twins brought up together. It has been suggested that as such separated twins are reared in an identical environment until adoption, and mostly in similar environments after adoption, one cannot be certain that the similarities found in their IQ scores are due to genetic factors only. It is, however, of interest that such twins actually can experience very *dissimilar* uterine environments. Also DZ (dizygotic* or fraternal) twins who are *brought up together during their entire childhood* have IQ scores very little different one from another than those obtained from non-twin siblings; both these facts, that is, the high correlation of MZ twin scores even when the children are brought up apart and the similarity between the correlation of DZ twin scores and ordinary sibling scores is exactly what one would expect if the genetic factor made a high contribution to the display of intelligence. However, Vernon (1979) does state that the data from which these correlations have been calculated, and which were collected up to 1965, 'are open to many difficulties of interpretation' (page 180). In addition, Adams, Ghodsian and Richardson (1976) analyzed data relating to the IQ scores of 136 pairs of twins, 41 MZ and 95 DZ of which 55 were same-sex, and 40 opposite-sex twins. They state that though the IQ scores of MZ twins had higher correlations than the IQ scores of DZ twins, the difference was not appreciable, and that because these findings *could* be of importance in relation to the debate on heritability and also to the meaning of test scores, they require very careful consideration.

Turning to evidence from non-twin data, the IQ scores of adopted and fostered children resemble more those of their biological parents than those of their adoptive parents; and the IQ scores of unrelated children brought up together have a relatively low relationship. Similarly, when the IQ scores of persons of different degrees of blood relationship are examined in relation to one another it is found that the closer such persons are in blood relationship, the closer are their IQ scores, even when they have been brought up apart from one another (Erlenmayer-Kimling and Jarvik, 1963). There is also a good deal of other evidence, such as from inbreeding among humans, and from the *difference* between parent–child IQs, that there seems to be a substantial genetic contribution to intelligence.

The inheritance of other personality characteristics: The possible relationship between physical characteristics and temperament

Behaviour is displayed and personality expressed through bodily activity. It would seem reasonable to assume therefore that there is some relationship between anatomical and physiological properties and behaviour. Williams (1960) in an article entitled 'The biological approach to the study of personality' outlines the very many anatomical, endocrinic and physiological variations which can be found in humans. He gives many examples of these, such as, for instance, that human stomachs and thyroid glands can vary sixfold in size; that the production of hormones can differ in different persons over a sevenfold range; and that the branching of the trunk nerves is extremely individualistic. It is obvious also that every person has a distinct respiratory, endocrine and nervous system. Similarly, the brain varies both in structure and in number, size and arrangement of neurons for each individual. Williams considers that the unique equipment which an infant brings into the world must be at least as important in determining his personality as environmental factors. Similarly, Mottram (1944) states that 'the endocrine organs are potent in determining our personalities'. Several studies, quoted by Hutt (1972), indicate how psychological differences between people are influenced by sexual factors, so that, for example, men are more susceptible to visual stimuli, but women to auditory stimuli; and women have a lower touch and pain threshold. It has also been observed that boys from birth are more vigorous in their movements than girls.

Mittler (1971) in reporting on examinations of twins in respect of a number of biological factors which may affect behaviour, states that, for instance, intelligence and cognitive skills (considered earlier in this chapter) 'are built on biological foundations'. He reports on studies of twins which have considered anthropometric data (such as height and weight), motor skills, and sensory and perceptual processes, as well as a number of physiological data, including brainwave functioning, sedation thresholds and the functioning of the autonomic nervous system. The conclusion can be drawn from these data that identical twins are more similar than fraternals in such factors and functions as height, electrical activity of the brain, autonomic functioning and basic sensory processes, and that these functions are unlikely to be affected by the fact that, as Mittler says, 'they [the identical twins] are treated in a more uniform way by their parents [than fraternal twins]'. Although one cannot categorically state that these functions are *not* affected by such treatment, it is unlikely that such functions are in the *main* determined by environmental factors (Vernon, 1969, for instance, suggests that brainwave activity could itself be affected by the *development* of intelligence).

Theories about a possible relationship between body build and personality have existed for a considerable time. In folklore there have been assumptions that fat people are jolly people; a vaguely related corollary of this is expressed by Caesar in Shakespeare's *Julius Caesar*, when he says:

> Yond Cassius has a lean and hungry look;
> He thinks too much: such men are dangerous.

As early as the second century A.D. Galen had related four bodily 'humours' to four basic temperaments. In 1925 Kretschmer extended his analysis of the bodily differences between the sufferers from the two major psychoses (schizophrenia and manic-depressive psychosis) to include normal persons, so that he delineated four personality types which were related to four types of body build. Later, in 1940, Sheldon developed 'somatotyping', that is, the study of the relationship between body build and temperament.

Sheldon's work has been heavily critized for a number of reasons, but it is possible that psychologists may not have given him the credit he deserves, for other work carried out in more recent years has, broadly speaking, confirmed many of his findings. Thus Cortes and Gatti (1965) have shown significant correlations between self-descriptions of temperament and body build in boys and girls in late adolescence. The Gluecks (1950), in a well-known study of delinquent boys in New York, found that the delinquent children, who had been matched in a number of important psychological, physical and socio-economic factors with non-delinquents, were nevertheless markedly more muscular and 'hard' in body type than other children, and showed Sheldon's associated temperamental characteristics, that is, they were assertive, impulsive, extraverted and aggressive. However, these delinquents came from homes where they were shown little understanding and affection, and the Gluecks surmised that these environmental factors interacted with morphological factors to produce the delinquent behaviour. (This matter is further discussed in chapter 7 in relation to the assessment of individual children.)

Constitutional psychology maintains that because there are basic differences between people in their psycho-physical make-up they tend to have different needs and so will tend also to express themselves differently one from another. They will also interpret life experiences differently one from another, and consequently react differently to their experiences.

Sheldon thought that the educational system, at least in the USA, was too much geared to an assumption that all children are more or less alike, and he thought it most important to note that children do differ greatly one from another, largely, in his opinion, because of their different body builds. He felt that the child with a muscular physique is best provided for in a competitive society where his assertiveness and social extraversion are appreciated.

Constitutional psychology has not been a popular form of study in recent years partly because there are real difficulties in knowing how the results of such studies can be interpreted, but also because the atmosphere of the times lays such great stress on the influence of the environment on the development of the human personality, so that work which attempts to see if there is some relationship between physical structure and psychological characteristics has not been taken up with much interest. Many textbooks of psychology ignore this topic altogether; it is given some attention here because, as is discussed above and in chapter 7, there is enough evidence about the relationship between physique and temperament for the knowledge which this relationship gives to provide an additionally useful tool in the assessment of the temperament of others.

Twin studies, longitudinal studies and work with animals in relation to the possible inheritance of temperamental characteristics

Another approach to the study of personality is provided by a comparison of specific personality characteristics as they manifest themselves in MZ* and DZ* twins, and by a comparison of MZ twins who have been brought up together and with MZ twins who have been brought up apart from one another. Although such investigations have been concerned with many different kinds of personality traits, two in particular, called 'types' by Eysenck (1976) and 'second-order factors' by Cattell (1965) have been studied fairly extensively. These two are 'extraversion' and 'neuroticism' (or 'anxiety' in Cattell's terminology). In Eysenck's hierarchial view of personality many different kinds of personality traits, habits of behaviour and specific responses can be grouped under these 'types', rather like generations on a family tree. Thus when I am out walking I may see someone I know; my *response* to this is to cross the road. This response arises from a *habit* of, normally, avoiding rather than seeking out other people; and this habit in turn springs from a more general *trait* of shyness, which in its turn comes from my having an introverted personality *type*.

Although we are not, in this book, concerned with the way in which psychologists study the dynamics and functioning of the adult personality, it is relevant to say something of the work of the psychologist Eysenck. Eysenck has offered some explanations regarding the inheritance of certain personality dimensions, and it is necessary to say something about the framework within which these explanations are structured.

Eysenck considers that personality *is* behaviour, that is, that in our behaviour we display our personalities. He considers it important, if we are to understand more about the human personality, that we should be able to identify and then accurately measure human characteristics which are possessed by all persons, though in widely varying degrees and strengths. Thus, everyone, however unintelligent, has some measure of intelligence. Similarly, everyone displays some degree of emotionality, and this emotionality can be seen to have at least two qualities, one being along the dimension of 'strong–weak' and the other being along the dimension of 'quick–slow'. So one can rename these dimensions respectively the neuroticism and extraversion dimensions. Again, much human behaviour relates to what might be called toughmindedness versus tendermindedness, which Eysenck calls the psychoticism (or 'p') dimension, and yet other behaviour springs from attitudes held about life, which might be measurable along a dimension called the radical-versus-conservative (the liberal) dimension. So, by identifying at least five major dimensions which are universally displayed in different strengths by individual people, and by finding means whereby the strengths of the dimensions for individual people can be measured, Eysenck maintains that a reasonably accurate profile of any one person can be built up. The neuroticism, extraversion and 'p' dimensions can be measured by a self-report test called the Eysenck Personality Questionnaire (EPQ).

Our main concern in this section of the chapter is the study of the possible genetic contribution to personality characteristics other than intelligence and ability. Eysenck has put forward theories which relate the behaviour which people display to specific biological differences between persons. We need not here concern ourselves with a detailed description of his work; we need only say that evidence obtained over many years from work in psychology laboratories seems to indicate that the theories have stood up reasonably well to experimental testing, though Eysenck himself views his work as being basically heuristic.

There is evidence from many different studies, including those by Eysenck and Prell (1951), Shields (1962) and Canter (1969, unpublished), of a genetic contribution to the score which an individual can obtain on the introversion–extraversion continuum, and also on the neuroticism continuum, though the latter is less clear. Canter of the Glasgow Twin Study indeed considers that her work favours strong support for a genetic factor in 'sociability and possibly extraversion, and it would appear that (for separated MZ twins) hereditary influences are most strongly exerted *after* separation'. She found that in some characteristics separated MZ twins were indeed *more* alike than those brought up together. She suggests that when twins are brought up together they 'adopt different roles, at least in the case of social behaviour or social extraversion, to stress their individuality, and that *similarities are only released* when they come to live separate lives'.

A longitudinal study of importance in relation to the possible inheritance of temperament, and also in relation to environmental influences on the formation of temperamental characteristics was commenced in 1956 (Thomas and Chess, 1977) in New York (The New York Longitudinal Study — NYLS). The researchers sought to explore systematically individual differences in children, and to examine the significance of these differences for children's future development. They had been impressed, as everyone must be who has had contact with new-born babies, by the very clear individual differences in temperament which babies show even during their first few weeks of life. They also found that as clinicians they were quite often unable to make any connection between a child's psychological development and the environmental influences to which he had been subject. They identified and scored nine categories of temperament, which they called respectively: activity level; rhythmicity; approach–withdrawal; adaptability; distractability; threshold of responsiveness; attention span and persistence; intensity of reaction; and quality of mood. These categories were studied in the same 141 children at each of the infant school, pre-school and early school stages, and some of the original sample were studied at later ages also. Thomas and Chess say that such temperamental qualities can be observed in a child only two months old, and these characteristics tend to remain constant in quality. Of course the child's behaviour is bound to change as he develops, but the instances which the authors give about temperamental consistencies which express themselves in different kinds of behaviour with changing age are exhibited in the following example: if the child wriggles at two months while his nappies are being changed he is likely at one year of age to be 'into everything'. At five a child who behaves quietly in infancy may dress slowly and be able to sit quietly and happily during car rides.

In discussing the origins of temperament the authors refer also to the work of other researchers, in particular that of Torgerson (1973) who investigated the same nine categories of temperament in 53 same-sexed twins, some MZ* and some DZ*, at two and nine months of age. From his findings Torgerson 'concluded that the results of this study show a strong genetic influence on temperament, and that future studies on this topic . . . should not ignore the significance of the genetic influence' (Thomas and Chess, page 134). From the NYLS two MZ* babies were adopted into two different families at birth and both babies showed 'strikingly similar temperamental traits in the preschool years' (page 135). At the age of sixteen the twins were again interviewed separately and the researchers found remarkable 'physical and behavioural similarities'. They comment that although the families of these two girls had had no contact with one another they were similar in socio-cultural 'characteristics and goals for their girls' (page 136). But it is nevertheless striking that the girls had similar interests for music and acrobatics, were similar in their gregarious social life and were both doing well in school. It is not often that siblings raised in the *same* family show such similarities. Thomas and Chess conclude from their longitudinal study that there is 'an appreciable but by no means exclusive, genetic role in the determination of temperamental individuality in the young infant'. However, they also state that environmental influences 'may very well accentuate, modify, or even change temperamental traits over time'. We discuss these influences later in this chapter.

There is some evidence from animal work that characteristics such as 'emotionality' are to an extent genetically determined. Emotionality in rats is indicated by the degree to which a rat cowers in its box and by the frequency of its defaecation and urination when in an unusual situation. Denenberg (1962) has carried out a series of complex breeding experiments with rats in which babies of disturbed and of normal mothers were fostered respectively by normal and disturbed mothers. Other kinds of variations of the genetic and rearing factors were experimentally controlled, and Denenberg found that the genetic factor seemed to have some influence on later emotional behaviour. He also found that the quality of interaction between the mother and child during the period between birth and weaning permanently affected the adult emotional behaviour of the offspring. Again, Searle (1949) found that it was possible to control the breeding of rats so as to produce some who were more, and others who were less, afraid of the maze apparatuses in which they were tested for problem-solving ability. The results of work with various breeds of dogs (Freedman, King and Elliot, 1961) have shown variations in the seemingly innate reaction to handling by humans of these different breeds. Perhaps more interesting still is work by Lindzey, Winston and Manosevitz (1963) with mice of different strains subjected to 'traumatic' experiences in infancy. They found that the *same* experience had different *kinds* of effects on mice from different strains. One recalls Freud's view that an experience which will harm one child will pass another by without apparent effect. Infant monkeys display behaviour appropriate to their sex even when reared by surrogate mothers, particularly in relation to aggressiveness and vigour (Harlow, 1965).

There is a good deal of evidence, then, to show that certain kinds of temperamental qualities are related to physiological and morphological* factors, and that they appear to be present from an early age. This does not mean that the environment has no effect on behaviour, nor that personality characteristics such as, say, optimism are not most probably due to the transaction of genetic and environmental factors, but it does seem from the evidence from various sources which has accumulated during recent years that innate factors may play a greater part in determining personality characteristics than had been previously conceded.

The effects of various environmental factors on the development of intelligence

As mentioned earlier in this chapter, the environment is not a unitary influence, that is, there are many separate and also many interrelated factors present in a child's environment which influence the development of his personality and behaviour. As far as intelligence is concerned, it is suggested by the so-called 'environmentalists' that persons are generally born more-or-less equal in innate mental ability, and that the differences in IQ scores found between people are due mostly to the unfairness and/or inadequacy of the measuring tests used. As far as differences in scholastic performance are concerned, most environmentalists consider that these differences are due to the diverse environmental situations in which different children find themselves, though most environmentalists also do not consider that poor *early* experiences in life need necessarily affect later achievement to any great extent. The burden of their argument rests very much on the notion that a better provision of educational facilities and an improvement in the general living conditions of many people could *greatly* enhance the achievement of most children who at present perform badly in school. There is some very recent evidence (Rutter *et al.*, 1979) to show that certain conditions in schools do tend to produce better scholastic results regardless of the social-class background of the children attending these schools (chapter 8). Also, Wedge and Prosser (1973) have shown that most children who are, as they call it, 'socially disadvantaged' perform very much worse in school than children from more fortunate backgrounds. Although Wedge and Prosser write that there is no general agreement about what constitutes social disadvantage, they themselves define a socially disadvantaged child as one who

(1) comes *either* from a one-parent family *or* a very large family, *and*

(2) comes from a family which is badly housed *and*

(3) comes from a family which has a low income.

They found that one in sixteen children in Britain suffers from these three conditions in combination, which, they say, is after all the equivalent of two children in every classroom! These children are, at the age of eleven, on average three-and-a-half years behind other children in reading. Wedge and Prosser state that 'one in six [of the disadvantaged children] in general was receiving special help within the normal school for "educational backwardness" compared with one in sixteen of the ordinary group' (with which they were compared) (chapter 7). In addition to suffering these disadvantages many of the children started life with further handicaps: many more than is usual had young mothers (it is known that children of young mothers are physically and psychologically more vulnerable than children of mothers of average age); the mothers of many were more likely to have smoked heavily during pregnancy than the average expectant mother; their mothers made fewer than the usual number of advisable visits to ante-natal clinics, and more such children were born prematurely than is usual. Yet, surprisingly, one in seven of these children was said by their teachers to have 'outstanding ability' in music, or science, or chess or sport, etc. A finding such as this is difficult to fit into a 'pure' environmentalist view of the causes of poor achievement.

There is sufficient evidence to indicate that children brought up in an institution from early infancy are backward in achievement and intelligence when they are compared with children from the same socio-economic background who were not brought up in an institution. Such children from even the best institutions are usually rather badly deprived of nearly all the factors which act as stimulants to the development of cognitive processes: the surroundings are often drab, the adult–child ratio is too low to provide the child with more than the minimum of adult conversation, there are seldom books to consult or people with time to answer questions. Though it is difficult to isolate any *one* factor among these several which may be crucial to the development of a child's cognitive potential, when all these factors combine together, as they do often for the child reared institutionally, the result is nearly always a depressing of the innate, cognitive potential.

Vernon (1979) has assessed the contribution which the many environmental factors make to the development of intelligence. When one considers the pre- and peri-natal factors which are, after all, the first environmental factors to affect development, it does seem that severe maternal malnutrition, prematurity, anoxia and other delivery complications, as well as family size (for the latter-born children of a *large* family) can all contribute to lowered intelligence. As far as birth order is concerned Zagonic and Markers (1975) found that in a family of over seven children the decline in IQ score from the seventh child to the last child is three times greater than the average difference between the adjacent siblings. There seems little doubt that as family size increases each subsequent child is likely to score lower than his preceding sibling.

Sameroff (1975) has pointed out that, as far as peri-natal complications are concerned, these are in various studies·'consistently related to later physical and psychological development only when combined with and supported by persistently poor environmental circumstances' and, he adds, 'evolution appears to have built into the human organism regulative mechanisms to produce normal developmental outcomes under all but the most adverse circumstances' (page 283).

Some of the most potent of these poor environmental circumstances referred to by Sameroff have already been considered; what other factors may affect the development of intelligence?

The development of language learning and thinking is, according to Bruner and his associates, related to the early mother–child relationship, and, as we see on page 206, the *kind* of language a child eventually comes to speak will affect how he responds to schooling, and this in turn can affect his progress at school. We may still ask, however, to what extent the quality of the early mother–child relationship affects the development of *intelligence*, which, it will be remembered, is not synonymous with scholastic achievement (page 95).

It is now known that the baby's brain develops very greatly in the first two years of life. Ritchie (1967) has described how the weight of a baby's brain increases by 350 per cent during this period, and by only 35 per cent in the following ten years. In the first two years there is a rapid growth in the cortical brain cells — that is, of the neurons*, and also a major change occurs in the interconnections between the brain cells, and by four years of age the last stage of dendrogenesis* is attained. It is, therefore, *not unreasonable* to suppose that experiences which occur during the first four years of life, and particularly during the first two years, might affect the nature of dendrite* growth and consequently of intellectual development. Russell (1979) also has stressed the importance for the developing brain of having many, particularly pleasurable, experiences involving other humans in the early months of life. There is evidence from animal work (Altman, Das and Anderson, 1968) that some aspects of animal brain development are affected by environmental circumstances. There seems little doubt that usually babies who are *grossly* deprived of stimulating interaction with an adult over a long period will not be able to achieve their intellectual potential, though there are exceptions even to such conditions (Koluchova, 1972). Again it is undoubtedly true that a warm and responsive mother, particularly one who responds with interest to her *baby's initiation* of joint activity, will stimulate the infant to further joint activity. Such effective interaction between mother and child is also more likely to make this kind of interpersonal activity a happy activity for the child, and will also satisfy his curiosity drive and so stimulate him to wish to learn. This, in turn, will have its repercussions later on the child's *attitude* to learning in school. However, it is doubtful whether such maternal responsiveness will *very greatly* enhance the infant's *intellectual* abilities. Newson (1974), however, stresses that it is possible that contemporary theorists in developmental psychology underrate the importance of such responsive 'social mediation' (page 256). In addition, it is clear that maternal responsiveness has considerable influence on other aspects of personality development (chapter 7).

It is not possible here to examine in detail all the separate environmental factors which may affect the development of intelligence. It is in any case difficult to isolate specific factors from other factors with which they almost inevitably interact. However, when one considers the various separate influences, some of which are more amenable to study and have been reviewed here, and others of which we have not examined, one is left with one major factor which encompasses nearly all the individual environmental factors, and that is socio-economic class. Sameroff (1975) concludes that 'socio-economic status appears to have much stronger influence on the course of development [not just intellectual development] than perinatal history' (page 274). Wedge and Prosser (1973) also make the point that the social class to which a child belongs is the 'single factor most strongly associated with his attainment' (page 54). Vernon (1979), too, considers that the conditions which, for example, surround the birth of the child are 'mixed up with social class and other factors' (page 100). In other words, the quality of life which a child experiences from conception onwards is in almost every aspect of his life so strongly related to the socio-economic class of his parents that this one, major, umbrella factor is the most accurate predictor of intellectual performance, and the single most influential factor on such performance. However, one also has to remember that it is very likely that the environment in which a child finds himself is a reflection of the genetic endowment he has received: in other words, the fact that a child's parents have provided him with a good environmental background because of their social class membership also means that most likely they have also provided him with a good inheritance. Indeed, it is not unlikely that the parental ability to provide a good environment in itself stems from the parents' genetic endowment. There is obviously a 'co-variance', or, as the layman usually puts it, an interaction, between the environmental and genetic contributions to intelligence, which often means that an advantageous environment goes with a favourable genetic endowment. However, as is discussed earlier in this chapter, one child in seven of the severely disadvantaged children studied by Wedge and Prosser (1973) was more able than half the non-disadvantaged children they examined. Thus it is clear that some children with outstanding natural abilities are able to transcend even very severe environmental handicaps. It also seems likely that other children, with lesser natural abilities but living in a more satisfactory environment, are able to achieve a similar level of competence because the stimulation, help and support they receive from infancy onwards enables them to make full use of their abilities. Jensen (1969) has suggested that the environment acts as a threshold variable, that is, it cannot enable abilities which do not exist to be displayed, but it can depress the natural endowment. Butcher (1968) has observed that whatever weight may be given to the genetic contribution to tested intelligence, society must accept the responsibility of acting *as if the environment were of crucial importance*. To this end attempts were made in the United States to remedy the disadvantages suffered by many children by means of the so-called 'Head start' schemes which sought to give such children during the pre-school period help in nursery school settings which would, it was thought, enable them to start school from the same level as more advantaged children; by-and-large such help did not achieve the purposes for which it was instituted, probably because too little help was provided too late, though these schemes were by no means uniform in character. The failure of these schemes, however, does not mean that intervention or compensation schemes as such are necessarily ineffective; there is now evidence (Vernon, 1979; Clarke, 1978) that very poor early experiences do not necessarily prevent a child from maximizing his natural potential abilities later in life, though the compensation required must be of a different calibre from the kind of nursery school teaching which was provided by the various 'Head start' schemes in the USA; but it has also become clear that early *intervention* is more effective than later compensation. In Britain the Halsey Report (1972) set out four objectives in relation to children who live in 'educational priority areas (EPA)', that is, for children who are socially disadvantaged. These four objectives are:

(1) to raise the educational performance of the children;
(2) to improve the morale of teachers;
(3) to increase the sense of community responsibility; and
(4) to increase parental involvement in their children's education.

It does seem that, particularly if parental interest can be aroused, this kind of intervention provides the best chance of remedying some of the unfortunate effects on a child of living in a socially disadvantaged environment. Possibly the best-known recent intervention programme carried out in the States to assist mothers to help their babies while at the same time drastically improving the babies' own environment is that of Heber and Garber (1975). Not only were the mothers given training in every aspect of child care, but the infants themselves from the age of three months were brought up in a stimulating environment for at least five days a week, although this kind of stimulation ceased when the children started school. They were compared at various ages on IQ scores with a control group of children and, though the special group mean IQ dropped once they ceased to have special stimulation, it was still 24 points higher than that of the control group, and also than that of their own siblings. There were several other advantages to the mother–child pairs as a result of this intervention. However, one does not yet know whether the effects of the training will remain with the children, and also, of course, the cost of this kind of programme makes it quite impossible to carry out with the total population of disadvantaged children. Other projects, such as the work carried out by the Red House Community in Denaby in Yorkshire (Department of Education and Science, 1975), are less elaborate and involved home visiting of families with children between eighteen months and five years of age. Perhaps one of the most useful approaches for preventing avoidable depressing of a child's cognitive abilities lies in another scheme tried at Denaby, which is to involve adolescents still at school with the work of the nursery group, so that potential parents learn how important is their own responsiveness to their child, and the initiation of parent–child activities in the development of infants and young children.

When one looks at remedial programmes it appears that, contrary to earlier reports, remedies applied after early infancy can effect improvements, though in general it seems that unless the attention given is very special, the earlier a change to a better environment is effected the better. Skeels' (1966) study of orphans tested at eighteen months, some of whom were then adopted into average homes and were compared with others who had had to be left in the orphanage, appears to indicate that at eighteen months of age removal to an average home background can produce remarkable changes. Skeels claims an average gain of 30 IQ points.

A study carried out in this country between 1975 and 1978 (Holmes, 1978) monitored the progress of three-year-old disadvantaged children who attended a special education pre-school unit for children in residential and day care, and compared these children's progress with similar disadvantaged children who did not attend the special educational unit. This study claims that effective intervention which 'can meet their [the children's] interrelated emotional and education needs . . . enables them to make a successful transition to an ordinary infant school' (page 10). It is suggested by the author that if this intervention prevents the need for special education later, then the cost involved in running such units can be recovered. The study found very great differences in school adjustment between children who attended the unit and those who did not, and this was so even for children who attended only one hour a day. Holmes found that the reliable one-to-one relationship which was established between child and teacher gave such children who had experienced very little personal relationship with an adult the ability in due course to learn more independently. The unit found that

(1) a very high adult–child ratio;
(2) stability for the child of place, time and routine for meeting with the adult; and
(3) learning with an adult sitting beside the child who also held conversations with him, in which she indicated that she remembered about yesterday and discussed what would happen tomorrow

all gave the child the opportunity to talk about his life with someone who listened, and who was interested, and who could also 'bear the anger and sadness involved' (page 8). The confidence so established also enabled the children involved to trust the school teacher once they started infant school, and greatly enhanced their own capacity to learn. Clarke and Clarke (1976) also comment on the efficacy of such adult–child interaction when they write: 'It is as if the [socially deprived] child himself had no way of internalizing the processes which foster his growth, whereas [normally] the parent–child system does possess this capability' (page 250).

Regarding the improvement which can be brought about by later schooling, the evidence from several studies seems to be that the effects of different teaching methods, and even such seemingly common-sense factors as the provision of small classes, have no major impact on the performance of children at school. These facts are, indeed, again borne out by a recent study by Rutter, Mortimore, Maughan and Ouston with Smith, (1979) called *Fifteen Thousand Hours*. The authors, using inner London schools as their testing ground, found that the major difference between 'successful' and 'unsuccessful' schools lay not so much in 'common-sense' differences as in the manner in which the school was internally organized. This study is referred to in more detail in chapter 8, but it does seem that what the authors call the school 'process', that is, certain aspects of the internal organization as well as the 'atmosphere' of the school, can have a marked effect on the examination results of the children attending these schools. They found that the least able children in the best schools did on average as well as the most able in the worst schools, and that, contrary to what is often said, in schools where children of ordinary ability did better than one might have expected the more able children also performed better.

the effects of the environment on intellectual ability and academic achievement are concerned, then it does appear as if both socio-economic disadvantages, coupled with parental lack of understanding of the importance of their role in providing stimulation from infancy onwards, can have depressing effects; it also seems that such effects can be remedied to an extent by removal of the child to a better daily environment, though this is not, of course, possible for the majority of children. However, the education of potential parents in the psychological as well as the physical aspects of child care would make the provision of a more helpful psychological environment much more readily available for the next generation. It also appears that certain particular good qualities in any school can help children of all ability groups to display these abilities.

One must, however, also remember, as discussed earlier in this chapter, that all the evidence indicates that the environment is not the sole determinant of how well a child is able to perform at cognitive tasks, whether these are IQ tests or school examinations. Clarke (1978), who considers that the provision of a good environment can do a great deal to remedy an early disadvantageous background, and who seems to place less emphasis on the genetic differences between persons than on the differences in the diverse environments in which we find ourselves, nevertheless states with caution that 'within limits human development *may be regarded as somewhat open-ended, at least potentially so*', and he adds that this means that one cannot deny the 'powerful influences of genetic and constitutional factors' (page 255). What seems of prime importance is for society to try to arrange matters in such a way that every child is able to display to the full whatever abilities he may have.

The effects of the environment on other personality characteristics

Although this chapter is called 'Influences affecting the formation of personality characteristics', it is possibly necessary here to remind the reader that psychologists are at present concerned more to understand about the *processes* of development than to find specific *causes* for development, for it has become evident in recent years that much more research is necessary into the processes of development before causes can be assigned to the factors which affect it. We have also to remember that a good deal of behaviour both of children and adults is situation-specific, and only in part affected by the 'core' personality which is formed in childhood (page 74). Nevertheless, because we are interested in the upbringing and education of children we are interested in knowing what kinds of factors in the environment are *likely* to affect personality development.

The effects of various kinds of handling of children by adults is discussed in greater detail in other chapters, where the development of language, the child's emotional, social and moral growth, and the adult's role in interaction with the child are discussed. At this point the effects of various kinds of environmental factors will be considered in a more general sense.

The development of a child's personality is clearly affected at various times by many different kinds of influences, and also by the specific period in each child's stage of development when the influence is being exerted. One can also consider each effect of the environment according to the degree of the child's personal involvement in it. It goes without saying that to some extent at least each child is influenced by the culture into which he is born, the nation to which he belongs, the social-class membership and the personality characteristics of his parents, and also his own experiences of life. Some of these factors involve him more deeply on a personal level, others less deeply. These influences are interdependent, so that each 'ring' in diagram 3 to an extent affects the rings inside it.

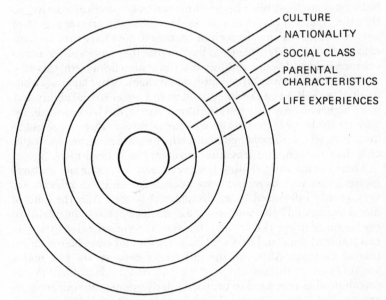

CULTURE

NATIONALITY

SOCIAL CLASS

PARENTAL CHARACTERISTICS

LIFE EXPERIENCES

Diagram 3: *Environmental factors which may influence the formation of the personality*

Sexual, cultural and social-class influences

It has been postulated by some writers, particularly by anthropologists, that the temperamental differences found to exist in men and women are due solely to cultural and not to biological causes. Some cultures do appear to rear children so that there are no discernible temperamental differences between boys and girls, for example, the girls become as aggressive as the boys. Other cultures produce boys and girls who are almost the mirror image of men and women in our culture, the men being 'feminine', and the women 'masculine' in temperament (Mead, 1935). However, such cultures are the exception rather than the rule, and there is some solid, biological evidence (Nash, 1970; Hutt, 1978) to suggest that the usual temperamental differences between men and women in fact are largely due to biological differences between the sexes, these being most likely strengthened by cultural traditions. Thus Hutt (*ibid.*) describes not only how males are more vulnerable to physical and psychological illness, but also how they are represented more often at the extreme ends of the scales measuring certain human characteristics than are females: there are, for example, more dwarfs and giants, more feeble-minded and geniuses among men than among women. There are other differences to which Hutt refers which have their behavioural repercussions: thus baby boys are from birth better equipped to be physically active, so that the greater measure of independence and the greater degree of aggressiveness which most societies permit to boys have their biological foundation. Girls differ from boys in that they have a lower auditory threshold and better auditory discrimination from birth; this may well be one reason why girls exhibit on average a better language ability than boys. Boys on the other hand have a better spatial ability and score higher on creativity tests than girls. Again, this biological ability may at least be *one* of the reasons why the world over there are so many more men who are mathematicians, why men are more mechanically able than women, and why most inventors have been male.

There seems little doubt, however, that, for example, cultural interests and various motivations, such as the desire to achieve, are very greatly influenced by environmental factors. Also the kind of moral feeling and behaviour which a child develops and the quality of the language he speaks, are all influenced to a considerable extent by cultural traditions and by social class norms and class-biased child-rearing customs. Although the differences between the two major social classes in Britain, the working and middle classes, are not as pronounced as they used to be, particularly among the younger generation, the effects of parental membership of a social class does still appear to influence quite a number of such behavioural variables which in their turn affect personality development. In chapter 5 the influence on the child's development of the linguistic code used by parents is examined, and we see that this has an impact on the nature of the interpersonal relationships which are formed; on the kind of self-discipline which can be evoked; and even on the way the child interprets his experiences. There is sufficient evidence from a number of different sources to show that the use both of certain disciplining techniques and of certain forms of language in the home can also affect the kind of morality developed in the child (chapter 5). The use of language both to explain to the child the consequences to others of disapproved actions, and to point out to him that such actions will usually be disapproved of in other, similar, circumstances, together with the use of a non-power-orientated disciplining technique, tends to produce in the child an inner moral control and a reasonably strong conscience (Hoffman, 1975; and Hoffman and Saltzstein, 1967). These are the child-rearing methods more usually used by parents belonging to the middle classes. By contrast, power-orientated disciplining methods and a 'restricted' code of parental language, which does not enable the child so easily to generalize from one situation in which he has transgressed to other, similar, situations, are techniques primarily adopted by parents from the lower working classes. These techniques are not as likely to produce moral behaviour which is self-regulating, but rather a type of behaviour which relies on external sanctions for regulation (chapter 5).

Studies which have investigated parental personality characteristics in relation to child personality growth are discussed in some detail in chapter 8. This is a complex area of research in which it is not possible to control influential variables, such as the strength and effect of possible, innate predispositions in their interaction with the various experiences of the child provided by his environment. Nor do we know yet which of a number of variables which often go together to form a particular child-rearing practice, such as, for example, the practice of providing a good model for behaviour *and* reasoning with the child instead of enforcing obedience, are more influential in producing a particular kind of desired behaviour or a particular kind of personality trait in the child. However, it does seem that where parents are warm, loving, autonomy-granting and respectful of their child as a valued individual, and when they are also able to enhance his self-esteem, and yet can be authoritative (not authoritarian!), the child has the best opportunity to develop his personality to the full. If, in addition, the parents provide a good model for behaviour, reason with the child about his behaviour instead of insisting on obedience, and if also they give him responsibility early in life, it appears that he will be likely to acquire pro-social tendencies. Mussen and Eisenberg-Berg (1977, page 3) define 'pro-social behaviour' as behaviour which 'refers to actions that are intended to aid or benefit another person or group of people without the actor's anticipation of external rewards' (see also chapter 5).

Of course, a child is subject to many direct influences from sources outside the family, of which school and television are the two most potent. In the USA children spend more time viewing television than in going to school (chapter 5) and these two activities together take up far more time than the time spent in the average family in interaction between parent and child. Both school and television could play a much greater part in fostering pro-social behaviour than they seem to do at present. And Mussen and Eisenberg-Berg (1977) also say: 'Socially responsible television programming can help raise the levels of helping and sharing among child viewers by decreasing portrayals of violence and aggression, and instead presenting more instances of exemplary pro-social behaviour' (page 160). Also in some cultures, for instance in the USSR, where children in elementary schools have to take responsibility for helping younger children, helping behaviour is generally increased (Whiting and Whiting, 1975).

Early experiences, especially the mother–child relationship

The possible importance of early experiences, particularly in relation to the quality of the mother–child relationship, must be considered in relation to personality development, though this matter is discussed again with regard to various aspects of development in chapters 5 and 7.

Bowlby's early paper (1944), which concentrated on the effects, as he then saw them, of maternal-deprivation experiences on later behaviour, stimulated much retrospective research into the early mother–child relationship. It is possible that in concentrating on early experiences researchers overlooked two related facts: one is that a child with a deprived early childhood will usually, though not necessarily always, also experience a deprived later childhood; and that even though experiences early in childhood are important, it is not impossible that the later years of childhood are also significantly important. As Clarke and Clarke (1978) write, 'the whole of development is important, not merely the early years' (page 272). This, however, does not mean that the early years may not be *more* important than the period of life after, say, five years of age, though in discussing here the possibly greater importance of the first five years it is not intended that later childhood experiences should be thought in the least unimportant.

In addition to the findings of retrospective research into the causes of behavioural and emotional disturbances, and to the emphasis placed on early experiences by the psychoanalytic theorists (chapter 2), the theory which states that the early years must be more important than later years rests also on the assumption that the plasticity of the infant's nervous system makes him very susceptible to new learning, and that such new learning is very impressionable and not easily overturned by later and different (better) experiences. In addition, a good deal of work with animals, such as that of the Harlows (1962) with rhesus monkeys and Denenberg (1962) with rats indicates that for these animals at least early infant experiences of a certain kind can lead to impoverished social and sexual behaviours and/or neuroticism. The extent to which such clinical, observational and animal-work findings can support the importance of early experiences in relation to *aberrant* human behaviour is considered in chapter 7. These many studies have focused attention also on the possible importance of sensitive mothering, and on the forming of attachments and bonding in infancy for the development of a child's full cognitive, social and emotional potential.

We discuss on pages 95f the importance of maternal sensitivity to the stimulation of a baby's sense of curiosity and desire to learn, and on page 172 such sensitivity on the part of the mother is discussed in relation to the forming of social bonds later in life. Much opposition has in recent years been expressed to the notion that the mother–child relationship during the child's infancy is of prime importance, for the responsibility this appears to place on the mother is very great. Many mothers do not enjoy looking after small babies and prefer to go to work or indeed have to go to work, and the idea that she should not go to work, unless another more-or-less continuously present caretaker can give her infant the kind of attention she could give him were she to remain at home, is not acceptable to many new mothers. It is not relevant here to enter into this controversy, for obviously many individual factors relating to specific family circumstances and personalities will enter into the decision which any particular family with a new baby will make. However, the matter is referred to, for the *desire* to feel that the early mother–infant relationship is not 'really important' will *not thereby make it unimportant!*

We discuss in chapter 5 the social nature of the baby. Because he is a social being he not only has a need to exercise, as it were, his faculty of sociability, but, as anyone knows who has observed the very evident emotional distinction which exists for the 'bonded' baby from 7 months onwards between those to whom he is bonded and strangers, the forming of bonding relationships has a strong emotional significance for him. Detailed observation of babies in interaction with their sensitive caretakers makes it evident that for the baby the regular and very frequent presence (though not necessarily actually *continuous* presence) of another person who understands his non-verbal cues and who can make his meanings explicit to himself is a satisfying experience. Such a familiar person can show him that the world is a pleasant, responsive and meaningful place. This kind of experience is emotionally, cognitively and socially a most important introduction to the world, and to the people in it. Such an introduction cannot be given adequately by a succession of strangers. It is helpful to imagine what is involved in a good emotional relationship between any two people, and then to consider what kind of early relationship provides a good model for such later relationships. It is clear that the opportunity to form a persisting relationship with one or a few responsive humans is important for the baby's social development; indeed, to experience loving, continuing and responsive, though not over-protecting, care from birth and throughout at least early childhood, is possibly one of the most valuable experiences any human being can have. The experimental evidence for this statement is discussed by Rutter (1978), Schaffer (1977), Richards (1974) and many other recent writers.

What such quality of caring means for the mother in practical terms is that she, or whoever is sharing the baby's caring with her, should not only as far as possible be continuous and regular in her caring, but have sufficient time to get to know the baby. What is important is not the *quantity* of interaction but the *quality*. The full-time, and even part-time working mother, particularly if she already has one or more children, though she may care for her baby regularly, often has little time in which to get to know him, and little time also in which to interact with him in a responsive and social manner. A sensitive mother (page 171) will *wish* to interact with her baby in this way; an insensitive or over-anxious mother will be debarred from doing so by her own personality.

However, we have to consider other factors in relation to the importance of such care as it affects the developing personality: one is that the child himself contributes not only to the bond-forming process, but that the quality of *his* contribution affects the quality of his mother's response to him. It is clear (page 91), as described by Thomas and Chess (1977), Dunn (1977), Bell (1968) and others, that from birth babies differ in temperamental characteristics, and these characteristics have their effect on the adults who care for them. To give an extreme example, it is very difficult to talk to and play with, say, a four-month old baby who never smiles or babbles. And, having said this, one can see how difficult it must be for the baby, who has not yet learnt to be sociable, to develop his ability to smile responsively and to transform his infant babbling into vocalizations (chapter 4) if no one responds to him.

Another question one wishes to ask is this: it is obviously highly beneficial for the baby to experience the kind of care we have described, but to what degree is the eventual adult personality affected if such care is absent, either in early childhood only, or throughout childhood? Also, can remedial action be taken in later childhood to rectify the missed early experiences?

The answer to the first question must, at this stage of our knowledge, simply be that we do not know the extent to which multiple mothering, or lack of responsive and sensitive care *by itself* affects the developing personality. We examine in chapter 7 what is known about children who have experienced multiple mothering from birth, but for many children the deprivation they suffer is not so gross, and it is very difficult to know whether any personality effects which they may show are *mainly* due to unresponsive mothering in infancy, or lack of parental interest in middle childhood, or to some temperamental idiosyncracy of their own. Unless a child is grossly deprived and/ or unless the personality defects he exhibits are pathologically abnormal, it is not possible to say whether or not the missed advantageous childhood experiences *directly* relate to particular personality characteristics subsequently exhibited. It is possible to say that extreme experiences can lead to identifiable behaviour, but Danzinger (1971) makes the point that although findings about such relationships are useful both in enabling us to try to avoid such extreme situations for children, and also because they give information about child development which is helpful in other ways, such findings do not tell us much in *detail* about the antecedents of *ordinary* levels of behavioural characteristics and their ordinary, though identifiable, antecedents. In addition, psychologists understand now that the adoption of a 'transactional' model, which allows for the continuously interacting effects of temperament and environment, while giving a more realistic picture of personality-forming causes, also acknowledges that we cannot say, except in extreme situations, what were the major influential variables which produce a particular effect. As Sameroff (1975) has written, 'linear sequences [between one cause and one effect] are non-existent, and (that) development proceeds through a sequence of regular restructurings of relations within and between the organism and his environment' (page 285).

However, having said this, the author wishes to stress again what many researchers have reiterated, and that is that even if experiences in infancy are not of supreme importance, because of a variety of factors, it is wise not to minimize the possible effects of such experiences. The factors to be considered are that

(1) the infant has an inherent ability to be social, which ability has, however, to be developed;

(2) the plasticity of his nervous system and the speed of the development of his nerve cells in infancy enable him to learn in a manner he will never be able to equal; and

(3) his emotional needs and sense of helplessness are such that responsive caring must be immensely comforting and anxiety-reducing.

It is also not unreasonable to assume in the absence of compelling contradictory evidence that experiences early in life, though not consciously remembered, will be influential on later development. There is a further point, and that is that although the concept of a critical, or closed, sensitive period of development may no longer be tenable as far as human development is concerned, it is possible to be aware of a particular child's special needs at special times. Thus the baby who especially follows his mother with his eyes has begun to be particularly interested in her; the baby who stops vocalizing and moving his arms when a stranger looks into the pram signals that he realises he is looking at a strange person; and the baby who, as we have discussed, is upset when, in the presence of strangers, his mother leaves the room, and continues to cry while she is out, has developed an internal representation of her, and a bond to her which is important to him emotionally.

We attempt to answer the second question, ie to what extent can later remedial action rectify missed early experience, in chapter 7 where certain special, mostly debilitating experiences, and their effects are also discussed.

Further reading

VERNON, P. E.: *Intelligence: heredity and environment* (W. H. Freeman and Co., San Francisco, 1979)

MITTLER, P.: *The study of twins* (Penguin Books, 1971)

KIRBY, R. and J. RADFORD: *Individual differences* (Methuen, 1976)

SECTION TWO

The Development of Behaviour

CHAPTER FOUR

The growth of the intellect

Cognitive growth as described by Piaget

We discuss in chapter 2 how it is useful for the purposes of study to think of the human personality as constituted of three basic, interacting forces: the intellect, the emotions and the will. In this chapter the development of the child's intellectual abilities will be considered, and in the next chapter the child's emotional and motivational growth and its accompanying social behaviour.

In recent years, however, it has become increasingly difficult to study development in such water-tight compartments, for it is very evident that certain non-intellectual aspects of personality, such as, for example, the growth of self-consciousness, affect quite potently intellectual development (page 67). We also discuss in chapter 2 some problems relating to the acquisition of knowledge, which is relevant to the subject matter of this chapter on the growth of the intellect, and Piaget's work relating to the development of the child's cognitive powers is described in chapter 2 from a *theoretical* viewpoint. The reader who has not yet read chapter 2 should read the section 'Cognitive–developmental theory, particularly the theory of Jean Piaget' (page 58) before proceeding with this chapter where the actual, ontogenic, cognitive development, as described by Piaget, will be considered. Other psychologists, among whom Bruner is an outstanding example, have described intellectual growth, and Bruner's work is referred to also in this chapter; but Piaget's work, because of its scope and depth, has had a wider influence, particularly on pedagogic practice, than any other comparable theory.

According to Piaget the baby under twenty-one months or so is at the sensori-motor stage — that is, his perceptual and motor apparatuses operate simultaneously. At first much of the motor activity is merely of a reflex kind; soon, however, the baby begins to discriminate between various objects in his world, so that at the end of the first month he will know, for example, what in his immediate environment can be sucked and what cannot be sucked. Co-ordination of hand and eye, of touch and sight, follows quickly, and some time between five and eight months of age the baby is able to act on objects outside himself and can think ahead, so that he is capable of forming intentions and behaving purposefully. By the time he is one year old he can perceive relationships; he notices events which are not dependent on his own actions, and he begins to have a rudimentary knowledge of causality so that he can make things happen. How often has one seen a baby of this age drop things from cot or pram, in the delighted knowledge that it will fall down for someone else to pick up!

The six months following a child's first birthday comprise a period of rapid learning and experiment, and by the age of twenty-one months he can, within narrow limits, foresee what actions will succeed, *without testing them first*. He is now able to *represent* things and actions to himself — he is 'adapting' — and this, says Piaget, is what *thinking* is really about. It is not necessary at this stage for the child to be able to speak in order to be able to think; his thoughts are really internalized actions. The first stages of thinking are thus wordless ideas about actions; however, the complexities of adult thought cannot, so it would seem, take place without a good language ability.

We will see, as we follow intellectual development through to adolescence, that in order to develop adult intellectual abilities the child has to learn to free himself from two influences which are dominant in childhood but which, with increasing maturity, become less powerful in governing behaviour. These two are

(1) the influence of the information about the world brought to the child by his perceptual apparatus — i.e. his senses — and

(2) the influence of the child's own viewpoint.

Piaget calls these respectively the 'percept-centred' and the 'egocentric' view of the world. (Egocentric is *not*, in this context, to be confused with emotional feelings akin to selfishness.)

We have seen that, according to Piaget, the small child has first to learn to use his senses in order to interact with people and things; he then has to learn to inhibit some actions and to internalize these, which is the beginning of thought. However, many actions during the first few years of life are novel to the child and have to be carried out before they can be internalized. Great reliance is therefore placed on the information which sight, hearing, touch, taste and motor activity bring to the child about the world. For this reason his interest is 'centred' on information obtained from his perceptual apparatuses, and he necessarily places far less reliance on his thinking processes for obtaining information about the world than do older children and adults.

It is also not possible for the very young child to understand viewpoints which are different from his own. In this context the term 'viewpoint' is not used to refer to an understanding of another's 'point of view', but in the more physical sense of understanding that objects and people in the world have an existence independent of the child's existence. It is thought likely that the newborn baby has no concept of anything being separate from himself; there are no objects, for everything is subjective, an extension of himself. He has to learn first that things exist in their own right, apart from himself. Until this happens the newborn child is entirely 'egocentric'; he lives, as Piaget himself says, 'in a universe without objects' (Piaget, 1968). It is impossible for the young child to understand the most elementary kind of causality, or to appreciate the permanence of things in the world without progressively decentring from his own viewpoint until, eventually, there is some appreciation that other things have an existence separate from himself. He learns to recognize objects viewed from different angles and distances, and so he appreciates his own separateness from other things and their separateness from one another in space. He learns also about permanence and he begins to have some ideas about causality; but all this is a gradual process. A child under seven years of age will find it difficult, as Piaget has shown, to appreciate another's physical viewpoint. For instance, Piaget stood a doll on a table and placed before it an object, such as a pencil lying diagonally to the doll's line of vision. He then asked children to choose from two or three drawings the one which represented the doll's point of view. Children under seven or eight years of age found it difficult to deduce the doll's angle of vision.

In a social setting, too, it is possible to observe the child's egocentric view of the world. A boy under seven who has two brothers, when asked if one of his brothers also has brothers, will say: 'Yes, he has *one* brother' — he cannot see himself as the brother of another child, because this would involve separating himself off as an object and seeing himself in another context — i.e. from his brother's point of view.

Piaget gives the term 'pre-operational' to this stage of cognitive development; this stage lasts from two to seven years of age approximately. An 'operation' in this context is an action which takes place in imagination (page 64). We have seen that this imaginative process successfully enables a child even before he is two years of age to internalize a selection of simple actions, and also that a child between two and seven is able to internalize his behaviour — that is, he can think to a progressively greater extent. Nevertheless this limitation in thinking is, by adult standards, so marked that Piaget (1968) considers that effective operational thinking does not start until the child is seven years of age. Children between seven and eleven thus learn gradually to internalize more and more of their actions, but even then such thinking, as we shall see later in this chapter, is of a 'concrete' kind; children during this period learn to replace action by thinking, but their thinking is still greatly tied to action.

A great aid in helping the child between two and about four-and-a-half years of age to develop his thinking powers is the child's increasing ability to use and understand language. This may explain why a small child who has much contact with older persons, such as the eldest in a family, or an only child, frequently seems to have better-than-average powers of thinking.

With the first use of language the child indicates that he understands symbolism: that is, that one thing — in this case a word — can stand for something else — for a person or for an object — and the actual use of a word helps him to represent a person or object to himself more easily in his imagination. (The development of language ability as such will be considered later in this chapter; here we are concerned with language only as a vehicle in the development of cognitive processes.)

Even during the first two years of life the child begins to learn through his use of language to build up a representational world; language enables him to rework, as it were, his internalization of action, so that his previous world of action and of wordless thought gradually becomes a world of symbols and of language. However, because of the slow development of language learning, thinking remains for the nursery child largely wordless, internalized action, and it is greatly affected by what the child perceives.

A child under two years of age can alter his *motor* habit if he perceives *visually* that the habit is unproductive. For example, a biscuit which the child has found several times hidden under a cup will quickly be retrieved from under a plate if it has been *observed* that the biscuit was hidden under the plate, but, in the absence of this observation, most children under two years of age, even if definitely *told* 'The biscuit is now under the plate', will continue to look under the cup. (One has, of course, to ascertain when carrying out such a test that the child understands the words 'cup' and 'plate'.) Such a simple experiment, and others like it, would seem to indicate that the force of visual experience is stronger at this age than that of verbal information. The Russian psychologists Luria and Yudovich (1960) have carried out interesting experiments of this kind into the relationship between a child's language and the development of his mental processes (page 136).

The thought processes of most adolescents and of adults seem to be as stable as the material world appears to be: our thoughts are consistent; we can consider relationships and entertain hypotheses; we can keep a number of criteria in mind when reasoning: we can use powers of thought to order, to classify and to think conceptually; and we can also argue deductively and inductively. These mental abilities in the child have to be developed when he is between about two and twelve years of age. The child under three thinks transductively — from particular to particular; his thoughts are still neither consistent nor stable and even at a later age they are dominated by what he perceives. Piaget has named the stage from about four-and-a-half to seven years of age the 'intuitive thought' stage: this is still part of a 'pre-operational' stage, but it is a substage in which children have been observed to make judgements based on their mere perception of a situation and not according to reason. If, in a now well-known experiment carried out first by Piaget, a quantity of water is poured from one glass into a *differently shaped* glass, a five-year-old observer will say that there is now a different *amount* of water in the second glass. Similarly if two rows of beads of equal number are laid out on a table in such a manner that the individual beads in the two rows form pairs, and the equality of number in the rows is clearly visible, when the beads in one row are pushed closely together then a child of five will say that there are now *fewer* beads in this row than in the other row. A six-year-old may solve one of these problems correctly but not necessarily the other. Seven- or eight-year-old children will mostly give the correct answers to a simple problem of this kind.

Children under seven years of age or so do not yet, according to Piaget, appear to understand the principle of the conservation of number and of property, nor the principle of a one-to-one relationship. Indeed, work by Beard (1963) shows that when the experimental situation is complicated, for example, by the experimenter pouring water from one glass into two smaller glasses, and later from these two into five smaller glasses, it becomes evident that even ten-year-olds not infrequently hold these principles rather tenuously; that is, they assume that more glasses must hold more water!

Piaget and other workers found that children at the same developmental stage (under seven years of age) cannot usually place a number of objects of different quality, or colour, or dimension according to a particular order or category, for example, pencils of differing lengths from the shortest to the longest. If a four-year-old is asked to perform such ordering he will arrange them in pairs first, and then compare the pairs. He cannot carry in his mind a large unit for comparison of individual items within the unit; but when a child has reached what Piaget terms the 'concrete operational' stage at seven or so, he will look at all the pencils, and then order them all from the shortest to the tallest without much, if any, trial or error action. Piaget says that children begin now to have an 'anticipatory' schema.

For the seven- to eight-year-old child thinking is different in kind from that of the four- to five-year-old. The child is now becoming progressively released from the dominance of the senses, though they are still very influential in guiding his understanding and behaviour. However, he is beginning to build up an internal consistency of thought, even if his logical thinking is still mostly based on a consideration of concrete objects.

One of the instances of the difference in thought is shown in the developing ability of the child over seven to classify objects. A child of six is able to make a collection — to pick bluebells in the wood to make a bunch — but he cannot classify according to criteria. Between seven and eleven he learns to hold several criteria in mind, classifying according to shape, colour, size, etc. Because the child is being freed to an extent from the excessive influences of external reality as far as his thinking processes are concerned, he can begin to build concepts — that is, ideas relating to classes, series and numbers; but his conceptual thinking is still tied to actualities — that is, to first-hand realities and not to abstractions. However, his mind is now becoming more systematized, so that he has an increased self-awareness, and he is able to 'turn round on his own schemata' as Bartlett expressed this human ability in another context (Bartlett, 1932). He can now begin to watch his own mind manipulating thoughts, though this ability is not fully evident until the child approaches the end of the 'concrete operational' period at eleven or twelve years of age. During this period he begins to learn not only about the conservation of quantities and to know about measurement of objects, but he also learns about the weight and volume of substances and of containers. Some kinds of measurements take longer to grasp than others, so that the measurement of objects is understood at about six years of age, but weight and volume not until about eight and ten years respectively. It is reasonable to assume that up to about six or seven years of age children have no real conception of measurement (Piaget, 1968a), and, from an adult's point of view, they have curious ideas about age: they assume that taller children and taller adults must be older than smaller children and shorter adults! The concept of time is also something which is learned slowly; the four-year-old understands only what morning and afternoon signify; by five he knows the days of the week, and by six or seven he can tell the time.

We have seen how it is only through *action* that the child begins to think; thoughts at first are wordless ideas, but, after the child leaves the sensori-motor period, thinking must be increasingly *verbal*, so that the internalization of actions carried out after the sensori-motor period has passed requires verbal ability of sufficient extent to enable increasingly complex actions to be expressed in verbal terms. The younger child under seven years of age, owing to immaturity and lack of experience with people and things, has been unable to internalize fully all his actions; the child between seven and eleven years of age increasingly experiences the world, and one would expect the internalization process to proceed fairly quickly, but Piaget suggests that because *verbal reasoning* remains a limited capability throughout the 'concrete operational' period, the process is in fact slower than one would expect. Indeed, children seem to use the same process for *verbal* reasoning at this stage as they did when dealing with *objects* during the 'intuitive thought' stage. For example, at that stage they could only deal with pairs of objects at a time, not with several, and now they can only deal with two verbal propositions at a time. Thus they cannot understand the puzzle which Piaget (1928) set and which appears in Binet's tests. The puzzle set was as follows: 'Edith is fairer than Susan; Edith is darker than Lily; who is the darkest of the three?' Curious replies are received from children under eleven years of age to such a puzzle; children will say things like: 'As Edith and Susan are both fair and Edith and Lily are both dark, so Edith comes in between Lily and Susan.' During this period children also find instructions couched in 'grid' verbal terms very difficult. If one asks, for example, that 'the fourth little girl in the second row should put up her hand', it is unlikely that children under nine will be able to identify themselves by this method. Proverbs too are seldom understood before early adolescence.

It is important to realize that, in addition to having difficulties with rational notions and conceptual ideas, the young child's percept-centred and egocentric view causes him to view happenings in the world around him differently from the way older children and adults view the world. Ideas about causality change from 'animism', in which life is ascribed to everything that moves, to 'artificialism', when children assert that everything is caused by people. As Piaget himself says (1968a): 'The young child constantly makes assertions without trying to support them with facts.' Small children think, for example, that the moon moves because they are moving (Piaget, 1951). They cannot imagine an ordered sequence of events, so that, when they give explanations about causality, cause and effect become confused. Teachers will be familiar with the kind of answers a child under seven will give to questions, such as the following, which Piaget (1928) asked: 'The moon grows. How?' 'It [it was a crescent moon] becomes the whole.' 'Why?' 'Because it gets bigger.' 'How does it happen?' 'Because we grow ourselves.' 'What makes it grow?' 'The clouds'; and so on (see page 64).

At this stage too children consider that inanimate things know their own names and that things which move have feeling. It may well be, though, that these conceptions are due not so much to a maturational stage through which the child is passing, but rather the fault of parents and teachers who, in our society, tend to encourage such anthropomorphic conceptions of inanimate objects. There is some evidence that in other cultures children do not necessarily go through this developmental stage (Mead, 1932).

From the age of twelve or so onwards new intellectual processes begin to become available to the child. He is now no longer restricted in his thinking processes by 'concrete' operations; he can set up hypotheses and predict what would happen if these hypotheses were true. This ability is in marked contrast to that of the child under eleven years of age who cannot entertain hypotheses which are not actually possible. If one wishes, for example, to demonstrate factors influencing the swing of a pendulum, and asks children to find the time period for the swing in relation to the length of the cord on which the weight is suspended, in relation to the weight itself, and in relation to the push given the pendulum, only children of not usually less than thirteen or fourteen years of age will appreciate the necessity of keeping constant all but one variable during the investigation (Beard, 1968). When a child can understand this kind of reasoning he has reached the 'formal operational' stage. He is now able to reason, using statements at an abstract level, and he can build new concepts. Proverbs are understood, and the relationships of numbers to one another, such as ratio, can be comprehended. The young adolescent is able to entertain ideas relating to the possible, rather than just the actual, and to think of the future instead of the present only.

One can readily understand that with these capabilities many other kinds of comprehension, apart from the rational and scientific, now become available to the young adolescent. A true understanding of history depends on understanding other people's viewpoints, in being able to hold a number of criteria in mind concurrently, and in having a concept of time which extends beyond the immediate past. The anthropomorphic view of God, which young children hold, can now change to one which is less egocentric. As we see in chapter 5, ideas about morality, and also notions about other persons' personalities and their motives for behaviour, are all facilitated by the capacity to deal with abstractions, and to be freed from the percept-centred and egocentric view of life. Such freedom is, however, relative; it would be too bold to claim that even mature adults were totally free from these two influences. The extent to which such freedom is realized depends not only on maturational factors, but also on the values and expectations of the society in which the child lives. Western culture relies to a large extent on the ability of its members to plan ahead, and to consider the possible as well as the actual, and in consequence conceptual and abstract thinking abilities are much valued. In contrast, members of primitive societies, and persons belonging to sub-groups in western culture where such abilities are not appreciated, may never reach this, the 'formal operational', stage of cognitive development.

In chapter 2 criticisms of Piaget's work are discussed, but the reader is cautioned against 'throwing the baby out with the bathwater'. What has been particularly valuable about his work, and that of the researchers who have been stimulated by it, is that far-reaching pedagogic implications can be drawn from these research findings.

It is clear now that it is important for schools to teach quite young children 'to think about thinking'. Donaldson (1978) repeats what has been expressed by Bernstein and others (page 130), that is, that some children come to school much better prepared for learning than others; Donaldson, however, makes it a matter of urgency that those who are ill prepared should be helped as early as possible after coming to school to make good their deficiency, and she also insists that *all* children can be helped to make more of their thinking powers than our practical teaching methods at present enable them to do. To this end she stresses greatly the practice of teaching children early to read, not just as a skill in itself, but as a tool to aid thinking abilities. When a child struggles to make sense of a sentence, he has to think about its possible meaning. As Donaldson puts it, 'those very features of the written word which encourage awareness of language may also encourage awareness of one's own thinking and be relevant to the development of intellectual self-control, with incalculable consequences for the development of the kinds of thinking which are characteristic of logic, mathematics and the sciences' (page 94).

This book is not about teaching, but it would be irresponsible in the context of a chapter on the development of the intellect not to introduce the reader to new ideas about how to help a child maximize his intellectual potential (problems in learning to read are discussed in chapter 7). Donaldson quotes experimental evidence which shows that many children do not know what is meant by this activity called 'reading'. Many of them have to be made aware of the *spoken* word before they can understand what the *written word* is. Such children do not realize that what they speak is composed of separate words, so that it is hopeless to teach the written word without a child understanding what a *word* is. Donaldson writes that 'awareness of this correspondence [between the spoken word and marks on paper], even of its existence, much less of its nature, should never be taken for granted'. So practice in speaking, in being made aware of the meaning of words, must, for many children, precede the teaching of reading. But, Donaldson writes, the *way* reading is taught can have an effect on a child's developing self-awareness, and, as we discuss in chapters 2 and 5, this developing self-awareness has important effects not only on cognitive functioning but also on interpersonal relationships. To this end Donaldson stresses the importance in early learning-to-read of allowing the child to pause rather than insisting on a speedy reply: if the child is to become self-conscious he must have time to reflect, and to become aware of thought processes, and this cannot occur if he is hastened into responding quickly. And he must learn to read not by looking at isolated words on 'flash cards' but by having new words embedded in meaningful sentences among words known to him. Also, because, as Donaldson reminds us, the spoken word is so different from the written word, the child must be introduced to the written word in the same form as the spoken word, and, she believes, this is a help also to the fortunate child who is already familiar, through being read to at home, with the style of written language.

The development of language

In considering the development of language learning in children we must differentiate between a number of aspects of such learning, many of which present problems which we are far from understanding. We wish, for instance, to describe *what* actually happens between the time when a baby first makes sounds and the time when a young, intelligent adolescent is able to, hold an interesting conversation. Then we are also interested in the theories of how this learning might take place; is it mainly by imitation or through a process of conditioning (pages 140–145), or through some other means? We are also interested in the *functions* of speech: it is obviously and primarily a tool for communication, but it also serves as a socializing agent, and it also obviously has important connections with the development of thinking abilities. One can also ask why the baby, who cannot know anything of any of these advantages which speech will have for him later, learns to speak at all.

Language learning as an aspect of child development is so fundamental and poses so many questions, that although it is impossible to deal with all these questions in this chapter, it is necessary to give the reader some idea of what is known to date about a child's first language learning. We must consider at least three major questions:

(1) how does the ability to communicate develop;
(2) how and when does the child make his meanings clear; and
(3) what is the relationship between language learning and other aspects of development, such as cognitive growth and social growth?

Language learning has been studied in the past not only as if it occurred in isolation from other aspects of development, but also as if it occurred as a mere vocal phenomenon having nothing to do with a child's other ways of behaving. Also, great attention was paid for many years to investigating how children come to speak grammatically. It is, indeed, difficult to account for the extraordinary ability every child has to form sentences which are not imitations but are *creations of his own*, and which are more-or-less grammatically correct, even when only a few words are put together. The fact that irregular verbs and irregular plurals ('Look, gooses!') are often used as if they were regular, indicating that small children have not imitated the word but employed a grammatical rule, has been of infinite fascination to psycholinguists, and in fact led Chomsky (1957) to propose his theory of the Language Acquisition Device (LAD).

Chomsky differentiated between 'surface' and 'deep' structures of sentences: thus the two sentences 'John is eager to please' and 'John is easy to please' have the same surface structure, but their deep structure is quite different. Again 'John gave his sister an apple' and

119

'John's sister was given an apple by him' have different surface structures but the same deep structure.

It is known that although the surface structure of languages varies from one language to another, there must be sufficient common ground between languages to enable translations to be made from one to another, and it is thought possible that all languages share a common 'deep' structure. It is suggested, therefore, that children may be born with a innate 'idea of language', and that they learn their own particular language by relating what is heard to the underlying structure. Work in Japan and in Russia has shown that children's speech development follows the same pattern in Japanese as it does in the Indo-European languages (McNeill, 1966), although the surface structures of the adult languages are very different.

A preoccupation with the developing child's acquisition of syntax has to an extent blinded psycholinguists to the many other questions about language learning which need to be answered; it has also prevented them until relatively recently from looking at language learning in the context of a child's total development. We discuss in this chapter in some detail the importance in the generation of language of the relationship between

(1) the baby's seemingly innate ability to pay special attention to speech sounds,
(2) his early ability to engage in social interaction with others and
(3) his own thought processes.

During his first year the infant's social–conversational skills increase greatly. It seems hardly possible for the baby to learn these skills, for they are too complex, they are acquired very rapidly, and parental behaviour seldom seems to be directed explicitly towards teaching the infant these skills. Schaffer (1978) suggests that both structurally and functionally the baby is pre-adapted in a highly specific sense to be a social and conversational being. Both the way his body is structured and the way he functions are conducive to social interaction; for example, in relation to the rhythms of his physical functioning, these include bursts of, and pauses in, sucking; looking at and looking away; sleeping and waking. Some of these rhythms relate to *intra*personal functioning, others to *inter*personal functioning, and they predispose the child in due course among other activities to vocalize and then to listen; to act and then to watch. Newson (1978) also quotes Trevarthen's work as showing that the neonate has within his many movements gestures which 'simulate adult communicative gestures' (page 34). So the neonate, as Wells, Bruner, Trevarthen, Richards and others have pointed out, is ready to communicate. However, this does not necessarily mean that such communicative gestures have meaning for the infant, let alone that the infant knows they have meaning for other people. Lewis (1963) has made the point that the meaning which language has for the baby himself springs from the meaning which a baby's first early distress and comfort sounds have *for him*. Lewis comments on the bodily condition of, for example, discomfort, of which the young baby is aware, and of the particular discomfort cries which he makes, and which accompany his bodily condition. Ricks (1972) has identified the cries of eight-to-twelve-month-old infants, and found that these have four different sorts of meaning: greeting, frustration, requesting and surprise. He worked with English, Spanish and Italian children and found that the same sounds indicated the same emotional–social states for all the babies (see also page 125). This relationship between physical awareness and accompanying sounds is important in establishing the meaning of language. As far as the baby understanding that his vocalizations have meaning for others is concerned, this understanding comes about largely because most mothers treat their babies from birth as if they were persons with whom one can communicate. A smiling baby is responded to differently from an anxious-looking or crying baby. In addition, sensitive adults, as Newson (1978) writes, respond in anticipation to 'actions-in-the-making'. The beginnings of a smile are attended to as if they were already a smile, so that, as Newson puts it, whenever a baby 'is in the presence of another human being . . . his actions are processed through a subjective filter of human interpretation according to which some . . . of his actions are judged to have . . . relevance in human terms . . . and are then reflected back' (page 37). So the infant's active, spontaneous behaviour, which has a temporal patterning to it, and to which adults are sensitive, helps this communicative process, and it becomes meaningful to the baby. We have referred elsewhere to the fact that, in relation to the child's toilet-training, the mother can make explicit to the child his own bodily cues and so enable him to attend to these cues in good time. Similarly, by having reflected back to him in an interpretative way the meaning of his own communications, often born out of his own physical states, he learns to understand the communicative functions of his own signals. Mothers also use what Newson (*ibid.*) has called 'intonational markers' which, to an extent, anticipate what is going to happen. About a toy which swings the mother might say 'It's going *up* and *down*' not only when the swing is actually going up or down but just before it does so, and one knows how much small children love this kind of anticipation. And this intonational commentary again helps to make more explicit to the child his own actions in relation to the words used by the mother.

So far we have discussed, within a social context, how an infant might learn to understand his own actions, and also that others know what he means by them. How does he come to use action deliberately to communicate? Glances, gestures and other actions in an interpersonal situation all 'stand for' something to be communicated, and to this extent are symbolic, as language is symbolic, though language is more abstract than other communicative symbols, for there is nothing iconic about language (Hamlyn, 1978). Lock (1978) gives the example of a baby raising his arms: at first the mother pushes her hands under the child's armpits to lift him, then gradually he comes to raise his arms in anticipation of her lifting him, until he reaches the stage where he raises them to indicate that he wants to be lifted up. Slowly the meaning of his crying, which indicates he needs something, is amplified by arm raising or other actions, which indicate *what* he wants. Babies use communicative means to say something about their *affective* state, while adults largely communicate in order to make a reference to something. Lock (*ibid.*) suggests that by using gestures or movements as well as, for example, crying, the baby of six months upwards has already bridged the gap between affective and referential communication: he cries to indicate that he is in an effective state, but uses gesture to say *what* this state is. However, even gestures have meaning only in a social context: when the child understands that his deliberate gestures have for others the meaning he intends, he also understands the nature of symbolism. This understanding in turn leads to language use rather than gesture use for communication. Clark (1978) has described how babies before they can speak point to objects to indicate some meaning about them, and it is often the names of the objects pointed at which are first verbalized in one-word utterances.

Functionally there is little difference, according to Lock (1978), between, for example, a child pointing at a cup indicating that he wants a drink, and saying 'cup'. At this stage the child has mastered the fundamentals of language, but he does not yet possess language. Language enables one to communicate unambiguously, in a structured manner, objectively and propositionally, with statements whose truth or falsity can be judged (Lock, *ibid.*); the baby who just says 'cup' is very far from doing this, but the first step towards mastering language would seem to be the joint use of word and gesture.

We have discussed the baby's ability to communicate his wishes and to name objects. In this connection it is interesting to note that, as Wells (1975) states, utterances by small children which relate to interpersonal functions actually predate those which relate to other functions by several months, though a child's 'receptive' vocabulary — what he knows — contains more names of things than words for use in interpersonal situations; however, his 'productive' vocabulary — words he can actually say — contains relatively more words to do with interpersonal functions. Hamlyn (1978) has suggested that language is, possibly, learnt in two *simultaneous* 'tiers': one tier tells us what language is about — that it is about meaningful sounds with which one can communicate with others about the world, and that one has to use a definite structure with which to do this — subject, verb, object. The second 'tier' is the *actual* language learnt for the society in which one is born; this, in the Chomskyan sense (page 120) is the 'surface' structure, though Hamlyn's first tier does not correspond to Chomsky's 'deep' structure. The second tier includes learning the names of objects, which is, suggests Hamlyn, different from learning to communicate wishes, feelings, and so on; and Lock (1978) also suggests that the ability to name objects seems to have a different history from the ability to learn to communicate wishes.

One can now see that the interaction between mother and child is the precursor of speech. The mother and baby work together to build up a pre-verbal communication system which must be constantly adjusted. Bruner has said 'the spirit of play seems to be a *sine qua non* of language learning' (1975). In playful interaction these necessary interchanges take place. It is clear that deaf, or partially deaf, babies will be affected by their hearing loss in learning to speak, but one would not necessarily have expected blind babies to have difficulty in learning to speak. However, Urwin (1977) has found that blind infants' restricted use of words at the early stages of language use is related to the social-interactional constraints which are of necessity imposed on them at the pre-verbal stage of development. During such early social interaction the baby learns about intentionality and reciprocity, what Schaffer (1978) has called 'the concept of dialogue'. It is clear that there is no intention in the activities of small babies, their actions are random; but soon the ability to differentiate ends from means is achieved, and the baby also learns to anticipate events. He learns that by joint activity, through reciprocity, certain actions are achieved: he drops a ball and someone else retrieves it; he lifts his arms and his mother picks him up; he speaks and she answers. Thus such maternal interactions with him not only help language development, but they also help his social development. We discuss in chapters 3 and 7 the advisability of continuity of care by a limited number of people in the child's early years. The pre-verbal communicative system which is built up between the child and his principal caretakers, and which is constantly adjusted as the child matures, is idiosyncratic to these limited relationships. It is difficult for strangers to understand the baby's personal cues for communicating. When he knows himself to be understood the baby's confidence in his powers to communicate are strengthened and encouraged, and this confidence spreads to other aspects of his activities. The great value to the growing child of the establishment of a realistic self-confidence has very probably been underestimated by parents and teachers (chapter 8); and it is possible that the roots of self-confidence are laid by these early mother–child social interchanges.

As far as the actual chronological development of language is concerned, early, involuntary babbling gives way, at about six weeks of age, to voluntary babbling. Lewis (1963) has described how the very young baby can respond to the speech of others not by making sounds himself, but either by ceasing to make sounds, or by making bodily or facial movements, which include smiling. When he is about three or four months old he will begin to make sounds in response to other people speaking to him, but these are not imitations of what is being said: the imitation lies in responding to the sounds of others by making sounds of his own. It is an imitation without similarity, though the similarity may exist for the baby. Slowly, aided partly by parental repeating of the noises the child makes, which have some approximation to proper words, he selects for utterance those responsive sounds which are the ones he hears. We have as yet no means of knowing what maturational developments occur at this time to bring about this ability, except that physiologically the child is dependent on the proper development of speech organs and of some brain areas; but this does not explain his ability to make the noises he *hears*. It is obvious that at this stage, too, that is, towards the end of the first year and throughout the second year, it is important for the baby to be in frequent and close contact with his mother, so that he can have the verbal experience which is so necessary for further development. Part of this verbal experience comes from the adults in his company *expanding* the child's own utterances. (By 'expanding' is meant taking a child's combination of words — 'Doggie out', for example — and expanding it: 'Yes, the doggie is going out', to which the child might reply 'Doggie going out'.) It seems, however, that *commenting* on a child's remarks rather than expanding them is even more helpful. Thus it is even better to reply to 'Doggie out' by saying something like: 'He wants to see if he can find any cats' than merely to expand the child's remark (Cazden, 1965).

We discussed earlier in this chapter in a general sense how the child comes to understand the meaning which his communications have for others. He has also to understand their communications to him. His receptive vocabulary is larger than his productive vocabulary so that he can respond to the speech of others with actions before he can do so with words. He waves when someone says 'Good-bye', or stops doing something when he hears 'No'. In this respect his accomplishment is little different from that of domesticated animals who are able accurately to respond to an (often) large number of verbal commands. It is here, with the growth of meaning, that emotion enters into language learning. Both child and animal are emotionally primed, as it were, to act or to desist from acting when they hear certain words. This requires not only some appreciation of the meaning of the word, but also an understanding of the situation in which it is spoken, and a particular affective relationship with the person speaking. It is not the word alone, but the pitch, the tone and the expression of the speaker which affectively convey meaning.

Relatively soon the child's own vocalizations evoke responses from others; he can get others to do things for him, as when he says 'Mamma' and his mother attends to his needs; and he can get them to change their facial expressions, because they are pleased with what he says. At some point in his development he begins to use words intentionally, and the processes which enable him to do this are probably very complex indeed.

During the second year of life the child's speech development progresses very rapidly and he passes through a transitional stage where his speech is mainly either an approximation to the adult speech he hears or an attempt onomatopoeically to give a name to something in his environment. During this year too a relationship is formed between speech and the baby's own actions, so that he himself desists from doing something after saying 'No' to himself. He also learns to use words as substitutes for action.

Although we do not understand how imitation takes place, and although theories which attempt to explain language learning by evoking an operant conditioning paradigm (page 142) have been criticized, yet it is *comparatively* easy to account for the acquisition of *early* speech by some such principle. What is far more difficult to explain is the ability of children to structure their speech grammatically.

We discuss on page 119 the problem which has been of such interest to psycholinguists, that is, how children come to learn in so brief a time what the syntactical rules of their native language are. It is agreed that this cannot be learned by imitation alone, for children use words with inflections they may never have heard before. It is also obvious that, as he develops, a child must be able to deal with an infinite number of possible sentences. It has already been stressed that the social and physical interaction between mother and child can be seen as a kind of prefiguration of linguistic interaction. However, in addition to acting out, as it were, with the baby the equivalents of the parts of speech normally used linguistically — subject, verb, object — most mothers also talk a good deal of the time while they are interacting with their baby, so that the baby from birth hears the words his mother uses to accompany the actions she performs. She also interprets his crying. We have referred on page 121 to Ricks' (1972) finding that during the second half of the first year a baby's cries have the distinct meanings of respectively, frustration, greeting, surprise or request. Ricks also found that the adult subjects in his investigation were well able to interpret these cries, even when made by *other* parents' Italian and Spanish children. When the baby first begins to speak, his mother's interpretations of his meanings, both when these interpretations are correct and when they are incorrect, are crucial to his language development. It is quite clear though that in whatever manner syntactical rules are being learned, their learning cannot be isolated from the meaning of what is being said, and, as Ervin-Tripp (1971) has pointed out, before the baby can express his own meanings he must know the meaning of what is being said *to* him. He could not learn to speak otherwise. It is impossible to separate semantic distinctions and the growth of the child's vocabulary from the way such distinctions and the newly-learned words are expressed. We will return to this question later.

Delaguna in 1927 formally noted what many people have intuitively understood about baby language, and that is that even the single word at the holophrastic* stage, spoken at the beginning of the second year, is often much more than just a name label; the example which Cromer (1974) gives is that of a child in his second year pointing to a pair of slippers and saying the single word 'Papa'. Later in the child's second year the two-word phrases made up of a verb and a noun or a noun and a noun can be used to express a variety of meanings: thus 'Mummy sock' can express, for example, relationship, proximity or identification. Indeed, Cromer (1974) lists fourteen different kinds of semantic relations to be found in early word phrases.

Cromer (*ibid.*) also reports Brown (1973) as finding that even though babies first use verbs without any inflectional endings, because of the situational context in which a verb is spoken, parents understand that the baby intends the verb to refer either to the past, or to be imperative, or to indicate an intention or to express present temporary duration, such as 'Fish swim'; and Cromer says that 'the first grammatical distinctions the child makes with verbs in his utterances' (following the very early use of words) 'are those which encode the types of meaning he had been credited with expressing [by parents and others] just prior to the acquisition of his new linguistic abilities' (page 211).

It has been suggested by a number of writers that only when the child gets to the end of the Piagetian sensori-motor* stage at between eighteen and 21 months of age is he able to create and use language, because by this stage he has begun to differentiate himself from other people and from objects, and so is in a position to comment objectively about the world. It is also at this stage that he has achieved some ability to internalize action (page 64). So language development seems dependent on three factors:

(1) the ability to internalize action
(2) social interactions and
(3) 'the grasp of consciousness' (the title used by Piaget for his latest — 1978 — book), which is seen in a rudimentary form in

this early differentiation of self from others and from objects.

Internalization of action is, according to Piaget, what early thinking is all about, and it is, of course, a cognitive ability. It is clear that the child's ability to use language develops *pari passu* with his growing cognitive ability. Although, as we have seen, most writers hold the view that the ability to acquire language is a very special human ability, and must be accounted for by some special human faculty, Bower (1979) has written that 'the processes and limitations of language acquisition are the processes and limitations of cognitive development in general, and there is nothing very special about language acquisition' (page 241).

Bower discussed the work of Greenfield (1975), which seems to show that the same kind of hierarchical complexity which underlies cognitive tasks given to children also underlies their comprehension and production of speech. In a series of simple but revealing experiments which involved motor tasks, using words and making a construction, Greenfield *et al.* have shown that there is parallel development in language growth and growth in other cognitive areas. One also has to remember that the processing of information by the child in order to enable him to comprehend what is being said to him has already progressed to a highly sophisticated stage by the time he himself produces language. It is not unreasonable to assume, therefore, that the child's ability linguistically to process information can be used in due course to enable him to produce language himself. We have simply no idea how a knowledge of all that is relevant in the world, including words, is stored and how it can be so effectively and speedily retrieved whenever it is necessary to act, think or communicate. Quite clearly this is a specifically human ability, related to man's highly developed cortex, and the human baby is, therefore, potentially ready from birth to be able to process information highly efficiently. As far as the use of words is concerned Bruner (1978) has said that 'there appears to be some readiness [rather] quickly to grasp certain rules for forming sentences, once we know what the world is about, to which the sentences refer'. And, he goes on to say, these rules are neither 'imitated' nor are they simple reflections of the world of concepts that the child has learned for dealing with the extralinguistic environment, though they are plainly related (page 65); he adds, later, that 'there may indeed be something innate about the child's ability so swiftly to crack the linguistic code' (page 83).

One has to confess that despite the child being a member of a species which can encode information so effectively, despite being exposed to language use, despite social interaction which prefigures linguistic interaction, despite the growth of consciousness and increasing cognitive ability, the fact remains that the acquisition of language to the degree of competence which a child of two-and-a-half to three years of age exhibits is a miraculous achievement. It is also a fact that the child at this age is enormously competent in many other ways too. What, indeed, marks out the young child from other people is the great flexibility and speed with which all kinds of learning, including language learning, is achieved. It is the task of all developmental psychologists, including psycholinguists, to discover, as Slobin (1966) has remarked, the exact nature of the total learning process which occurs during the acquisition of the use of language.

Language and social development

Language, as we said at the beginning, is a social tool, enabling communication to take place between people. We know that the baby's cries of comfort and pleasure are different from his cries of discomfort, so that quite early in life the baby is communicating and expressing meaning, but meaning is expanded by the normal concomitants of adult speech, and the manner, gesture and intonation of others all convey meaning. Thus when his mother smells a rose and conveys her pleasure at the scent and sight of the rose, the word 'rose' is not only a neutral sound symbolizing a particular flower, but is in addition a sound relating to something pleasant (Lewis, 1963). So learning to speak means learning about the quality of objects as well as learning what the symbolic equivalent of an object is.

It is usually said that the young child talks but does not communicate; what he talks about are mostly his own needs, and he is motivated to use speech to satisfy these needs. To this extent his speech is a kind of communication, but not in the sense in which the word is usually employed. Piaget (1926) considers that the speech of a young child is relatively 'egocentric' when compared with adult speech, particularly when he is playing with other children. This view implies that for the young child communication is not a necessary function of speech; apart from speaking to satisfy their needs, children repeat words and phrases to themselves for the mere pleasure of talking, or a child talks to himself as if he were thinking aloud, or he speaks because the presence of another person serves as a stimulus for his monologue. This does not imply, though, that such speech is non-social. Indeed, Vygotsky (1962) has concluded that a young child's speech has a high social function, but that it *appears* to be egocentric because children do not realize that their private world is not shared by others. He has shown that 'egocentric' speech is social in origin, and that it is thus of help to the child in organizing his behaviour. Vygotsky thinks that Piaget's 'egocentric' speech possibly links speech and thought, because when the child speaks to himself he is thinking aloud. Piaget has agreed with this view in part by stating that it is possible that egocentric speech may lead to 'inner' speech which helps the development of logical thinking.

It has been established (Smith, 1926) that a child's vocabulary increases tenfold between two and six years of age. Fry (1979) gives even more surprising figures when he states that at two years of age the child has a vocabulary of 200 different words, at two to three years 1,000 and at four years 2,000. (The average adult vocabulary consists of 4–5,000 words.) There are, however, large individual differences in the size of vocabulary attained at different ages. Qualitatively this increase implies a deeper understanding of words, which makes their individual meanings more precise and extends the range of meanings available to the child. Between three and four years of age an important stabilization process occurs: speech becomes grammatically more correct, the number of unintelligible words decreases, and by the time a child starts school he has a fairly comprehensive repertoire of intelligible language. The child's social development is reflected in his speech, so that the kind of words he uses changes: more pronouns of the second and third person are added and fewer of the first person are used. Also the number of emotionally toned words decreases (McCarthy, 1954) and slowly speech becomes more and more 'socialized speech', as Piaget terms it. The child now really exchanges his thoughts with others. This exchange of thoughts and ideas cannot occur, however, until a child is able to take a mental viewpoint away from his own, egocentric, viewpoint, and until he can adopt the viewpoint of his hearer, who is not chosen at random but selected because the child wants to communicate with a specific person. Piaget's studies (1926) indicate how the proportion of what he terms 'egocentric' speech to socialized speech decreases with age, and how the number of emotionally toned phrases also decreases.

Lewis (1963) has said that 'children do verbal deeds to each other, deeds which matter more and more in their lives'. A child of seven or eight years of age is already something of a social being, and the use of language is part of the continuing socialization process. Between this age and eleven or twelve years of age the 'group' made up of peers normally becomes more and more important to him. His membership of a peer group is one of the two important social forces influencing him, and it is by the use of the right language that he confirms his membership. (The other social force of great importance is, of course, the influence of adults in school and at home.) By belonging to a peer group he realizes that basically language exists in order that people can communicate with one another. Often the language of such a peer group is special and secretive, and the junior child exhibits great loyalty to the group in preserving the secrecy of the group language.

At this time too the child's individuality emerges strongly, and it is shaped in part at least by the reactions of others to him and by his feelings and reactions to others. He forms attitudes which are expressed increasingly by language rather than by bodily movements and by physical activity, such as fighting. Rules of behaviour, whether social or play, cannot be understood without the ability to use language adequately (chapter 5); rules now become important to the child, and hence through his understanding of rules and his need to have rules at this age, language brings together the child's cognitive and orectic* functions. It does seem, however, that children do not use language to talk about their *feelings* until early adolescence (chapter 5).

One aspect of language learning which has not been investigated until relatively recently is children's specific non-understanding of apparently simple language. Mention was made earlier of how very young children understand before they can speak, but it has come as rather a surprise to investigators in recent times to find that such words as 'less' are not understood correctly in the context of a sentence. Thus Donaldson and Balfour (1968) found that children under four-and-a-half years at least were unable to give a correct response to the word 'less', and in the set-up devised by the experimenters children up to this age responded to 'less' as if it were 'more'. Similarly Cromer (1970), in seeking to test Chomsky's ideas about the deep and surface structure of language, found that only children over six-and-a-half years of age were able to understand a sentence such as: 'John is easy to see'; all younger children interpreted this sentence to mean that John was the actor — i.e., that John was doing the seeing!

We discuss earlier in this chapter how the child's understanding of language precedes his ability to use it himself, but Donaldson (1978) makes the valuable point that understanding is not an all-or-none affair. Over a period of time children learn that words have subtly varying meanings according to the context in which they are spoken, so that they often completely misunderstand what is meant by familiar words spoken in an unfamiliar context. Donaldson quotes Laurie Lee's deep disappointment with his first day at school when, after having been told 'to sit there for the present' he sat 'there' all day but the present never came! It is important for adults to realize that children do not always understand what we mean even when we speak using relatively simple language.

Language and social class

Any consideration of language development, particularly in relation to social growth and cognitive development, must include reference to the work of Bernstein. Bernstein (1961 and elsewhere) studied the differences between the language used by the two major social classes in Great Britain — that is, the working class and the middle class — and he considers that these differences have crucial effects on a number of aspects of child rearing, with consequent differences in personality and moral and cognitive development. He put forward the view that these differences also reflect differences in the values held by people in these social classes. Such differences are probably narrowing now as the divisions between the classes are less clear-cut, but they still exist. Bernstein has emphasized that for a child from a lower-working-class background the first experience which he has of middle-class language is when he starts school at five years of age, whereas when the middle-class child starts school he enters a basically similar milieu to that experienced at home. Speech, says Bernstein (1961), 'marks out what is relevant — affectively, cognitively and socially'; so that what is relevant in the lives of members of the different social classes is reflected in their speech. He has suggested that two different forms of language use are current: a 'restricted' code used at times by the middle classes, but all the time by the lower working classes, and an 'elaborated' code used exclusively by the middle classes. The restricted code is rigid; it is predictable; it does not easily differentiate between people; and it does not aid heightened perception or awareness; it exists largely for the present, and it is highly stylized. It is in some respects similar to infant speech, in that it is used to express feelings and enhance social solidarity with the listener. The restricted code is based on shared assumptions and shared identifications, and it assumes that social solidarity is more important than individual experience. The middle classes use the restricted code when talking to strangers about the weather! It is a language which is descriptive rather than analytic. With the restricted code a great deal of meaning is conveyed by gesture, pitch, stress, etc., whereas the 'elaborated code' emphasizes the exact description of experiences and feelings; allows for subtle discriminations by appropriate adjectives and adverbs; makes possible the analysis of relationships and enables the speaker to sustain concentration on particular themes. Also it is not predictable; it points out differences rather than obscures them; its range is wider, so that the number of stimuli to which a listener can respond is greater, and it allows for the *verbalization* of feeling. With the use of the elaborated code the speaker does not take the listener for granted.

A child from a middle-class home learns both languages; the child from a lower-working-class home mostly learns only the restricted code. It is suggested that because the mother from a middle-class background uses the elaborated code with her children, her attitude to her children and the responses she evokes in them will be quite different from the attitude which a mother from a lower social class may have towards her children. There is a difference between being told: 'I'd rather you didn't do that, dear' and a peremptory 'Stop it!' In the former sentence the words express important, but delicate, feelings.

Restricted language does not allow for the expression of such subtleties and thus an awareness of human relationships on such levels does not come so easily to the child who is unused to this type of speech. The sentence: 'I'd rather you didn't do that' not only asks the child to stop its activities, but implies that the activity worries or aggravates the mother; that she is asking, but not necessarily demanding, the child to stop; it therefore also implies a degree of respect for, and a granting of autonomy to, the child, which is absent from the peremptory 'Stop it!' Of course all mothers and teachers from all social classes at times say 'Stop it', but it is not the only or invariable way of asking a child to refrain from an activity, and whereas the child from a middle-class home can understand both ways of being spoken to, the child from a lower-working-class background can usually only understand the one form.

In addition, by normally using elaborated language the middle-class mother uses a particular situation to teach a lesson which is much more widely applicable than merely to the situation about which she is speaking; the kind of words normally used by the working-class mother specifically direct the child to the *one* instance. So the child's thinking may be more centred on the present and what is expedient rather than on general principles and a consideration of other people's feelings. The use of restricted language also reflects a lack of interest by its users in long-term aims. Vernon (1969) has said that because the lower working classes in particular normally have little control over their economic future there is little point in their planning or thinking of distant goals (chapter 7). This lack of interest in the future is reflected in their use of language. In a study reported in 1973 which sought to examine the effects of social class differences in the relevance of language to socialization, Bernstein found that whereas both middle- and working-class mothers placed greater emphasis on the use of language in interpersonal aspects of socialization than in the use of language in socialization into basic skills, this emphasis was more pronounced for the middle-class mothers.

Bernstein has suggested that by internalizing the language, and the feelings which accompany the language, the child becomes more and more self-regulating, and that the type and degree of self-regulation which is achieved depends largely on the language form used. Briefly one can say that elaborated language habitually used by parents tends to lead to the formation of greater inner control and a more acutely sensitive conscience than the use of restricted language does. The use of elaborated language in disciplining the child means that the mother is largely making a personal appeal to the child and is respecting his individuality. She hopes the child will himself internalize the rules of behaviour and the result of the breaking of such personal rules will be a feeling of guilt. An 'imperative' rather than an 'appealing' mode of control means that through the particular language use external rules are assigned, and shame rather than guilt is produced in the child when these are broken. Turner (1973) found that when given a picture story task in which they had to choose an appropriate mode of control, working-class children of five and seven years of age more frequently chose controls of an 'imperative' kind, and the middle-class children of an 'appealing' kind.

The use of the restricted code also reflects both for the parents and the children a rearing system which relies for the control of behaviour more on strength and dominance than on inner restraint. In chapter 7 more specific consideration is given to the question of how a child coming from a linguistically deprived home background is affected by being spoken to in elaborated language when he enters school. However, it seems clear that the expressions used to indicate what kind of behaviour is acceptable, the feelings which are subtly expressed in sentences longer and, in structure if not in word use, more complex than the child has heard before — these are all relatively strange to the child and they make the receiving and giving of communications difficult for him. An older child will thus experience a correspondingly greater difficulty in expressing himself in English, and his thought processes may not lend themselves so easily to logical, clear, deductive thinking. Because linguistic ability is basic to educational success, such children are quite severely handicapped from the beginning of their school lives. Evidence exists from a number of studies (Bernstein, 1958, 1960; Jahoda, 1964) to show that when young adults from working-class backgrounds are tested on verbal and non-verbal intelligence tests, their verbal scores are always grossly depressed when compared with their scores on non-verbal tests, a difference not found when young adults from higher social classes are tested. The result is that a potentially high intelligence is to a greater or lesser degree unable adequately to use the medium of words in which scholarship is expressed.

Bernstein's work has not been without its critics, and Rosen (1972) among other criticisms suggests that we still do not know very much about working-class language; but, he says, we do know that 'working class speech has its own strengths . . . [and] that there is no sharp dividing line between it and any other kind of speech . . .' (page 19). He also says that the middle class pay a price for the acquisition of their language with 'loss of vitality and expressiveness'. However, speech and language-use are not synonymous, and the evidence which now exists regarding different cultural linguistic styles and their repercussion on a variety of aspects of behaviour is too great to dismiss.

Language and thinking

It is necessary before thinking can take place for a child to be able to make a mental representation of objects and relationships in their physical absence. When a child thinks, he must be able to evoke an image of a kind without direct sensory stimulation. Although the child at the early, sensori-motor* stage of development, before he is twenty-two months of age or so, is beginning to be able to think in this way, his understanding of the world is so limited that he is not even quite sure that objects exist if they cannot be experienced sensorily. For this reason it is very important for young children to have a great deal of sensory experience with many different kinds of objects, materials, colours and textures. At this level thought is internalized action, and only through action can the early thinking processes develop. This internalized action Piaget has called 'an operation', and his theory of the development of thought is outlined in chapter 2.

Piaget has suggested (page 63) that the beginnings of thought during the sensori-motor period are independent of language. When the child first starts to represent actions to himself (page 115) and thus 'short-circuits' movements, he is using the power of thought. There is some disagreement whether thinking beyond this stage of development is dependent on language development. Flavell and Hill (1969) state the view that "linguistic ability does not appear to be either synonymous with, nor a necessary pre-condition for, cognitive processing". They say that this applies to the 'middling levels of developmental maturity' as well as the sensori-motor state of development, though they also state that it is uncertain whether the ability to engage in the more advanced forms of thinking is independent of linguistic ability. They suggest that linguistic symbols provide one kind of material, suitably coded, for thinking, and that this serves as an '*intra*personal communicative function', as opposed to the usual *inter*personal function of language. However, the notion that even the 'middling' developmental stage of thinking, that is, Piaget's 'concrete operational' stage (page 64), is not dependent on language would seem difficult to maintain, though psychologists other than Flavell and Hill are undecided whether language is *necessary* as opposed to being *useful* in aiding the developing thought processes (Herriot, 1970). Although it may be possible to understand concepts of conservation and causality without using words such as 'more', 'less', 'alive', etc., the ability to manipulate such concepts in order to develop a certain and sophisticated understanding must, one feels, depend on the ability to be able to express this understanding in the appropriate words. It has been found that five-year-olds who understood the word 'middle-sized' were better at discriminating between three shapes of increasing size than the children who did not understand the word properly (Spiker, Gerjeroy and Shepard, 1956). Britton (1970) comments on the need to be able to classify and to form concepts of classes in order to name objects. He says that there is an 'hierarchical relationship between word meanings which has the most far-reaching influence upon thinking'. Thus a child will know the colour red, but then learns to distinguish between scarlet and crimson, and later to subdivide the scarlet into vermilion and pillar-box, and the crimson into blood-red and wine-colour. It is certainly difficult to understand how the comprehension of the abstract terms which are used by adolescents and adults who have entered the 'symbolic' stage of thinking can be developed without language, for there is no equivalent to these terms in the material environment.

Bruner considers that children must be able to internalize 'techniques' such as the language of their culture if they are to progress to the symbolic thinking stage. He confesses (1964) that he cannot suggest how language becomes internalized as a programme for ordering experience, but suggests that it probably depends on interaction with others: one might venture to speculate that the 'intrapersonal communicative function', to which Flavell and Hill refer, can only come into play if the *inter*personal function of communication takes place fully and in a stimulating environment. Bruner indeed lays great stress on the role of language in enabling the child to progress from 'enactive'* to 'symbolic'* thinking. He suggests that the role of language becomes increasingly powerful as the child grows, particularly between the ages of four and twelve. During this period language becomes a tool for the translation of experience, for once language can be used in this way the child is no longer tied to the immediate, but can represent the past and speculate about the future. Language, says Bruner, has 'features of remoteness and arbitrariness' (1964); and these features enable an integration of behaviour and of thought to occur, which, he suggests, is not possible without such a tool. Bruner has also put forward the following ideas about the development of language and thinking, which he divides into four stages:

During stage 1 the child speaks a language which embodies a power of organization he cannot achieve in thought. (By this Bruner presumably means that children use words in speaking which they cannot manipulate in thought.)

Later, during stage 2, the child achieves in thought what he can achieve in speech.

During stage 3 he extends the range of his power of organization by first verbalizing more complex experiences and then contemplating these verbalizations.

Lastly, during stage 4, his powers of organization in thought come to exceed his powers of organization in speech (Britton, 1970).

Examination of the thinking powers of deaf children should help to establish whether or not language and thought are as intimately related as Bruner suggests. Research work with children who become deaf before the period of language acquisition indicates that many kinds of thinking processes are possible for the deaf, but in Furth's study (1966) nine out of twelve deaf children were inferior to hearing children in aspects of thinking. However, children with such a severe degree of deafness are treated so differently from hearing children in a number of ways that one cannot be completely sure that it is the absence of hearing spoken language which accounts for the difference in thinking abilities, though Furth, in an earlier (1964) study wrote that the deaf children he has studied performed similarly to hearing children on tasks where verbal knowledge would seem important in order to do well. This is not what one would expect if language importantly influences thinking abilities.

Vernon (1969) considers that symbolic thinking is totally dependent on the quality of speech models and communications which the child receives from parents, teachers, older children and contemporaries. Many other psychologists also hold the view that more than any other single factor the quality of speech which a child hears acts continuously on the development of his mental powers from the age of six months onwards. Vygotsky (1962) and Luria (1961) seem to have shown that 'inner' speech is of importance from an early age in helping the child to plan and order his actions. Such internal language abbreviates trial-and-error learning and thus makes problem solving more effective. Britton (1970) has put Vygotsky's view in this way, that in 'inner speech words die as they bring forth thought'. Language is, according to Vygotsky, an internalized regulator of behaviour, but it seems clear from experimental work that such regulation by language can only occur after considerable experience with language. Luria gave children of three years of age a rubber bulb and told them to press it whenever a red light was flashed, but not to press when a blue light came on. Inhibiting the action — i.e., *not* pressing when the blue light came on — seemed impossible for children of this age. Later they were told to give themselves the audible instructions "Press" or "Don't press". The inhibition of the negative function of 'Don't press' was such that the children didn't press at all to either light, or they pressed all the time regardless. By four-and-a-half years of age children were able to give themselves instructions overtly to press or not to press, and to obey these instructions, and finally, at five, they were able to give themselves instructions silently. Burke (1966) has said that the 'essential distinction between the verbal and the non-verbal is the fact that language adds the peculiar possibility of the negative', and it can be seen from Luria's experiment that action and not words is predominant in a young child's life: the force of language which enables the *negative* command to inhibit action is not sufficiently strong before about four years of age to prevent *positive* action from taking place.

Another advantage which the use of language gives human beings is that, as Turner (1977) has pointed out, it 'enables a person to transcend the here and now, and is therefore concerned with possible rather than actual worlds and with the hypothetical rather than the verified' (page 257).

Herriot (1970) says that 'the present condition of the field of language and thinking is utterly confused' (page 157). There seems to be no *absolute* proof at present to indicate that the *quality* of language which a child hears affects his thinking processes: it may be that language reflects but does not necessarily determine cognitive growth, and that other factors, such as an increasingly long short-term memory span, may be as influential as language in affecting thinking processes. However, we discuss earlier in this chapter Bernstein's classification of the language used by the two major social classes in this country and how a familiarity with the 'elaborated code' makes it easier for children with a middle-class background to feel at ease with the language used by teachers when they come to school. It is too soon to say that such children are not advantaged when starting school because of their familiarity with this particular way of using the English language. It is also again worth quoting Donaldson (1978) who has written that 'those very features of the written word which encourage awareness of language may also encourage awareness of one's own thinking and be relevant to the development of intellectual self-control, with incalculable consequences for the development of the kinds of thinking which are characteristic of logic, mathematics and the sciences' (page 95).

Learning

Harry and Margaret Harlow have posed the following problem (1949): 'How does an infant, born with only a few simple reactions, develop into an adult capable of rapid learning and the almost incredibly complex mental processes known as thinking? This is one of psychology's largely unsolved problems.' During the past twenty years the Harlows have attacked this problem in their own way, but before we consider the value of their work for an understanding of human learning we must look at the various kinds of learning which have been identified.

Children come to school in order to learn, and teachers hope to help them to learn: this is what teaching is about; but we have to think of learning as being an activity which is much wider than school learning. From the time a baby is born he begins to learn; indeed man is *par excellence* a learning animal. He comes into the world far less well developed than other animals, and he is forced to rely on his ability to learn, for he has few, if indeed any, inherited modes of behaviour. This ability enables him to develop greater flexibility of behaviour than any other creature, and this flexibility expresses itself in all aspects of his behaviour. A theory of personality development based on the view that man is primarily a learning organism is considered in chapter 2.

We can understand, therefore, that learning involves diverse activities, such as learning to control our emotions; learning to conform to society's needs of us; learning a skill; learning to think conceptually; as well as learning facts. We know that different kinds of learning, sometimes combinations of different kinds of learning, are responsible for different aspects of what is learned. One of the most difficult things to learn is 'how to learn'! This is, possibly, from the point of view of academic achievement, one of the most important things a child can learn, particularly in the primary school, and it is also possibly one of the most neglected subjects of teaching, as well as of research into teaching methods. The emphasis in schools, even in the upper forms of grammar or comprehensive schools, is on instruction; the development of individual learning ability is seemingly neglected both by the schools and by research workers. We will consider later the specific factors affecting a child's ability to learn in school. It is necessary first, however, to look at learning in the broader context of 'learning to live'.

Learning, from infancy onwards, can broadly speaking be of four types, though experimental psychologists may argue that fundamentally all four can be reduced to a classical conditioning paradigm. It does seem, though, that one can distinguish between

(1) imprinting,
(2) imitation and identification,
(3) classical conditioning and
(4) operant conditioning.

Imprinting

Imprinting is a form of learning which has been extensively studied during the past 45 years, first in birds, and later in animals and humans. Imprinting experiments and observations seem to indicate that the kind of behaviour which at one time was thought to be entirely instinctive can actually only be displayed if the correct learning experiences occur at 'critical' times, that is, during special and usually short periods early in an animal or bird's life. The basic difference between imprinting and other forms of learning is that it appears to occur without any *ordinary* kind of reward. Behaviour learned as a result of imprinting experiences was at first thought to be irreversible and quite different in many respects from other kinds of learning, though it is possible, as Hinde (1962) maintains, that the differences between imprinting and other forms of learning are due more to the particular conditions in which learning takes place than to any intrinsic differences between kinds of learning, but such learning does appear to be limited to certain periods in an organism's life, and to be dependent also on innate mechanisms of a particular kind. Imprinting is a kind of amalgam of an inherited tendency to behave in a particular way, and experiences occurring at the right time in early life which are necessary to enable this kind of behaviour to be displayed. Thus Lorenz (1935) found that newly hatched ducklings 'instinctively', or so it seemed, followed their mother, but if during the critical period soon after hatching they heard Lorenz making the appropriate 'quacking' noises, then they followed him, and continued to follow him and not the mother duck at all. The importance of these experiences lies not only in the kind of necessary behaviour which the *baby* bird or animal displays, such as following the mother, but in the fact that lack of the appropriate experience in babyhood has repercussions on the later social and sexual behaviour of the adult. Thus Lorenz and others have found that if a baby bird or animal had been imprinted onto an unnatural object, it found difficulty in relating to others of its species later in life. Many farmers know the problem which a hand-reared lamb has in being assimilated into the flock once it leaves the farm kitchen.

In chapter 3 evidence is reviewed which indicates that humans are particularly sensitive at certain periods of life to particular kinds of experiences, and that their later development may be affected if these experiences are missed. We know from animal work (Scott, 1962) that the greater the effort which has to be made by a baby animal or bird during these critical periods (for example, in making an effort to follow rather than, say, cling to the mother), the greater appear to be the lasting effects of imprinting experiences. Although the human baby is unable to make any real effort to attach himself by physically following his mother or even by clinging to her, as primate babies do, he is able to smile and he is able to follow her visually, and the 'visual following response' may be the human equivalent of the *actual* following response of animal and bird babies. Attachment behaviour to one particular person is thus thought to occur through a process akin to imprinting, and probably occurs before the baby is six months old; at this age he knows well and smiles at familiar persons, but he begins to be unresponsive to, and often shows fear in, the presence of strangers, if a familiar person is not present. It is thought important that babies should have the opportunity during this period of becoming attached to one major caretaking figure.

Because imprinting experiences appear to have greater relevance to the behaviour of animals who must come into the world with more innate drives determining their behaviour and with fewer opportunities for learning than humans, it is not thought that strictly classical imprinting plays much part in human learning, though one should not dismiss the importance for later personality development of imprinting-like experiences in early life which have been enjoyed, or, more important, have *not* been enjoyed.

Imitation and identification

When we consider imitation it becomes difficult to say what exactly takes place when a child imitates, beyond saying the obvious, that he can be observed to mimic the actions of another. Some psychologists have stated that the ability to imitate is innate, others that imitation can be explained in terms of learning theory. Thus several theories of imitation have been put forward, and it is clear that to account for the occurrence of imitation is very difficult, particularly when no obvious reward is given to either the child or the person on whom he is modelling himself. As we shall see later, though it is maintained by some psychologists that learning without any kind of reward can and does take place — and indeed imprinting appears to be a form of learning of this kind — most psychologists consider that in more ordinary forms of learning a reward of *some* kind is always present even if this is not overtly discernible.

Aronfreed (1968) has suggested that affect* has a strong mediating role in influencing the occurrence of imitative responses; Bandura's ideas (1968) include a reference to the need of the child to see that the act he is about to copy is an appropriate guide for behaviour for himself. If one sees this awareness of 'appropriateness' as a kind of affective reward, that is, that the carrying-out of a new but appropriate act brings a feeling of satisfaction, then it is possible to see the place of reinforcement* in imitation. This view is not unlike Mowrer's (1960), that imitation is a kind of 'empathetic' learning: the child experiences 'intuitively' the satisfactions experienced by the person on whom he is modelling himself. This assumes that the child will not only be aroused by these feelings, but that he will also anticipate that he too will be rewarded by such desirable feelings if he imitates. Although this theory *describes* the kind of anticipated satisfactions that may initiate imitation it does not *explain* what occurs; indeed it may not be possible clearly to define the affective features which bring about an awareness of 'appropriateness', or the 'empathetic' feelings which seem to suggest that satisfaction will be experienced if another person's behaviour is imitated. Certainly the ability to imitate has been observed in the first few weeks of life by, among others, Melzoff and Moore (1977).

It is possible that imitation of acts for which no obvious reward is given cannot easily be distinguished from 'identification' which is a form of imitation. Identification is a kind of behaviour whereby an individual models himself unconsciously, or partially unconsciously, on another person, incorporating part of that person's personality into himself. When a child identifies with another person then that person is usually someone with whom the child has a close emotional tie, and in early life such a person is normally a family member who ministers to the child's needs. Freud's 'Oedipal'* theory attempts to explain both sex-role identification and how, through such identification with the parent of the same sex, a child adopts the values, ideas and ideals of the parent. In this way identification aids the development of the personality, and the formation of the superego (chapter 2). Freud has also postulated that this is indeed how societies are able to pass on their cultural norms from generation to generation. Sears (1957) has suggested that in the absence of a nurturing adult a child, by imitating the actions of that adult, 'reinstates' her, even though she is physically absent; and also by such imitation a kind of self-administered reward is obtained. Although in early childhood identification will be mostly with close and nurturing adults, this process continues in later childhood, when the child may identify with an admired teacher or a loved peer.

Identification is an extremely complex phenomenon to test experimentally because, whereas one can offer a child *behavioural acts* for imitation and then observe the extent to which such acts are imitated under various conditions, one cannot for experimental analysis offer the more subtle aspects of a model's *personality* for imitation.

A great deal of experimental work with children has been carried out to try to discover under what conditions children will imitate, what kind of actions they will readily copy, and whether they learn other people's behaviour even though they do not imitate such behaviour immediately. There is good evidence that learning through imitation takes place extensively in childhood.

Although we do not fully understand the processes involved in imitative learning and identification (Sluckin, 1970), some practical advantage can be taken of the outcome of experimental work with children. Thus Bandura (1962) found that children will copy aggressive behaviour very readily, though less so if the model being imitated is seen to be punished for his aggression. This finding would appear to have some relevance to the kind of TV material which children see, where the hero is often shown to be as aggressive as the villain, and he is never punished but always rewarded in some way for his successful violence!

Classical conditioning

Classical conditioning, which was first discovered by Pavlov in Russia, is a form of learning in which a natural response to a normally natural stimulus, such as the sucking movements a baby makes when his mouth comes into contact with nipple or teat, is, either fortuitously or through a deliberate training procedure, evoked by an unnatural stimulus, because the natural and unnatural stimuli are closely associated in time and space. Thus if, for example, a baby is regularly picked up just before feeding, as indeed most babies are, then he will after a little time begin to make sucking noises and particular movements of the mouth on being picked up and before the bottle or breast is presented to him. The baby has become 'conditioned' to make the response of sucking to the 'conditioned' stimulus of being picked up, and he will continue to make such a response, at least for a time, even if the teat or nipple is not always presented after he is picked up. The situations under which classical conditioning may take place have been fully studied in many different kinds of conditions, and it seems irrelevant here to say more than that there is little doubt that babies through a process of classical conditioning do learn about the sequences of events in their lives, particularly about those events which relate to their needs. (In chapter 2 the social-learning theory of personality development, which is based on conditioning paradigms, is explained.)

Operant conditioning

Operant conditioning employs a different paradigm: here a part of a baby's or animal's existing behavioural repertoire is used in a new and particular situation; in an experimental set-up this situation is selected by the experimenter. The behavioural act is not a natural response to a natural stimulus, as in classical conditioning, but it may be any quite arbitrary piece of natural behaviour which the experimenter, or, if we are considering the social training of a child, the parent or teacher, is interested in encouraging. The natural behavioural act is 'reinforced', which in most circumstances means that it is rewarded; and consequently the likelihood of that piece of behaviour being displayed again is increased. In our discussion of language learning (page 125) we show how those natural early sounds which a baby makes, and which approximate to 'Mamma' or 'Nanna', are reinforced, mostly because the adults in the baby's life show pleasure when he makes them, or because the baby is rewarded in some other way when he repeats the sounds. As a consequence these sounds are more likely to be repeated than other sounds. Notwithstanding the fact that the training of animals and the socialization of children through a system of rewards (positive reinforcement) and punishments (negative reinforcement) is usually based on aspects of operant conditioning techniques, for various complex reasons the methods employed in such training programmes meet with less success than parents anticipate, particularly so far as punishment is concerned (chapter 8).

The two forms of learning most applicable to the child as far as social and school learning are concerned are probably imitation and operant conditioning, and of these two operant conditioning is of the greater importance in relation to teaching. Although no contemporary psychologist would today state with certainty *exactly* what effects reward has on behaviour, it is possible to make some general statements which may be of help to teachers. Skinner (1938) has shown how an animal can be trained to perform complex acts (he has taught pigeons to play 'ping-pong'!) by waiting until the animal performs a particular act which the experimenter knows is to be part of the final act he has planned for training, and then when, quite by chance, the animal performs this act, immediately rewarding it. The act is thus reinforced. The training schedule continues in this matter until progressively a succession of acts has been established by rewarding those pieces of behaviour which fit the predetermined pattern, and ignoring those which do not fit it. It has been suggested that this 'selective reinforcement' is as effective in the home and in school with human children as in the laboratory with birds and animals. Teachers must be 'observer-detectives' and if possible reinforce immediately those aspects of a child's behaviour which the teacher wishes to strengthen, ignoring as far as possible those aspects which are not desirable. The question of rewards and punishments in relation to social behaviour is discussed in chapter 8; here we are more concerned with the strengthening of a child's school learning ability.

If one considers the principles underlying operant conditioning as they are applied to teaching-machine programmes one can learn a great deal about how these principles might be used in classroom teaching without the use of machines. The programme on a machine is designed to teach a subject in very small steps. There are at least two reasons for this: one small step in a process of learning can be understood more easily than several steps explained in quick succession; and by making sure that one step is understood, and telling the learner that he was correct in the answer he gave to the machine, the learner is being positively reinforced. We know from animal work that this strengthens the response just emitted; in other words, learning has taken place. The principles underlying teaching-machine programmes also show how important it is for learning that children be allowed to progress at their own pace; in addition the active participation in self-generated learning, rather than the passive attention demanded by an instruction session, seems to be a relevant feature of learning. So, by observing the four principles of

(1) contriving a situation in which a child is more likely to be right than wrong,

(2) telling him immediately that he is right,

(3) allowing him, with supervision, to progress at his own pace and

(4) ensuring that he actively takes part in the learning procedure,

the teacher is maximizing the child's chances of learning. Successive positive reinforcement is also cumulative as far as motivation for learning is concerned.

Adherence by the teacher to these four principles motivates the child by giving him success in learning through enabling him to understand what he is doing. His interest and attention must, however, be continually aroused and he must be able to memorize what he learns; but a poor memory may mean a lack of interest in the subject learned, or a lack of attention, or both, for what has not been attended to cannot really be remembered. So interest, attention, memory and motivation are all linked. It is easier, of course, to interest a child if something new he is required to learn is linked to some everyday experience he has had in his life outside school. Most primary schools teach with this principle in mind, but, although more difficult to put into practice with secondary-school subjects, one feels that more could be done to bring academic subjects to life in this way for older children than is at present being done in many secondary schools.

Sears and Hilgard (1964), in an article on the teacher's role in the motivation of the learner, say that a good teacher utilizes and arouses in the child three different motives for learning: he seeks to arouse curiosity, he stimulates a child's desire to achieve, and he uses the child's wish for a warm relationship with his teacher to activate his learning abilities. Of course only a basically affectionate teacher can do the last, and only a teacher who is himself interested in the subject he is teaching can do the first. Although a good teacher can also stimulate the child's wish to achieve success by learning, this is possibly more dependent on social class and cultural factors than on the school situation. Undoubtedly the need to achieve is present in children from quite an early age when they find they have a competence in the performance of some task (Heckhausen, 1967). Indeed, White (1959) has suggested that the need to master the environment directs persistent behaviour, and one may assume that children experience a *need* to become increasingly competent in dealing with their environment. In addition, Western middle-class values place great emphasis on the need to achieve, and many studies have found that the drive to achieve, particularly in children from middle-class homes, acts as a powerful impetus to learning (McClelland, Atkinson, *et al.*, 1953). The findings from a number of investigations indicate that children from such homes show more responsibility in school, and a higher degree of aspiration than children from working-class homes. It is, therefore, likely that children whose parents set a value on achievement will be able better to take advantage of the teaching they receive in schools, and this may be *one* of the reasons why children from middle-class homes in Great Britain have in the past won grammar-school places out of proportion to their number in the population.

Learning to think, learning to learn and problem solving

Thinking in relation to language development is considered on page 134 and the development of cognitive processes from birth to maturity is reviewed in chapters 2 and 5. We must, however, consider here how the *ability* to learn to think develops. Harry and Margaret Harlow (1949) trained both monkeys and children to choose small objects on a board by showing them a sample of the object, and they then rewarded them by enabling them to find something edible if they chose the right object. By elaborating the training series it was possible for monkeys and children to learn that the relevant clue was, for example, not the shape of an object, but the colour, or the size. They were shown a blue object and they had to select all the other blue objects regardless of how they might differ from one another in other respects. The next test might involve not the colour of the objects, but their shape; thus all the round objects might have to be selected regardless of other criteria. One test consisted of nine objects on a tray; monkeys were given a sample similar to one of them and they had to pick out *only* those objects, but *all* those objects, which were in some relevant way like the sample. In a more difficult test they were given a sample which had nothing obviously to do with the objects, such as a triangle which *represented* the colour red and a circle which *represented* blue. At least one animal learned this sign language almost perfectly. Thus both the monkeys and the children in the Harlow experiments were not learning to solve *one* problem only, but they developed what have been called 'learning sets'. The first solution is based on a random, trial-and-error method of discovery; but as opportunities for learning continue to be provided, random choices cease and deliberate choices are made. There is good evidence to show that what has been learned in this way is retained for considerable periods of time. By these methods children 'learn to learn'. The Harlows suggest that children build up learning sets by learning to solve increasingly difficult problems. At first they try previously learned habits and also new ways of responding, then they discard those responses which are unsuccessful and retain the useful habits which have been formed. As children continue successfully to solve many problems of a certain kind, new habits are established which are then brought into operation whenever they appear to be relevant. Thus the ability to solve problems is established and a 'set' is built up which enables further learning to take place more easily and rapidly. Humans have the advantage over animals in that they can use language, and words have the function of calling forth particular learning sets which are appropriate for certain problems.

At the beginning of this chapter the cognitive development of the child is described, and in particular Piaget's scheme of how this development takes place. It is suggested by both Piaget and by Bruner that the highest stage of thinking is reached when a child in early adolescence comes to be able to think conceptually, and Piaget and Bruner both describe how this stage is gradually reached. Psychologists are not agreed whether all learning, including the ability to learn to think conceptually, is basically a form of simple conditioning — that is, learning ever-increasingly complex response 'sets' by association — or whether some kinds of learning are of the conditioning–association type, and other kinds of learning are due to insight or understanding which, presumably, depend on the development of cognitive structures. Thus simple rote learning would be an example of the former kind of learning, and complex problem-solving an example of the latter kind of learning. There is little doubt that the young child finds the solving of abstract and conceptual problems difficult, and that a good deal of his learning is of the 'associative' type, that is, he learns the correct responses to make. Piaget would maintain that the child under seven years of age has not yet developed the cognitive structures which enable him to *understand* what he is doing. He can at this age do many school tasks, such as simple arithmetic, by learning the correct procedures; for example, he can learn his multiplication tables, and so multiply, but he *may* not at all know what is meant by multiplication! However, it does seem, as we discuss on page 67, that both the way schools attempt to teach understanding as opposed to rote learning, and the way also experimenters have approached the task of testing what young children understand, has insufficiently taken into account young children's often idiosyncratic limitations in understanding the way *language is used*. Although there are clearly limitations to a young child's conceptual abilities, we now know that these abilities are not as limited as Piaget's early work led us to believe; it is the task of the school and of parents to build on the ability which is present, by fostering understanding while at the same time developing the child's great skill in associative learning. A great deal of rote learning can be achieved in early childhood, and most of it can be taught while giving enjoyment to the child; nor need this be done at the expense of fostering the child's ability to understand eventually what he is learning. However, it is important that all this must be done using language which has meaning for the child.

However, whether someone learns with or without understanding depends not only on the age of the learner, but also upon the *type* of learning which is taking place. Most learning involves a mixture of habit and insight, and diagram 4 shows how learning tasks can be scaled from those which depend entirely, or almost entirely, on acquiring the right responses which become habitual, to those which are entirely, or almost entirely, dependent on the ability to form concepts. It is obvious that a great deal of what we have to learn in life does not depend on using conceptual thinking powers.

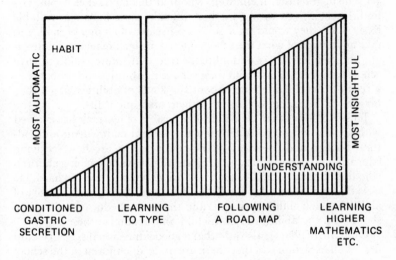

Diagram 4: *The scaling of learning tasks according to degree of understanding involved*[1]

We have considered two factors in relation to conceptual learning: one is that its development can be seen as a result of developing *maturity*, and the other that the use of such learning powers is dependent on the *kind* of material being learned. There is, however, a possible third factor which we have to consider when discussing conceptual learning, which is that the power to think in conceptual terms may well be an ability which some children simply do not possess, or possess only to a very limited degree, and that this ability, at least at certain limited levels of intelligence, may be independent of intelligence.

Jensen (1969) has suggested that not only is there evidence that this may be so, but that if such evidence were to be fully substantiated this could have important implications for educational practice. Jensen

[1]Reproduced from Hilgard, E. R. and R. C. Atkinson: *Introduction to psychology* (Harcourt Brace Jovanovich, 1967) by kind permission of the publishers.

and others have produced fairly convincing proof that some children have a high *associative* learning ability — that is, they are good at rote learning — but these children also often have a low *conceptual* learning ability: they have difficulty in learning material which requires insight and understanding. Jensen considers that children who are disadvantaged either because their home life is unstimulating or because they lack particular abilities, or for both reasons, are not able to take advantage of the traditional classroom situation which puts great emphasis on cognitive learning. However, many basic skills necessary in life can be learned by associative learning methods, and Jensen suggests that if children, who find this method easy but who find the cognitive learning method difficult, could be taught suitable basic skills, they would leave school conscious of having been able to take advantage of what the school offered, instead of feeling inadequate and helpless. It is undoubtedly true that many children leave school feeling hopeless about their scholastic abilities and probably as a result generally depressed about the kinds of abilities which they may be called upon to exhibit in their subsequent life.

Jensen believes that the traditional system of learning has evolved without taking into consideration the natural endowment and cultural backgrounds of many of the children who are now receiving education. Teachers must, he suggests, find ways of teaching children who find the traditional, cognitively orientated method too hard. He feels that schooling takes too little advantage of the great diversity of abilities which children exhibit, and that a good educational system should tap the abilities of each child and maximize these.

One can, of course, also add that a good educational system would first of all ascertain whether there are, indeed, children in the school who have a low conceptual learning ability, and at least maximize whatever conceptual ability such children have, in addition to teaching them other kinds of cognitive skills which they can, probably, more successfully employ.

Further reading

DONALDSON, M.: *Children's minds* (Fontana, 1978)

TURNER, J.: *Cognitive development* (Methuen, 1975)

GREENE, J.: *Thinking and language* (Methuen, 1975)

LOCK, A.: *Action, gesture and symbol: the emergence of language* (Academic Press, 1978)

BRUNER, J. and A. GARTON (eds.): *Human growth and development* (Clarendon Press, 1978)

CHAPTER FIVE

The development of moral, social and emotional behaviour and the child's growing perception of his social world

Preamble

In this chapter we shall be interested in such factors as the growth of moral knowledge, moral behaviour and moral feelings; the development of conscience and altruism, of empathy and sympathy; how and when various kinds of other emotions become available to children; how the ability to understand the behaviour of other people develops, and how children's friendships grow; and in several other allied topics.

In our consideration of children's total development it has in the past been customary to separate out various aspects of development because in this way these aspects can be better studied; and social development has been regarded as being a separate kind of study from moral and emotional growth, and from the development of an understanding of other people. However, it is now clear that social behaviour cannot be separated from the emotional factors which affect our relationships with other people, and these relationships in part rest on a particular moral code which is recognized in the society in which we function, so that the acquisition of moral knowledge and feeling, and the emotional responses we make to other people's behaviour and needs are all closely interrelated. Rather than discussing 'moral development' it is more helpful to look at the development of what is now termed 'pro-social' behaviour. This will include aspects of interpersonal behaviour and also of the development of a 'caring and sharing' attitude, so interestingly described by Mussen and Eisenberg-Berg (1977). For example, one is concerned to know how altruistic behaviour develops, and how it may be encouraged, and it seems likely that feelings of empathy are a necessary part of altruistic behaviour, which is itself part of moral behaviour. Similarly, moral behaviour rests on decisions made in particular situations, and this, as Kohlberg has said, is related to intellectual ability, to moral knowledge, and to the ability to anticipate events.

Heredity and environment

When we look at the origin of the kind of social, emotional and moral

149

behaviour exhibited by any one child we have to take into account both the congenital and the environmental factors which influence behaviour. In any consideration of the development of social behaviour assumptions must not be made that only the environment shapes behaviour. In chapter 3 the congenital influences on temperament are reviewed and we also discuss in that chapter the longitudinal study described by Thomas and Chess (1977) in which they observe that in the first few weeks of life children display an individuality in temperament which tends to remain constant in quality and seems to be independent of early parental handling and parental personality. Such characteristics are modified by the influences of home, school and society generally, but these influences play upon unique material and so produce unique effects.

Consideration of these influences involves separating not only early experiences from later experiences, but also appreciating that social influence may well be a two-way process — that is, that the child may influence the parents as well as the parents influencing the child. Bell (1968) makes the point that a correlation between parent and child behaviour only indicates that a relationship exists, it does not show the direction of the relationship; and too often the assumption is made that the influence can only be uni-directional — that is, from parent to child. In chapter 8 we discuss the question of how different children in the same family may each evoke different behaviour towards them from their parents, and there seems little doubt that the characteristics of any one child have some effect on the behaviour of the adults, both parents and teachers, with whom he has to do, and this in turn affects the child; extremely assertive children, for example, will evoke responses from adults which are normally unusual for them. Another example is provided by children who are primarily interested in material things and in being active; such children are not as susceptible to social training as those who are more concerned about their relationship with other people and who are more desirous of pleasing others. That this may well be a congenital factor is discussed by Scarr (1965), who comments on children's differential social responsiveness and sociability from an early age. However, we must also remember, as Hoffman (1975a) writes, that the effect of parental handling on the child is still likely to be more potent than the child's effect on the parent, though the subtle but possibly strong effect of a small baby's specific kind of social responsiveness on those who take care of him may have been underestimated.

Moral, social and emotional development

What precisely do we mean by moral, social and emotional development, and what is involved in such development? The socially and emotionally mature person is a competent member of his society, and before any child can reach this competence he has to learn many skills and habits. He has to learn how to differentiate between approved and disapproved behaviour, and he also has to learn both how to understand others and how to react appropriately to their behaviour. He finds that he feels guilt, love, anger and other emotions, and he learns that some of these feelings may be displayed and others must be controlled. The sanctions which operate to control and shape his behaviour change as he gets older, and as this occurs his awareness and appreciation of the world in which he lives become wider and keener. With increasing age he becomes more involved with other people; his feelings can be assailed more easily and his emotions aroused more readily by what people say and do. In comparison the baby who appears to be aware only of his own needs cannot be offended, and even though he may be very hungry he will only be aware of his acute need for food; he will not think malignly of the adults who seem to be denying him his need, whereas the eight-year-old who is thwarted will most likely feel resentment and hostility.

We will consider later how children learn with increasing understanding to interpret other people's behaviour, and we also review in subsequent chapters how adult handling may affect children's development (chapter 8). In this chapter children's social and emotional development will be studied in rather more general terms; we shall be concerned with reviewing what is known about the development towards social and emotional maturity of children growing up in our culture, and also consider the various factors which influence this development.

Moral development

In most modern psychology books what in the past has been termed 'moral' behaviour is now more frequently referred to as 'pro-social' behaviour. Mussen and Eisenberg-Berg (1978) have defined pro-social behaviour as 'behaviour which refers to actions that are intended to aid or benefit another person or group of people without the actor's anticipation of external reward'. In this chapter the term 'moral' will still be used, however, for it is a term which is not only in current use, but has also been used in philosophical writings for a very long period of time; however, the more modern term 'pro-social' is certainly from some points of view a more acceptable term.

It is clear that as a society we are by no means certain what we mean by 'moral' behaviour beyond agreeing with one another that certain kinds of 'core' behaviours, such as stealing, murdering or raping are immoral; but beyond a tacit disapproval of such violent misdemeanours, we do not seem definitely to be able to say what kinds of moral attitudes and behaviour we wish to inculcate in our children. In chapter 1 it is shown that previous generations were much more certain both about what they meant by 'moral' and about how to produce moral people. They were probably wrong about the latter though certainly convinced about the former. Today we are uncertain whether much behaviour which was previously considered moral, is in fact moral at all; very often so-called moral behaviour is confused with rule-following behaviour which it suits a particular society to inculcate in its members. We do not even know with any certainty what causes moral behaviour, or for that matter, rule-following behaviour, to develop as differentially as it does in different children from the same culture and society.

The question of what constitutes morality has been a subject of great interest to philosophers for many centuries, but empirical investigations of how human beings develop moral concepts are of relatively recent origin.

A discussion in depth of philosophical definitions of morality and of moral behaviour is out of place in this book. The reader interested in such concepts in relation to education is referred to either Wilson, Williams and Sugarman (1967) or Kay (1969) or Peters (1974). According to Kohlberg, whose work we will be considering, justice is the ultimate value. We can also say that true moral behaviour seems to arise from a conception of morality which is based on a consideration for the feelings of other people, and an appreciation of their needs and rights, and that it stems from an informed conscience. Because an awareness of other people's feelings is part of how one defines both empathy and sympathy, it is hardly possible to discuss the concept of morality from a developmental viewpoint without discussing how empathy and sympathy develop. Similarly, moral knowledge is intimately bound up with the ability to make judgements about the nature of behaviour and its ethical bases and appropriateness, and this in turn relates to an understanding of the personality of other people which underlies their behaviour. So developmental psychologists are naturally interested in knowing how this understanding develops during childhood.

It will already be clear that, as Brown (1965) has pointed out, in order to understand the development of behaviour which displays morality one must differentiate between moral knowledge, moral behaviour and moral feeling. These three aspects of morality do not necessarily develop or exist together, and they each appear to be learned in a different way. Also these different aspects of morality sometimes support one another, and at other times are not closely related. Thus moral feeling, which in itself can arise either from conscious understanding, or from having feelings of guilt, the reasons for which are not necessarily consciously understood, can influence moral behaviour. However, a number of studies have shown that there is no consistent relationship between, for example, resisting temptation and feeling guilty (Bandura and Walters, 1963). Similarly, moral knowledge may influence moral behaviour, but though there is usually a relationship between these two factors it is not necessarily a close one, as the classic study by Hartshorne, May *et al.* (1928–30) has shown. One has to realize that when people act morally they are not necessarily displaying a fixed, inner personality trait, such as *their* honesty, or *their* kindness. Kohlberg (1964) suggests that moral action requires a decision to be taken in a particular circumstance, and this decision is related to a person's intelligence, his moral knowledge, his ability to anticipate events and to various other factors. This does not mean that people have no moral values which act as a basic guide to their behaviour, but it has become clear in recent years that the reason why people behave in particular ways in specific circumstances does not only depend on some straightforward, universally applicable guide which in some manner they carry within them and which informs them on all occasions how to behave. Harding (1978) has suggested a model of the person which has six components:

(1) the self which experiences a unique individuality;
(2) the self which plays various individual roles, which is influenced by
(3) 'social reality', that is, that society has certain expectations about certain roles, such as what it is like to be a father, or a civil servant;
(4) the self which a person would like to be, and
(5) the self which he hopes is the way others see him; and, finally, there is
(6) the concept of identity, the degree to which all these notions of the self fit together and function effectively.

It is not unreasonable to suggest that even though the person subsumed under all these 'selves' may hold a number of values, how these values express themselves in behaviour will depend on which particular self is in operation at a particular time. If all moral behaviour, and, indeed, all behaviour to a greater or lesser extent, involves a decision-making process, then the decision made by a child or adolescent at any one time will be influenced also by

(1) the age of the child;
(2) the culture in which he lives;
(3) the specific situation;
(4) his personality, which is made up of his temperament, and the emotions involved with his having a conscience and an ego-ideal*, and which will include such feelings as guilt, altruism and empathy.

In addition, his moral *knowledge* will influence how he makes his judgement about what may be the right action to perform.

Many members of the teaching profession consider that what has been termed 'character training' is at least as important as intellectual training, and that the teacher's role in this training is particularly relevant. This long preamble to a discussion of moral development seems necessary, for it is important to show that questions of character training and of moral education are questions of great complexity; but the fact that we are faced with a complex problem does not mean that it is of insuperable difficulty.

As will already be evident, a full discussion of all the aspects of moral development is hardly possible here, but it is hoped that the main interconnecting strands can be drawn together to give the reader some concept of how, in a broad sense, the growth of moral behaviour can occur.

Major influential theories of moral development

When considering the development of all aspects of human psychological growth we are basically concerned with three major factors:

(1) what the processes of development are,
(2) how these change with increasing age and
(3) how development may be influenced by both internal and external events.

Reference has been made to the fact that it is difficult to separate different aspects of development, for instance, cognitive and affective growth. When considering moral development in particular, it is necessary to consider both these aspects of development, for, as we have noted, the stage of cognitive growth which a child has reached will determine the degree of complexity of moral judgement he can make, and the stage of moral feeling he has reached will show to what extent he has internalized the values current in the society in which he lives.

Apart from the group of social-learning theorists, the individual theorists who have had the greatest impact on our understanding of children's moral development are Freud, Piaget and Kohlberg.

Freud's ideas regarding moral development have concerned themselves with the internalization of moral feelings and with the development of the conscience, which includes the growth of a sense of guilt. These are the negative aspects of morality; however, he also had something to say about the positive aspects of how children come to assume the values of the people whom they love.

It is relatively easy to account for prudential behaviour, that is, for behaviour which makes sure one isn't caught doing a prohibited act and, therefore, at times desisting from doing what one wants to do because one is most likely to be caught; it is far more difficult to account for moral behaviour in the absence of the prohibiting authority, or when the likelihood of being caught is remote or even non-existent. Freud's view was not dissimilar to that of other theorists, such as the social-learning theorists, in that he rejected the notion that feelings of guilt were present from birth; his view was that young children are amoral and that they are, indeed, initially restrained from striving for pleasure, which is prohibited, through the exercise of parental authority. Because of the child's helplessness and his dependence on others he comes to fear the loss of his parents' love; this fear engenders 'social anxiety' which is not a true conscience, for at this stage the child merely fears the consequences of being discovered; but already this fear is tied not only to the fear of an externally applied punishment, but also to the more subtle fear of loss of parental love. Social-learning theorists similarly associate the child's knowledge of his dependence on his parents with his fear of their disapproval, and the consequent anxiety which is evoked acts as a restraining force. Social-learning theorists suggest that because early in the child's life he inhibits prohibited actions in the parents' *presence* this inhibition becomes associated with the tempting thought of performing the act and also with the anxiety evoked by the temptation, so that later this anxiety is likely to be evoked by tempting *thoughts* when the parents are absent. This is why an innocent child sometimes looks guilty when a wrong-doer in school is asked to own up: it might so easily have been the child himself who committed the misdemeanour, and the mere thought produces punishment in the form of guilt feelings from the superego*. Freud also considered that the child's need to identify with the parent of the opposite sex at the Oedipal* stage of psycho-sexual development was instrumental in the formation of the superego. So for Freud both the fear of loss of love — that is, 'social anxiety' — and the desire to take on the norms and values of the same-sexed parent, contribute to the development of the superego. (These ideas of Freud are discussed more fully in chapter 2.)

In Freud's theory the anxiety associated with the previous inhibition of action will usually result in the child desisting from doing what is disapproved. The reward, as it were, for desisting lies in release from anxiety. It may be doubted, however, whether this explanation by itself is adequate to account for the strong inhibition most older children and adults feel when they are tempted to act in ways which they know to be prohibited. Freud considered that a second, more powerful, emotional experience was required additionally to account for the development of a true conscience. He suggested that as well as having feelings of anxiety about the possible loss of parental love, the child also feels strong aggressive feelings towards his parents

155

whenever he is prevented in their presence from doing what he wants to do; but he cannot express these feelings outwardly because of fears of being punished for being aggressive, and also because of his erotic feelings for his parents (chapter 2). Thus the aggressive feelings which cannot be externally expressed are turned inwards and become a kind of self-punishment which is experienced as a feeling of guilt in relation to the act which evoked the feelings of aggression, and these emotions also become associated with tempting *thoughts*. Thus one can see that to the strength of the anxiety produced by the thought of losing parental love is added the strength of the inward-turned aggressive feelings, and these together form sufficient emotional force to act in most cases as an inhibitor to prohibited behaviour. Freud also used his idea about inward-turned aggression, which is, of course, the aggression initially felt towards the parents, to explain why children who have had a gentle upbringing often have a severe conscience, and why children who have had a harsh upbringing often do not have a strong conscience: if parents are loving and kind it is all the more difficult for the child to express his aggressive feelings towards them, so that the strength of the internalized, self-punitive emotion, which becomes the conscience, is all the stronger. (Parental handling in relation to child personality characteristics is considered in chapter 8.) Freud also postulated constitutional differences between children which make some children more prone to anxieties of all kinds, including moral anxiety.

The idea that proneness to anxiety is, to an extent at least, a constitutional factor would be supported by Eysenck (1960), but he would also consider that a person with an introverted personality is likely to have a stronger conscience than a person with an extraverted personality, the degree of introversion–extraversion also being determined in part by constitutional factors.

As far as the positive aspect of morality is concerned, that is, the passing on from one generation to another of the values and norms of the society, it is obvious that many adult values are explicitly taught, but many values can only be inferred by children, and in any case explicit teaching does not by itself ensure that children incorporate into their personalities the moral precepts they have been taught. Again, the force of emotional factors is at the base of Freud's explanation: that part of the superego which he termed the ego-ideal is formed at the time of the resolution of the Oedipus complex*. (Sometimes in his writings Freud made a distinction between the superego and the ego-ideal, at other times he treated them as synonymous. See *New Introductory Lectures on Psychoanalysis*, Pelican Books, 1973, page 96.) This occurs at about the age of four when the child identifies with the parent of the same sex; this identification by the child arises in part from fear of losing the parent, which Freud thought all children who have formed a relationship with a caretaking adult experience: by taking into oneself part of the personality of another person one is to an extent safeguarding oneself from the complete loss of that person. The act of identification, which is a form of imitation, is in itself a common process: teenagers in their admiration for sportsmen or pop stars behave like them, and a universal way of expressing a desire to be like another, admired, person is to incorporate some aspect of that person's personality into one's own personality. Freud, however, linked the young child's fear of losing his parents to his erotic feelings for his parents (chapter 2) so that the process of identification at the Oedipal* stage is most likely a more powerful kind of process than later kinds of identification. The child who has never experienced such a relationship does not fear its loss and so there is often no internal prohibition present.

Piaget (1932) has approached his study of moral development basically in two ways: one was to see how children's understanding of rules of behaviour becomes modified with age until, as Piaget says, genuine moral development has taken place; the other was to see how children learn to understand with increasing age the reasons for behaviour where a question of morality is involved, that is, how they come to understand other people's intentions, and thus how well they learn to make moral judgements. Within both these approaches lies the concept of justice: how does a child's idea of justice change with increasing age?

According to Piaget and other workers who have replicated his work, the young child under four-and-a-half years of age does not usually play co-operatively, but he plays often in parallel with other children (chapter 6). As he approaches five years of age he begins to be aware that other children, whom he sees at play, have rules by which they play, but these rules have no importance for him. Moral growth cannot proceed faster than language understanding (chapter 4) and the idea of rules having to be enforced cannot be comprehended without the language structure which explains this, nor without being able to see another's point of view. Thus, although the child is by no means wholly egocentric at this age (chapter 4) he is still, according to Piaget, largely at the egocentric moral stage. After five years of age or so, children begin to become keenly aware of rules; indeed, rules assume a great importance, being thought of as sacred, emanating from adults, and being unalterable and everlasting. The child is now entering the second stage, called by Piaget variously the stage of heteronomous morality or moral realism or the authoritarian stage. The child does not know how the rules are formed or who formed them, but he appears to think that rules, even of childish games, have always existed. Children at this stage find a certain security in the seeming unchangeability of rules, and this is the age when they play a lot of games with rules.

After eight years of age the child accepts that it is permissible to alter rules, provided that the other players in the game agree. The child is now entering the autonomous or reciprocal or equality stage, that is, the third stage. Piaget's final stage, the stage of equity, is reached at twelve years of age. This is the stage of mutual respect, co-operation and of a consideration of the rights of others, and represents the achievement of a true understanding of the nature of rules, and this stage is the one which, according to Piaget, is the most relevant to the question of genuine moral development.

Children are not, of course, consistent in their handling of rules, just as they are not consistent in their comprehension of the conservation of quantity or number (chapter 4). There is little doubt, however, that just as they become released from the dominance of the senses they also become released from the necessity of a slavish adherence to rules.

Concurrently with the child's changing view about the importance of rules is a growing sophistication in the ability to make moral *judgements*. Piaget has investigated children's ideas of justice and fairness, how they view punishments, and their understanding of such concepts as lying. He has asked children what is bad about telling lies: before eight years of age children say it is worse to lie to an adult than to a child; also the enormity of a lie is directly related to its size, so that a lie about a completely improbable happening, which would most likely not be believed and be treated as a joke, will be considered by the child of this age to be a 'big' lie and so a much more culpable act than to tell a 'small' lie which, however, might well be believed.

Young children under eight are also mostly concerned with fairness and retributive punishment, rather than with people's needs and an assessment of intent. Piaget has suggested that before seven years of age children do not judge the gravity of an act by the intentions of the agent, but by the amount of damage done. This percept-centred view of life means that for such children it will be more naughty to break a big jug while helping mother to lay the table than to break a small jug while trying to steal some cream from the larder. Again the size of the damage done, like the size of a lie told, is important, and not the intention behind the evaluated action. Because children under seven are so percept-centred, most of their evaluations will be dominated by what is immediately visible. It is difficult for them to understand motives for behaviour which cannot be easily and actually perceived, so that only what is quite obvious can enter into consideration (chapter 4). After seven years of age children begin to judge more by intent and not so much by consequence, and at twelve years of age Piaget considers that there is a real change towards concern for motive and intention. It has been said that this ontogenic* development mirrors the phylogenic* development of man's ideas of jurisprudence.

There is much evidence for the direction of development and for the definite stages of thinking in relation to moral questions which Piaget has described, though recent work does question whether children are as incapable of taking the intentions of an actor into account as Piaget's findings seem to suggest (page 167). However, he does not deal with the problem of conflict which so often arises when decisions of a moral nature have to be taken. The problem of conflict is discussed on page 161. Also research on adolescent moral judgements (Loughran, 1967) has found that some adolescents still make authority-based judgements (Piaget's second stage) and that half the judgements made by adolescents in one study were based on equality, the third Piagetian stage. It is the examination of moral judgements made by children between ten and sixteen years of age with which Kohlberg's work has been mainly concerned. He has also concerned himself very much with the problem of moral dilemmas and how these are resolved by children between these ages.

Kohlberg, in one of his papers (1974), describes how his own four-year-old son refused to eat meat because he thought it bad to kill animals, but later, when he heard a story of how Eskimos kill seals, became angry and said: 'You know, there is one kind of meat I would eat, Eskimo meat. It's bad to kill animals, so it's all right to eat Eskimos' (page 6). Kohlberg suggests that this episode illustrates

(1) that children can generate their own moral values, for this little boy had decided entirely on his own not to eat meat, and
(2) that these values have universal roots, for most children believe it is bad to kill, though it is also clear that such beliefs are not universally and consistently maintained. (The question of the universality of such beliefs is discussed below.) This inconsistency is also illustrated by the young child's desire for reciprocal justice, which Piaget has described, so that though it is bad to kill, nevertheless it is all right to kill Eskimos if they kill seals!

Kohlberg considers (1974) that 'there is a natural sense of justice intuitively known by the child' (page 5). He believes his work has shown him that a child's basic values do not come from outside himself, though this does not mean that external factors cannot influence the expression which such values take. This 'natural sense of justice' has universal roots, and Kohlberg's cross-cultural studies, he considers, have demonstrated this. He has carried out work in Taiwan, Turkey, India, Mexico, Great Britain and Israel, as well as in the USA. His work has demonstrated that children move through definite stages of moral development in an invariant order, which is akin to Piaget's stages.

Kohlberg has outlined three basic levels of moral judgement, and these can be related to six stages of development. As far as the *cognitive* processes are concerned which are involved in the making of moral judgements, one can say that, broadly speaking, Kohlberg's stage 1 is equivalent to Piaget's concrete operational stage, and his stages 4, 5 and 6 are equivalent to the formal operational stage of Piaget.

During the past few years the findings of a number of research projects, while supporting the hierarchical nature of Kohlberg's first three stages, have not been able to support his findings in relation to his last three stages. Kohlberg himself in his more recent writings has suggested that stages 5 and 6 do not appear until early adulthood. He has also now added a seventh stage which can develop after the experience of crises in life, and at a more mature age. Critics of his work include Peters (1974) who among other criticisms questions the logical relationship between Kohlberg's six stages and his possibly narrow definition of what is called 'teaching': the fact that a sense of justice is universally found among children does not necessarily mean that it is 'natural' and untaught. Kohlberg's work is still developing, and it is important more for the stimulation to research which it has generated than for the findings themselves.

According to Kohlberg each successive stage of moral development makes distinctions ignored by previous stages; comes closer to finding a universal basis for values; generates a more stable hierarchy of choice, and, he writes, 'finally, each stage comes closer to a decision made on principles of justice' (1974, page 9). He says that one can see the development of the concept of moral values in relation not only to human life, but also in relation to law, conscience, love or concern for others, authority, trust, contract, liberty, property rights, truth and discipline. Of interest to teachers is Kohlberg's concern with moral education, which, he says, can rest on the universality of the stages which he states exist, meaning thereby that one of the roles of moral education lies in 'stimulating movement to the next stage of moral development' (page 9). Kohlberg also considers that another important aspect of moral education is that it enables children to become more aware of their own values and also enables them to understand other people's values. However, he is quite clear that this does not mean teaching that such values are relative, and that any one man's principles are as good as another man's principles. By viewing *justice* as the ultimate moral value Kohlberg is able to differentiate between different levels of values, so that, as he says, being honest does not merely mean that one doesn't cheat, lie or steal. 'It means recognizing a number of vague and sometimes conflicting *rules*' (1974, page 11); but if one applies the moral *principle of justice* then one doesn't cheat because cheating is an unjust action towards someone else. He says that there are exceptions to rules but not to principles.

Discussions on this level can be encouraged with older children; indeed, Kohlberg himself is continuing his research by initiating discussions with adolescents, particularly by giving them moral dilemmas to discuss (Mason, 1979); but how can younger children be stimulated to move from one moral stage to another, for it does not follow that all children in all classes and societies inevitably move on to higher stages of moral development. We discuss in chapter 8 the possible relationship between various child-rearing methods and personality development; however, it seems appropriate following a discussion of the theoretical questions involved in moral development to say something here about the practical issues also.

Mussen and Eisenberg-Berg (1977), in examining the antecedents of 'pro-social' behaviour, have come to the conclusion that there is no single determinant which has an overriding influence on the development of such behaviour. 'Each antecedent functions as part of a complex matrix of factors that exert their influences simultaneously' (page 159). They conclude that altruistic children come from nurturant parents, who are themselves good models of pro-social behaviour, who 'use reasoning in discipline, maintain high standards and encourage their children to accept responsibilities for others early'. They also found that such children are relatively self-confident and active, and that they are 'advanced in moral reasoning as well as in role-taking skills and empathy' (page 159). They also found that children are more helpful if they are happy or successful. Explaining to the child why one should help others encourages pro-social behaviour, and receiving direct rewards for helping can also be an encouragement. We will return later to the question of the powerful effect of explanation, particularly of explaining to the child the consequences of his behaviour to others. According to Mussen and Eisenberg-Berg parents and teachers should also help children to reflect on their own and other people's feelings.

The importance of so understanding other people's feelings raises relevant and interesting issues regarding moral development which have already been briefly mentioned. As we have seen, moral development involves much more than just the growth of the intellectual ability which enables adults eventually to make decisions about moral behaviour. Why are people motivated to *care* about other people, particularly people with whom they have no close emotional involvement? And, even if we cannot say categorically *why* they are so motivated we should be able to say what are the processes, and what is the order, in which a sense of caring for others develops. The Freudian psychoanalytic school would suggest that the sense of caring springs from the operations of the superego* (chapter 2). It is suggested that though the superego has its origins in the child's relationship *with his parents*, the restraints which the superego operates become transferred on to other people, particularly on to persons in authority. However, this does not seem entirely to account for the often very strong feelings of empathy and sympathy which apparently one human being can feel for another. Kohlberg's system rests on the principles of justice (page 160), so one would like to know not only in what order and when various non-cognitive aspects of the development of the eventually mature sense of justice come to the fore, but why human beings should be motivated at all to take the interests of others into consideration in their own behaviour. Hamlyn (1978) writes that 'the recognition of other persons (and their existence) is very much a matter of the recognition of them as sources of feelings and attitudes of various kinds, which fit in with, or conflict with the child's own in a great variety of ways' (page 101). Perhaps one can do no more at present than speculate on the process which occurs and on its origin. Darwin (1872) has shown that facial expressions, particularly those of fear and anger, when observed by another primate of the same species,[1] will evoke the feelings associated with these expressions. This ability to communicate at least some of the grosser feelings clearly has a biological basis and is of survival value. One can speculate further that the ability which humans have to be able to understand the finer feelings of others in due course developed to serve social purposes. By being able to be empathic and thus motivated to behave, at least at times, as if the empathic person were acting in his own interests rather than in the interests of the person whose feelings he is experiencing, the survival of the social group tends to be safeguarded. For social beings altruism in individual members of the group has biological advantages for the species; and one of the mechanisms through which altruism may be developed is the ability to feel empathy. Hoffman (1975a), but also with Saltzstein (1967 and in other writings), has referred to the powerful effect in relation to the internalization of moral restraints of 'induction', that is, of making clear to the growing child the various possible consequences for others of his behaviour rather than concentrating on showing the child the punitive consequences for himself. The conflict which normally exists between selfish desire and the need to control the outward expression of one's own desires is minimized if the disciplining adult makes the well-being of another person something to be desired by the child. Thus one way of capitalizing, as it were, on the biologically given ability, at least as far as the grosser feelings of others are concerned, to be empathic, is to make the child aware early in his life of the needs of other people and the consequences to others of his own behaviour. This matter is further discussed in chapter 8.

---

[1]Darwin also discussed the expression of emotions in animals other than primates.

The processes underlying the development of social awareness and social growth

Social learning is different in kind from the learning of skills, or learning by rote, or learning to solve problems. The young child has to learn by a process of association which deeply involves his emotions; he has to learn to associate parental disapproval with certain types of behaviour, and his emotions are evoked because he feels unhappy if his parents show their disapproval, whether by physical punishment, or verbally, or by their attitude towards him. The process of social development involves the development of an awareness of oneself; an awareness of other people as separate entities with unique feelings and personality characteristics, motives and intentions; it also involves an understanding of social relationships, which includes, *inter alia*, the child's own relationships with other people; and an understanding of the adult social world in general. This is a very considerable programme.

Many writers, Mead (1934), Horney (1950), and more recently, Lewis and Brooks (1975) have emphasized the importance of the development of the *self* in social relationships. (In chapter 4 we discuss the relationship between cognitive development and the growth of self awareness.) It is considered most probable that the very young baby has at first no awareness of a distinct differentiation between himself and the people and objects around him, and that learning to differentiate himself from others could be said to be the child's first social act. It is certainly during the first two years that the child changes from being a biological to being a social being, and this necessitates his developing some kind of concept of himself as separate from others. Lewis and Brooks (*ibid.*) suggest that the child has to learn both that he is a being separate from others, and the categories by which to define himself. One could add to this that the child must also eventually come to understand in due course not only that he is separate from others but that he himself is a unique being with a continuing history, despite the fact that he has different thoughts and different feelings at different times. Lewis and Brooks-Gunn (1978) suggest that the first two concepts about oneself are learnt in the first year of life. By eighteen months of age children are not only able to label pictures correctly as to gender, but they can also label pictures of themselves correctly, and by this age they also know something about age, and that they themselves are young. The nature and quality of the infant's concepts of his own sex and age seem to have an effect quite early on his relationship with others: Lewis and Brooks-Gunn (*ibid.*) report work by a variety of researchers which indicates that infants prefer to look at other unfamiliar *infants* rather than at unfamiliar *adults*, and toddlers and older children prefer to play with same-sexed children. This relationship between increasing knowledge of oneself and increasing knowledge of others can further be seen through the connection between what is valued about oneself and also what is valued about others. In this way, the authors point out, preferences about others are built up. How and why we like some people and not others will affect the assessments we make of them. We return to this aspect of social perception on page 166.

Through observation of young children in contact with others it seems that a rudimentary concept of other children's separate existence from themselves comes into being by about two to three years of age. As far as understanding something about their own unique continuity is concerned, here Hoffman (1975b) remarks that it is possible that only between the ages of six and nine years does the beginning of a sense of such continuity truly emerge, and that this sense develops markedly during early adolescence.

Hoffman (1975b) and Feshbach (1977) have both suggested the processes whereby awareness of other people as beings having a separate and unique identity might come about. In part this growing awareness is due to cognitive processes, in part to affective processes. The cognitive processes involve

(1) a realization that other people (and objects) have a permanent *existence* outside one's own perception of them, and this means
(2) understanding that others have unique personality characteristics, 'life circumstances and inner states' (Hoffman, 1975b, page 612), which continue outside the immediate situation in which they are observed. It also involves, according to Hoffman,
(3) the ability to be able to appreciate the role of another person.

By at least one year of age children 'can retain a mental image of a person' (*ibid.*, page 611), and so have a concept of people as permanent 'objects', though a number of recent studies (Lewis and Brooks-Gunn, 1978) indicate that infants by three months of age appear to come to expect certain kinds of behaviour from their mothers which they do not expect from strangers; this, however, does not mean that the child has a concept of the permanence of his mother when she is out of his sight. As far as understanding the *continuity* both of himself and others as unique persons is concerned, we have seen that a complete sense of self-identity is not achieved early, and it is probable that a sense of other people's continuing identity is similarly not achieved before the ages of six to nine years. This question is discussed again more fully on page 166.

The affective process of a child's developing awareness of others can be said to start from the presumed biologically given feelings of distress experienced when others of the same species are fearful or distressed. Hoffman quotes Simner (1971) reporting two-day-old infants crying when other infants cried (and Simner gives reasons that in his view this was due to the infants' distress and not due to any other cause, such as imitation). Thus Hoffman suggests that such feelings of empathy in the first year of life probably precede a *cognitive* awareness of other people. It appears that another's distress can evoke a sympathetic resonance long before another person's identity can be conceptualized. This 'sympathetic resonance' is probably the beginning of the first of three stages in the development of the affective aspect of awareness of others. In the first stage, when self-differentiation is still far from complete, Hoffman assumes (1975b, page 615) that another person's distress is reacted to *as if it* were the child's own distress. He quotes a charming example of a year-old child who when himself distressed sucked his thumb and pulled his ear; when he saw a sad expression on his father's face he himself looked sad, sucked his thumb and pulled his father's ear!

Slowly the young child becomes more aware of other people as separate identities, and is able to give a more pronounced sympathetic response to the other's distress; but he still feels at this stage that other people's feelings are *identical* with his own. One should mention in this connection that the notion of empathy, as well as having a cognitive, role-taking component as we have discussed, has a two-level affective component: some people and most young children can only feel for another person what *they themselves* would feel in similar circumstances, whereas with a more developed form of empathy a person is able to feel what another person is feeling, even if he himself would not have such feelings in the same circumstances. Researchers have not always clearly differentiated in their work these two aspects of empathy.

The second stage of this affective process of the development of awareness of other people is reached, according to Hoffman (*ibid.*) at between about two to three years of age, when the child is forming a growing cognitive sense that other people have inner states and feelings different from his own. This can be seen when children are observed at this age taking the role of others, or indicating that they know a *particular* toy will comfort another child, whereas a younger child under two or three will attempt to comfort another child by simply giving him his *own*, comforting, toy. Hoffman also makes the interesting point that the child has to learn that although other people can have, and often do have, different needs and feelings from his own, yet all human beings, and particularly humans of the same age and sex, are likely to have very similar feelings; so that one has to learn that it is probable that others will experience the *same* emotions as oneself in a particular situation but also that it is possible that their emotions may be somewhat, or even very, different. However, a child as young as two or three years of age can really only be concerned with what other people may feel in an *immediate* situation. It is only when a child has the cognitive awareness of another's existence as a sentient and continuing being that he can experience, and so respond to, another person's general condition. It has already been suggested that this does not begin to happen until about six to nine years of age, and only in early adolescence are the corresponding feelings well developed.

It is, of course, obvious that during middle and later childhood his ability both to feel empathy and sympathy, as well as to understand something of another person's inner being, develops; also his appreciation increases of the many and various situations in which other persons can find themselves and the concomitant emotions which they can experience. Children are better able to identify the emotions of other children than those of adults, and ten-and-a-half year old children in one research project (Rothenberg, 1970) were significantly better in identifying four emotions — anger, happiness, anxiety and sadness — in adults than were children of eight-and-a-half years. Children under six are able, as we have seen, to have empathy for others when these others are either very similar to the child himself, or are placed in a situation with which he is familiar. When the situation is unfamiliar, or the person assessed very dissimilar to the child, then only by middle or later childhood can the child be truly empathic. Of course, even some adults never reach this stage of development, and always remain largely impervious to the feelings of others.

However, in addition to being able to have empathy and sympathy for others, the child as a developing social being, as discussed on page 163, also has to be able to make reasonably accurate assessments of other people's personality and character; to gain some understanding of how other people think; to learn something about the adult social world; and he will himself also form social relationships which will be of great importance to him throughout life, so that he has to learn to understand the nature of such relationships.

The study of how adult people are able to interpret the behaviour of others, why some people are better at doing this than others, why even so-called professionals, for example, psychiatrists and psychologists, are often so wrong about the meaning of other people's behaviour, is a complex one. We know that it is not only the behaviour of the person being assessed which is relevant, but certain characteristics of the person doing the assessing, too, enter into the validity of the judgements being made. Such factors as, for example, similarity of culture, class and education, make the understanding of each other's behaviour easier for each of the two people concerned; it is also known that certain people, such as highly dogmatic, or strongly punitive people, are less able than others to assess objectively other people's characteristics. There are great methodological difficulties in the study of person perception by adults, and these difficulties are even greater when we study the development of person-perception in children.

As discussed on page 120, much evidence now exists to show that even small infants are perceptive social beings, in that they very early in life show an interest in people. They attend to faces and speech sounds within a few days of birth, and by two months of age show a greater interest in what people do than in other objects in their environment (Trevarthen *et al.*, 1975). Bruner has repeatedly made the point, particularly in relation to language development (chapter 4), that babies appear to be 'primed' to be social beings, apparently being biologically ready, as it were, to attend specifically to the activities of other human beings; but it is also clear that a great deal of social learning must take place during childhood, through relationships with other people, in order that the child may become a *competent* social being.

In recent years a number of writers have described the findings of research work relating to the various aspects of social development outlined above. Thus, in relation to what the child understands about other people's *thoughts*, Shantz (1975) writes that by six years of age a child can understand that other persons have different thoughts from the child himself; by middle childhood he knows that another person can have thoughts about the child's own thoughts; and by ten years of age, or so, 'children evidence ability to infer what another is thinking while at the same time infer that the other is thinking of what the child himself is thinking' (page 289, *ibid.*).

As far as children's understanding of other people's *motives* for behaviour and the intentions underlying their behaviour is concerned, the early work in this field was carried out by Piaget, who sought to discover children's understanding of the motives underlying moral behaviour. This is discussed later in this chapter. The difficulty which a young child has in making realistic assessments of the motives for behaviour are probably due to a number of factors: there is not only his more percept-centred orientation to happenings when compared with the older child's orientation, but possibly also, as Williams (1967) has suggested, the young child may have a difficulty in separating ends and means, so that there is an undue concentration by him on means when making intention-judgements. When one combines this difficulty for the young child of separating ends and means with his higher degree of percept-centredness one can see why it is that the young child, as Wood (1978) found, is able to link observable means to an observable end, but finds it much more difficult to make inferences about the causes of other people's behaviour, feelings and thoughts which lie outside the immediate field of observation. A point brought out by Farnhill (1974) in relation to Piaget's work on children's moral judgements is that children from early in life have their attention drawn to the importance of 'good' (moral) behaviour, so that when young children are asked to make judgements involving intentions where 'goodness' or 'naughtiness' is involved, as they were by Piaget, the moral outcome is so important to them that the notion of intentionality seems to them less important; but this does not necessarily mean that they cannot ever take *intentions* into account. Farnhill asked one set of children with average ages of six, seven and nine-and-one-third years to assess the intention behind another child's (filmed) behaviour, and then to say whether they would choose this child as a helpful member of a co-operative group. The control group of children were asked to give their views about the same kind of behaviour in *terms of moral judgements*; Farnhill found that the first group of children differentiated significantly more between malicious and accidental conditions in the filmed child's behaviour than the second group of children who had had to make their assessments in terms of moral behaviour. Wood's work (1978) also did not involve children giving accounts of intentionality in relation to *moral* behaviour, but in relation to everyday interpersonal situations. Although she found that the young child relied a good deal on immediate observation in order to make his assessment, even the six-year-old child was quite able to make simple interpretations of behaviour, but mostly within the total context of what was observable. Thus the six-year-old would say that one man in a film laughed because another had been told off, both kinds of behaviour being observable in the film; indeed, most children under eleven years of age did not give reasons for such behaviour which related to the personality characteristics of the actors. The older child, however, made comments such as: 'He is laughing because he is the sort of man who is glad when someone else gets into trouble.' We can see that the child between seven and eleven years of age gains the ability to appreciate that a variety of actions may culminate in the same result. This seems to enable him also to realize that one action can be seen to have originated from a number of possible causes. Also, the child's increasingly accurate concept of time makes it possible for him to look into the past for reasons for any particular piece of behaviour which he is observing. The young child is very concerned with notions of first-hand reality, so that concrete and observable events are uppermost in claiming his attention.

Gottlieb, Taylor and Ruderman (1977) referring to the younger child's preference for making judgements in relation to the *outcome* of any event as opposed to discussing the intentions of the actor, found that children adopted one of three strategies depending on their age: the youngest focused either on motive *or* outcome, but they couldn't move their perspective from one to the other; the middle age group could move their attention when asked to do so; and the oldest group considered both motive and outcome, and used both to make their evaluation of responsibility. Harris (1977) found that when he presented children with five different situations based on Heider's (1958) five levels of criteria for assessing culpability, ranging from the actor and an event being associated only by physical proximity, for example, a man sits on a chair and it breaks (level 1), to an event (level 5) being fully and intentionally caused by the actor, he found the youngest children quite unable to differentiate between the stimulus events and their relationship to the actor's culpability.

Understanding the causes of other people's behaviour is closely linked to being able to make assessments of their personality traits and characteristics. As Rogers (1978) has recently pointed out, the function of the adult ability reasonably accurately to assess other people's personalities is to enable adults to interact with others successfully; and, presumably, the child's ability to make such assessments fit the child's social requirement at any one particular age stage. But the child's social needs and relationships change as he ages, and his understanding of other people must change too, and one assumes that these two changes occur *pari passu*. We have also seen (page 167) that at least in one experimenter's work (Farnhill, 1974) the type of assessment a child is called on to make will affect the kind of judgement he will make. Again, different situations will affect the nature of the judgement made, as is the case when adults make such judgements about other people. In addition, the degree of a child's understanding of a situation will influence his ability to make sense of other people's behaviour within such situations; Wood (1968) found that when children of between five and fifteen years of age were presented with four different filmed interpersonal situations the younger children were much more easily able to understand some situations than others.

A child's personal involvement in an interpersonal situation will also affect his judgement; many teachers will be familiar with this kind of description given by a six-year-old: 'I used to like her, but I don't now because her dog bit me.' Again, the relationship a child has with a person whose behaviour he is trying to assess will affect at least what he says about such behaviour to others: thus the five- and six-year-olds in Wood's study (1968) frequently referred to their parents' willingness to play with them. Children long for admirable traits in their parents and want them above all to be fair! The comments made by the seven- to nine-year-olds also indicated that they found satisfaction in joint activities, and a happy relationship with their parents, and these satisfactions became the chief focus for describing their parents as people; the ten- to twelve-year-old group referred in their descriptions of parents more to the kind of discipline parents upheld. At a later age the degree of parental understanding and helpfulness once again becomes important in children's descriptions. Whether only a free description of others by the child is called for by the experimenter, or whether children are 'prompted' by being asked specific questions which elicit descriptions which might not otherwise be given, the descriptive terms used by most children seem to range from physical descriptions of appearance given by the young child to, at nine years of age, descriptions which imply an understanding that people vary in mood and exhibit different traits at different times. By this age, too, people are no longer seen as if they were objects; also a person's *behaviour* in Wood's (1968) research was described by children of nine and over *as if* they were aware that behaviour is an indication of personality, but few conclusions were overtly drawn about behaviour as an indicator of underlying personality characteristics. Also how another person behaves *towards the child* in the middle childhood period still largely determines the child's assessment of him. By early adolescence the personal attractiveness of a described person, their attitude to others, and, occasionally, the feelings which people evoke in the adolescent, are used as descriptive terms. Now, children comment on the relationship between personality variables and behaviour, and descriptions of others are, by and large, much more objective. By fifteen years of age children's descriptions of others include a great deal of criticism not included in the thirteen-year-olds' descriptions, and the fifteen-year-olds are also very ready to be self-critical.

As has been suggested earlier in this chapter, the relationship a child has with other people affects the way he will describe them and, presumably, this in turn is a reflection of the way he thinks about different people in his world. The relationships we form with other people throughout life are the network of our social world, and in large measure the success we have in these relationships determines how happy our life will be.

Reference has already been made in chapter 3 and in this chapter to the young infant's propensity to become a social being. Attachments to other people are sought very early in life. It would seem that such attachments normally lay the foundation for later social relationships (page 106). However, both different kinds of early attachments and different social relationships later in life vary qualitatively from each other. In order to form deep, and possibly also less deep, personal relationships of good quality later in life, an attachment of a particular quality, what psychologists have called 'bonding', may have to be formed with another human being within the first two or three years of life. This point has been made by many writers (see Rutter, 1978), though Clarke and Clarke (1976) suggest that there is insufficient evidence, and some contrary evidence, for such a 'critical period' in the forming of bonding attachments. This matter is discussed more fully in chapter 7. In this chapter we are concerned with the *processes* involved in the formation of early relationships.

For most small babies the mother (or whoever is the baby's principal caretaker, here referred to as mother) will be the person to whom he first becomes attached and forms a bond. The bonding process does not seem to depend on the fact that the mother provides for the baby's physical needs, such as food, warmth and comfort, nor on the fact that she spends more time with him than anyone else, but that she normally has the time, the opportunity and the desire to respond to his social advances, and to initiate such advances herself. In all normal circumstances it is the mother who has the opportunity to relate to her baby in this way, but Schaffer and Emerson (1964) have shown that when the mother does not respond to her baby in this manner, the baby can and will form a bond with whoever it is in his environment who interacts regularly with the baby and who does respond to him, and who also initiates interaction with him. Thus it seems that quite early in life the baby seeks and finds satisfaction in personal relationships. Schaffer and Crook (1978) list four maternal 'approaches' as they call them, of which mothering as a form of 'interlocution' is the approach which is of particular importance in social development. They stress the 'basic mutuality of mother and child' (page 59) and the importance of this dyadic* relationship in the socialization process. The mutuality starts with the mother allowing herself to be paced by the baby's pattern of alternately sucking and pausing to suck, and when he pauses she is active, by, for example, talking to him, thus enabling him very early in life to learn that interactions with others are paced over time. This leads to the older infant interacting with his mother by taking turns with her in vocalizations long before he can hold a proper, verbal, conversation. Collis and Schaffer (1975) have shown in a similar manner that the mother follows the baby's line-of-regard when he is looking at something: when this happens it is the baby who is initiating an activity which, as Schaffer and Crook say, the mother 'converts into a dyadic experience' (page 62). In order to do this adequately she has to exhibit a degree of sensitivity to the baby's activities which not all mothers are able to accomplish, though what precisely is involved in being a sensitive mother is not easy to define. It is possible that even the most so-called sensitive mothers are not able to be equally responsive to all their babies, so that, as Dunn (1977) has pointed out, what one may really mean by 'sensitive' in this context is 'how this mother gets on with this baby' (page 75). However, Ainsworth, Bell and Stayton (1971) say that the sensitive mother is a person who *cannot* ignore or reject her baby; she responds correctly to his cues and signals.

The bonding process should not, however, be thought of solely as a one-way process. The literature on attachment makes little reference to the fact that the mother also becomes bonded to the baby (Robertson, 1977). It is the forming of this *two-way* relationship which, in part at least, makes it possible for mothers to cope with the many disturbing, trying and, at times, distressing aspects of a child's growing up, for which strangers cannot be expected to have the patience and love; and the baby who has a mother who is bonded to him is highly unlikely to become an abused baby.

If the mother gets on well with her baby, the baby not only experiences and so learns that social behaviour relates to reciprocal interaction, but in due course that his intentions can be understood by other people, and that he in turn can understand other people's intentions. Bruner (1978) has described how the 'turn-taking' vocal interactions, together with the mother following the baby's line-of-regard when he is interested in an object, lead, by six months of age, to 'co-ordinated cycles of eye contact and calling, controlled principally by the mother, of course, but increasingly by the infant' (page 77). Now the child can learn to exchange objects in play and soon to play various social games. This relationship is further discussed in chapter 4.

Thus the infant's propensity to make social relationships is developed by social interchanges with, usually, his mother and one or two other people in the family whom he sees often and regularly. As his memory becomes more efficient he is able to store a mental image of people he sees often and to develop a concept of their permanent existence (page 181). His attitude to strangers in the first year is an interesting indication of the stage he has reached in his relationship to people he knows: as Dunn describes this (1977) a ten-week-old crying infant is mostly pacified by the sight of a stranger, but an eight-month-old baby who is distressed because of his mother's absence may well become even more distressed if the stranger attempts to comfort him.

Thus the development of social relationships in part at least normally grows from the bonding to one or two special people early in life, through an appreciation by the baby of the difference in his relationship between such people and others whom he does not often see; and this difference in the quality of the relationships is clearly a difference which is a *felt* difference, that is, it is emotional in quality. At the same time the small baby will exhibit an interest in other infants, and in other people which is not particularly emotional in kind.

In what ways, if at all, is the quality of these early emotional relationships, and the quality of parental handling of a child in infancy and childhood, connected to his social behaviour exhibited towards other people? Lieberman's work with three-year-old children (1976), as well as studies with older children, show that the securely attached child even at three years of age interacts with other children in a more responsive way than the child who is less securely attached to at least one emotionally close adult. Longitudinal studies (Roff, 1961 and also 1972) also show that there is a relationship between good later adult social conduct and mental health and acceptability by peers in childhood. However, though such a relationship has been shown to exist in a number of studies, one cannot say that the earlier behaviour is a *cause* of the later behaviour. Indeed, even under one year of age some infants are clearly preferred to others by their peers (Lee, 1973), so that it is possible that temperamental differences (chapter 3) which make for acceptability by peers in childhood may be the reason also for happier social relationships later in life, but it also seems that children of authoritative* (not authoritarian) parents are socially more competent than children brought up by either permissive or authoritarian* parents. There is certainly a relationship between the *quality* of two-year-old children's interaction with their mothers and their peers (Eckerman *et al.*, 1975) though the *nature* of the interaction, as discussed below, is clearly different.

Small children's interaction with one another is related more to the use of toys and other objects than is a small child's interaction with adults, which is centred much more on emotional and affectional interchanges. Between three and six years of age the nature of children's interactions with one another changes clearly more than it changes prior to three years of age. More social play, as opposed to the alternate use of objects without any real interaction, can now occur, and social play includes the increasing interchange by four years of age of affection. Also children of this age give in more to one another, and give each other approval, too.

As Piaget has shown, and as is discussed in the chapter on play, children from school age onwards begin to play with one another more positively even if not yet co-operatively; and differences appear in the nature of play according to the sex of the children. Such sex differences appear in quite young children. (The changing nature of social interaction as it manifests itself in play is discussed in detail in chapter 6.)

Children's friendships

What do children of different ages seek from their friendships with one another? It seems that already by four years of age children give, and therefore, presumably, seek to obtain from others, affection, approval, attention and acceptance (Charlesworth and Hartrup, 1967). Children are also enabled through friendships to make an assessment of their own characteristics when compared with the characteristics they know others to have. What children say to one another, how acceptable they consider themselves to be to their peers, and the frequency with which they are asked to become a friend or join a group all affect their self-concept and self-esteem.

As children get older their expectations regarding what their friendships might give them increase and also change. Hartrup (1978) says that with increasing age egocentric expectations, such as that the friend is seen as a help *giver* (at age seven) give way to 'sociocentric notions' (page 152), that is, the friend is seen as loyal and committed. Their expectations are now empathic in nature, so that older children will expect their best friend to be the *recipient* of help from them, and they will expect also that the friend shares their interests and values, and that a certain intimacy will exist between them (Hartrup, *ibid.*).

Foot, Chapman and Smith (1980) have investigated children's friendships from a number of viewpoints. They report that girls seem to tolerate, possibly even seek, a higher level of intimacy with friends than boys; a further, though related, sex difference is that girl friends 'match their amount of talking very much more closely than did boy friends'. Children of both sexes, as one would expect, display more affection — laughing, smiling, looking, talking — when with friends than with non-friends (Foot *et al.*, 1977), though there is more difference in the degree of both laughter and smiling when exhibited by boys when compared to girls. The degree of reciprocal interaction between friends is also, clearly, much greater than between non-friends. The notion that reciprocity is an important aspect of friendship in children as well as among adult friends can be seen not only in the frequent exchange of looks, smiles and in the engaging of mutual laughter with friends, but also in children's expectations that confidences will be respected by friends (Gabral *et al.*, 1977). When we look at other sex differences we note that there is a same-sex preference for playmates and friends; curiously, it appears that little girls under seven years of age prefer larger play groups than boys, but this preference changes after seven when boys prefer the bigger groups, the beginnings of the adolescent boy 'gangs', and girls prefer single, best friends, or a few friends.

There seems little doubt from a number of studies that when children are attracted to one another and form friendships, qualities of generosity and a desire to share with, and also to give help to others, are evoked; in addition, children learn to cope with aggressive feelings more easily than they can do at home, and they also have opportunities through friendly interaction to be democratic, affectionate and tolerant in behaviour. Brady-Smith, Newcombe and Hartrup (1980) and others have found that the existence of friendship between children evokes social responsiveness. Hartrup, as described by Foot, Chapman and Smith (1980), suggests that peer relationships provide 'a full repertoire of social experiences', and such relationships are most helpful if peers are similar in 'social and cognitive capacities'. However, playing at times with both older and younger children as well as with same-age peers enables a child to learn to seek help, give help, and also to learn to stand up for himself, respectively. There is a relationship between children being socially active and being able to role-take effectively; and, as discussed on page 161, such socially active children are also better than others at moral reasoning. Whether such children have a 'natural' propensity to feel for others and understand other people in an intuitive way, or whether the quality of their early relationship with their mother has developed such feelings or enhanced a given potential, we do not know. A transactional model would suggest that both factors might operate to produce children who are initially somewhat more sensitive to other children and so are approached more often by them, and thus become socially more active, which, in turn, would give them more experience in learning to feel for, and understand, others. Pronounced individual differences in liking by others can be shown to exist from the first year of life. In the study by Lee (1973) of babies under one year old the baby who was most preferred by the others was responsive and non-assertive.

There are two further aspects of the socialization process which we must consider, even if only briefly, before looking at children's emotional development, as far as this can be separated from the interpersonal and moral aspects of their relationships with other people: one is the difference in our society in the socialization process, according to whether a child is born male or female; the other is the child's growing understanding of his own and the adult social world.

We have already reviewed in this chapter some sex differences as they operate in the choice of friends, and the relationships with friends; and in chapter 3 such differences as they affect the formation of the personality are discussed.

We have seen (page 163) that a baby in his second year is aware of gender differences, and as Hutt (1978) comments, this knowledge about himself 'is the first aspect of his identity that the child is aware of this' (page 194). It seems that two-year-old children know their own gender and also that of other people, and by three years, and often even earlier, they use the correct language to differentiate gender. In all normal circumstances, that is, where biologically there is no doubt about a child's sex, his gender is the most personal aspect of himself to be noted from birth. We do not know what his personality will be like, but we do know that he is a boy, and this inevitably influences our behaviour towards him. It is not surprising that so-called sex stereotyping is so pervasive in our society. However, if one allows for the fact that a child is seeking to establish a sense of identity from early in life, one way of doing this is through identification (chapters 2 and

175

4) with the parent of his sex; so it is understandable that sex-related behaviour should continue from one generation to another. Clearly, the precise nature of such behaviour will change with changes in fashion about what is appropriate and desirable about sex-typical behaviour in any one society at any one time, but the fact that different behaviours are thought to be appropriate for the two sexes inevitably influences the social development of children. There are, in addition, biological differences other than the overtly sexual ones between the sexes which, in our society at least, have socialization consequences: these biological differences include a greater sensitivity to certain properties of sound, and earlier neural programming of aspects of language in girls; and greater visual-spatial abilities in boys 'enhanced by cerebral asymmetry' (Hutt, 1978, page 196). These differences will have their social consequences: it would seem thus that a somewhat greater desire to communicate, and an interest in the personal rather than the impersonal, differentiate a girl's social attitudes from those of a boy. We have seen that this differentiation has a natural foundation, but partly through the child's own desire to establish his identity, of which his sex is an important attribute, and partly because of society's notions about what is appropriate sex-typical behaviour, a child's biological sex is socially reinforced. Hutt (*ibid.*) reports a study by Sternglanze and Serbin in 1974 in which the authors discuss the behaviour of males and females in American television programmes for children; they comment that not only were very few females portrayed in such programmes, but the males were shown as 'aggressive, constructive and helpful, females as deferential and passive' (page 189). And Hutt quotes the authors as saying (1974, page 714) that 'female children are taught that almost the only way to be a successful human being if you are female is through the use of magic'. Apart from the influence which such television presentations most probably have on children's gender concepts (and American children spend more time viewing television than going to school!) society's expectations about male and female behaviour means that, for example, a greater degree of aggressiveness and independence is usually permitted to boys than to girls. It is not too exaggerated to say that the whole socialization process is orientated around the gender of the child.

Children's understanding of the adult social world

A child's social world is, clearly, made up by the people with whom he comes into contact, and by the quality of his relationships with them, whether these relationships are of an intimate kind, or friendly, or largely role-related; these relationships will be influenced by the concept he has of himself and of the people with whom he interacts, and by his own personality, which will affect other people in their interaction with him. All these conceptions and relationships will change in their quality as he grows up. We have discussed earlier in this chapter how the development of his self-concept and his understanding of other people progresses through childhood. However, in addition to understanding people's motives and intentions, and being able to describe their personality characteristics, he has to learn about the nature of people's relationships to one another, about the world of work, about social class and race, about the world of school, newspapers, politics, finance, industry, entertainment and sport. The total social world has many features of which only a few have been mentioned here; unhappily we know very little about *what* children understand of these many facts of social life, and we know even less *how* they come to understand them. It is interesting that as a society we have been much more concerned to develop a child's intellect than his understanding of people, and his sensitivities and sensibilities; similarly, as researchers we have been more concerned to know how cognitive growth comes about than what and how a child knows about people and society. It would seem, however, that the young child's knowledge of the adult social world is very circumscribed. For most children their first encounter with this world is when they go to school; by going to school most children first begin to understand the roles which various people play in social institutions. Here they meet other adult authority figures, apart from parents, and many older children; and they may begin to understand something of the hierarchy within adult authority structures. Going to the shops is another contact with part of adult society. What do children understand about the roles played by different people in society, and about the various conventions and structures through which society functions?

Furth in a study carried out in 1974/75 and reported in 1978 with primary school children from three different types of school — village, small town and large town — investigated children's understanding of societal roles. Furth writes that only a 'few children showed a developed sense of individual differences and personal understanding'; and only these few children could describe how personal qualities and the societal demands of a role interact (page 248). Most of the children, even in the older age range, had only superficial ideas about what it was like to be a headmaster, a policeman or a teacher. When they were asked how someone had come to take on the role he now occupied they said that he had decided to *have* the occupation. 'A builder gets up in the morning, he looks for a place to build something' (page 249). And some of the older children saw 'the government as a kind of supreme employment agency' (page 249). Furth was impressed by the fact that for the younger child the adult world of work, and the roles people occupy at work, have two major characteristics: they are stable (a bus driver is still a bus driver when he gets home); and anybody can be anything merely by choosing to occupy a role. However, once having chosen a role very strict rules are attached to such roles. These ideas, that is, that the holder of a post *is*, as it were, that post, and that rules govern the behaviour of people occupying roles, is what one would expect according to Piaget's theory: children at the concrete operational stage (chapter 4) have difficulty in simultaneously holding in mind more than one concept, that is, it is difficult for the child to think of one person simultaneously occupying the role of bus driver, father, husband, pigeon-fancier, etc. (One five-year-old in a study by Hartley *et al.*, 1948, said he is 'Jewish when awake but American when asleep'!) Young children are also strongly affected by the importance of rules in governing behaviour (page 157 and chapter 4).

The roles which people occupy are designated by younger children in terms of what people do, so that a headmaster is someone who can smack children, and who blows a whistle (Furth, 1978, pages 247–8). Similarly, young children do not see such roles as also being professional posts. Furth reports many five- to seven-year-olds thinking like this boy (page 247): 'They [teachers] teach when they are in school and when they are not at school they earn money to buy things.'

When Furth asked children to tell him something about the community in which they lived he found the children's comments 'singularly child-centred, regardless of age' (page 250). Some referred to the personal while describing the community: 'A town needs bricks to make houses, Dad is a building worker.' And he found that primary school children's ideas about government were equally poor.

Furth also investigated children's concept of the function of money and what shops were for. He found that for most of the five- and six-year-olds one function of a shop was to give money. They saw the giving of change as an important way of getting money! By seven or eight years the giving of change is understood, but even at this age children are only beginning to understand that the shopkeeper has to use the money he gets to pay for goods from the factory. This is only understood properly by the nine- to eleven-year-olds, though even at that age children are not clear that only some of the money the shopkeeper gets goes to buy further goods. Furth suggests that children suffer from a moral confusion over this question, for it seems to them dishonest to take money from the till for their own use! He says that 'only a few children (14% of the 8–11 year olds) showed systemic understanding of the principle of buying and selling' (page 246).

Furth suggests that there are, between the ages of six and eleven, four stages of societal understanding: what he terms the playful (stage I), the functional (II), the part-systemic (III), and the systemic-concrete (IV).

Stage I he sees largely as a Piagetian egocentric stage (chapter 4): the child does not appreciate the individual differences between people and the roles they occupy; people become what they are because they just want to occupy a particular role, but once having taken on a role they are strictly governed by the rules of the role. The use of money is poorly understood at this stage, and money is seen as freely available. At this stage, too, as Piaget has shown, the children will argue both transductively and inductively; and they also focus very much on the 'external aspects of a role' (page 253) such as the wearing of a uniform. This, again, is in keeping with what is known about how young children describe people — it is the external attributes which are of importance to them.

Stage II still exemplifies largely the concrete emphasis on what constitutes a role, but now the functions which a holder of a role engages in come somewhat more to the fore. By stage III, when children are between seven and ten years of age, they are beginning to understand the difference between the person occupying a role and the role in society; but, as Furth writes, the failure to understand, for example, personal profit, shows that children at this age still have major difficulties. By stage IV, at the ages of ten and eleven, Furth comments that there is a 'sufficient grasp of societal structures to avoid the major logical inconsistencies found in stage III' (page 253) but there is still no real understanding of society.

We can see from these descriptions of children's developing understanding of society that just as the development of cognitive growth, as described originally by Piaget, depends on the child's increasingly complex structuring of the non-social world as he encounters it, so he also structures for himself the social world. The notions of assimilation* and accommodation* can be used to describe the growth of understanding the social world as they can be used to describe the growth of understanding of the intellectual world (chapter 4); but whereas children receive specific help, especially through schooling, to make sense of the cognitive world they encounter, they normally have to structure and restructure their social world without much help from adults. Perhaps we should, through role-playing activities, discussion and other similar activities, enable children sooner to gain a better understanding of the social world they will enter as adolescents. Such role-playing activities can also aid pro-social development.

Emotional development

It is obvious that the child's understanding of, and interaction with, his social world inevitably involves his feelings about other people, and the happenings which affect him in interaction with them. It is very difficult to study young children's emotions except in highly specific circumstances, such as observing their distress when mother leaves them, or their fear when confronted with strangers, or when they find themselves in specific circumstances which are new and strange. We cannot question small children about their subjective feelings. It is clearly also not possible to arrange experimental situations where most of these emotions can be methodically studied; and even if it were ethically possible to study, for example, distress, we cannot study most *positive* emotions except, again, in an anecdotal way by noting a small child's pleasure when he is reunited with his mother; though one can, of course, observe actions which give expression to the emotions one assumes are experienced while carrying out the actions, such as when a child offers a comforting object to another child who is in distress, or expresses pleasure when given a new toy.

The range of emotions experienced by humans is very wide and also very deep. What is meant by this is that very many different emotions which vary from one another qualitatively, such as love, fear, rage, contentment, to mention a few, can be experienced, and mostly to highly varying degrees. We know almost nothing in detail about when children feel many of these emotions, nor do we know to what degree they are experienced at different ages. Not only do ethical considerations preclude many otherwise fruitful forms of study of emotions being carried out, but most probably individual differences are greater in this area of human experiences and behaviour than in any other area. In addition, even a young child of four years of age will already have learnt to amend the expression of his feelings in the sole presence of strangers. There is a further problem, and that is that much emotional growth and change most probably occurs at a level which is not usually observable in behaviour.

The psychoanalytic school has been concerned with the emotional development of the child (chapter 2). The emotions which the small baby experiences very early in life relate largely to his physical comfort and discomfort. Freud postulated that the feelings which are evoked during the first four to five years of life are very strong, and how a child is able to deal with the emergence of these feelings has important repercussions on his later behaviour. We will return to a discussion of these ideas when the feeling of anxiety, which is so prevalent in most children, is discussed (page 183).

Obviously the developing awareness of the self as a separate entity (page 163) must come about through experiencing a variety of emotions. It is clear that the very small baby has intensely strong feelings, though in saying this one is not saying that the baby is *self-consciously* aware of his emotions; and he is unlikely to know before about three months of age whether his feelings of comfort and discomfort originate from internal or external factors. Spitz (1963) outlines how, in his view, the feelings which the baby has become, with maturation, definable emotions: at three months the ego* comes into being and this enables the child to relate expressions of emotions to sensations experienced and stimuli received. Spitz suggests that the deliberate smiling response is one of the earliest of these expressions; most other first emotions are, however, negative and relate to discomforts experienced. At this age the child's emotions are still largely unspecified and undirected. Between about three and six months of age the expression of emotions acquires a communicative function, and the emotions now become progressively integrated with facial and behavioural expressions. The baby can now express delight and anger, in relation to feeding, and he becomes increasingly more vocal in expressing his emotions instead of expressing them with a variety of bodily movements. One must assume that emotions are now experienced also more subjectively. Usually at about eight months of age (page 172) the child begins to have a concept of the permanence of objects and people, and he experiences anxiety in the presence of strangers if there is no familiar person also present. His distress in the presence of strangers can, therefore, be of a dual kind: absence of mother and unsureness of the potential actions of the strangers.

By eight months or so a child can also exhibit reciprocal affection, and by thirteen months of age spontaneous affection. From this time onwards anger at being disappointed, affection for other children, and temper tantrums when things do not go right for him can all be displayed. Although a child of eighteen months may well show his annoyance with other children by hitting and pulling, there is very little hostility in his actions. By this age, too, he is likely to be jealous if the occasion warrants it. It is often difficult for parents to understand why an older child should be jealous of a new baby when even more attention than usual is paid to the older child in order not to make him feel neglected, but such a child's limited appreciation of the world around him — that is, his egocentric and percept-centred view of the world (chapters 2 and 4) — implies that he can only understand what is important to *him* and what *he* can perceive, and what he perceives at any one moment is simply that another child is receiving attention. This is because only a very much older child can take the past into consideration when making evaluations of the present, and, therefore, feelings of jealousy will inevitably arise between children in a family however much the parents try to allay such feelings; nevertheless every effort should be made to minimize the occasions when such feelings may occur.

Bodily feelings and instinctual drives sharpen self-awareness throughout childhood, yet children speak little about their feelings. We do not know for certain at what age and at what stage children can think about their own feelings reflectively, though Jersild (1955) observes that children seldom mention before adolescence that they wish they could learn to cope with their emotional difficulties. Biber and Lewis (1949) have suggested that small children use language more to express ideas than to express feelings, and it is possible that before seven or eight years of age the affective and cognitive aspects of experience are not always fully differentiated. Certainly Wood (1968) found that when she asked children under thirteen years of age to describe other people they seldom mentioned how they felt about others, but at fourteen years of age children were remarkably more willing to discuss the feelings evoked in them by others. It is possible that children develop cognitively more rapidly than they do affectively or, alternatively, that in our western culture they feel themselves to be prevented for subtle reasons from expressing their feelings before they are about fourteen years of age.

On page 164 we discuss the development of empathy, and the importance of this for social interaction. The various non-cognitive aspects of development can be seen in interconnection with one another, and Erikson's theory of development (1969, chapter 2) which incorporates the social, emotional, psycho-sexual and physical aspects of development, provides a useful *framework* for their study. It must, however, be mentioned that there is only tenuous experimental support for Erikson's theories, though much incidental support for what he describes comes from casual observations of children and adults. Erikson outlines how in his view during the first three psycho-sexual stages the developing ego* has to establish trust, autonomy and initiative. Erikson has tried to link the timetable of the organism with the structure of social institutions (chapter 2). Thus the two- to three-year-old strives for social and physical mastery — at this age he seeks to establish his autonomy as a separate being, and he is very fast developing his social, motor, manipulative and verbal skills. Other people are seen largely as existing to meet his needs. He uses the pronoun 'I' for the first time, but his language is still too inadequate to express his feelings, and he is often frustrated and exhibits temper tantrums. Also his desires are strong, his newfound abilities require expression, but he has not yet learned to control his desires. This lack of control, added to the explosion of new abilities, may cause adults to demand more of the child at this age than he can give. He has to *learn* to control the expression of his strong feelings and his strong desires. Often, too, his lack of bladder and bowel control during the early part of this age stage seems inconsistent with the other skills exhibited, particularly in many two- to three-year-olds with good language ability (chapter 4); however, the muscles involved in bladder and bowel control are among the last to come under conscious control. Adults involved with children at this age stage can best help them by being sensitive to the cues the child gives prior to relieving himself, and, by telling him when he should go to the lavatory, give back to the child, as it were, his own cues, thus helping him to learn to identify them in good time. This is a conflict-filled period, and patience and understanding on the part of adults helps the establishment of a secure self-concept for the child.

The next stage, three to five years approximately, is the time for testing reality, and for showing *initiative*, which is indeed Erikson's major term for this period (four to seven). Feelings of guilt arise, and the child can also feel his limitations very much at this age. It is also the time for much imitative behaviour. Possibly imitation of others is one of the processes by which the more refined feelings which other people experience come to be understood empathically, for by copying other people's behaviour their emotions can be experienced vicariously. Loevinger (1966) has called this age stage the age of the opportunist: the child understands the rules he has to obey but obeys them to gain advantages. His moral behaviour is really only expediency-behaviour (page 244). It is also at this age that he begins to internalize* the actions of loved adults, and this enables him to reinstate them, as it were, within himself, when they are physically absent. In this way their absence can be better tolerated. He also begins now to internalize parental morality, for at this age he is very much aware of his need for parental love, and he fears the withdrawal of his parents' love (page 155). Feelings of guilt also now exist at the thought of misbehaving (page 155). Lidz (1968) has summed up the needs and major characteristics of this age by stating that children at this age want to manage their 'major resources'; they want to manipulate and communicate; they want to find solutions to problems and to explore; from adults they require consistency in behaviour and verbal responses. They need support and encouragement.

During the next period the most important emotional experience for most children is starting school, except for the children who have already been to nursery school. In chapter 8 the many anxieties which the majority of five-year-olds experience when they first start school are discussed. Undoubtedly many children coming to nursery school for the first time, even if they are accustomed to being away from mother from time to time, will experience the same anxieties to an even greater extent than children starting school for the first time at five years of age. Many such anxieties are inevitable and are overcome in the normal process of growth, but it is often difficult for adults adequately to assess childhood fears and anxieties because the degree of emotion revealed by children is probably only a poor indication of their true feelings. It is possible that we often make it difficult, for a variety of reasons, for children to express their feelings freely. One cannot stress too greatly how much the understanding of a child's thoughts and emotions within a framework of a supportive discipline can help the child himself to cope with his fears and anxieties.

Feelings of anxiety, defined by Jersild (1955) as painful unease of mind concerning impending or anticipated ill are present to a greater or lesser degree throughout most of life for most people. Undoubtedly, too, there are great individual differences (page 156) in how much is suffered by different people. However, although the world for the child of seven years of age and over is more manageable and better understood than before seven years of age, the child's greater ability to reflect on his own thoughts and behaviour, his greater awareness of other people and of their relationship to each other, and to himself, can make life at times very anxious for many children.

Nevertheless, before ten years of age a child mostly seems to lead a relatively happy and balanced life: he is approaching the end of the 'latency* period', as Freud termed it, during which period neither the earlier disturbing pregenital drives nor the even more disturbing later genital drives affect his emotions and his attitude to life (chapter 2). At twelve years of age this balance is beginning to be upset. Previous physiological changes have been largely changes in growth only: now hormonal sex changes occur which have their counterpart in the changes which occur in emotional feelings and social attitudes. These changes cause some anxieties, and new feelings of insecurity arise from an inevitably greater knowledge of himself and of other people, but the twelve-year-old still tends to retain the poise and social charm of his earlier years. However, he is beginning to discover himself and needs to understand his experiences, but it appears that not until he is about fourteen years of age can the young adolescent fully reflect on his feelings.

It has been mentioned earlier that the child of eighteen months of age or so will show his displeasure if he is frustrated, but that any attacks he makes against other children are not hostile in intent. Nevertheless, as his feelings develop and as they express themselves in actions, he must learn, at least in our culture, to control such actions if they are likely to hurt others. The young child is mostly angry because *things* don't behave as he wants them to, and there are consequently frequent occasions when he feels frustrated. However, by the time a child is about eleven years of age most angry feelings are engendered not by frustrating objects but by people. Being teased, unfairness, siblings taking their property, people lying to them, sarcasm and bossiness, all these are factors which make the pre-adolescent angry. Children seem to vary greatly in the amount of frustration, leading to aggression, which they are able to tolerate.

Much has been written about a child's need for love but little about its ability to give love. The ability to give and feel affection is largely dependent on the amount of affection a child is himself receiving. Many studies have shown the importance of a child receiving warmth and love throughout childhood, and the anxieties, depressions and general emotional impoverishment which can follow when children are denied these experiences. The development of feelings of affection has largely been studied in the negative: children who have been deprived of such affection have been observed, and the early work of Bowlby (1944) and others appeared to indicate that 'maternal deprivation' early in life has powerful unfortunate and irreversible effects on the developing personality. However, later work has shown that its long-term effects may not be as disastrous as earlier workers had indicated, and that, in any case, the term 'maternal deprivation' can cover such a wide range of experiences over such a long period of a child's life that it is a somewhat meaningless term to use. (The effects of depriving experiences are reviewed in some detail in chapter 2 and in chapter 7.)

In chapters 3 and 7 we discuss the possible importance, in relation to the formation of personal relationships and moral behaviour, of having the opportunity to forge a close bond with at least one other human being early in life. As discussed on page 139 we cannot say with certainty that a 'critical' period exists in early childhood during which such a bond should be formed, nor can we say if a child who has no opportunity even later in childhood to form a lasting and affectionate relationship with another person will *never* be able to form such relationships later in life; but many writers (Rutter, 1978; Mussen and Eisenberg-Berg, 1977) consider that, as Mussen and Eisenberg-Berg put it, 'strong early attachment appears to be a major antecedent of early interest in others' (pages 169–70). It does seem reasonable to assume that the emotional effect of experiencing from infancy onwards unselfish love, and the support of at least one more or less consistently present adult who understands the infant's nonverbal cues of communication and who is reliable, responsive and demonstratively affectionate must have an influence both of an emotional kind and as a model for the building of relationships later in life, and consequently also affect a child's social, emotional and moral behaviour.

Further reading

DANZINGER, K.: *Socialization* (Penguin Books, 1971)

WILSON, J., N. WILLIAMS and B. SUGARMAN: *An introduction to moral education* (Penguin Books, 1968)

KAY, W.: *Moral development: a psychological study of moral growth from childhood to adolescence* (George Allen and Unwin, 1969)

SCHAFFER, H. R.: *The growth of sociability* (Penguin Books, 1971)

PETERS, R. S.: *Psychology and ethical development* (George Allen and Unwin, 1974)

MUSSEN, P. and N. EISENBERG-BERG: *Roots of caring, sharing and helping* (W. H. Freeman and Co., San Francisco, 1977)

McGURK, H. (ed.): *Issues in childhood social development* (Methuen, 1978)

CHAPTER SIX

Play

Play is a very curious activity: Millar (1968), Winnicott (1971) and Garvey (1977) have all pointed out that play has no extrinsic goals, it is different from, yet similar to, 'non-play', and children who play are engaged in a voluntary activity which is neither planned nor out of control. It is akin to dreaming, but also related to reality. It fulfils many purposes. Winnicott (1971) has commented on the high pre-occupation of the child when he is playing, and how hard it is for the child to leave off playing when asked to do so. It is also very difficult to intrude into a child's play. Play is a twilight area of life, and the child is often in a near-withdrawal state while playing.

In discussing play we are interested in the purposes of play; in how these purposes are expressed during childhood; in the manner in which play changes with age; and in individual and cultural differences.

It is a pity that the word 'play' conjures up ideas of useless activity and carries with it overtones of disapproval. So often parents ask a child in the primary school: 'What did you do in school today?' and the answer not infrequently is: 'We played.' Many parents still feel that the child can play at home, but school is the place for work. However, for the young child there is little difference between work and play, so that when parents ask this question, as so many seem to do, and the child replies that he spent the day playing, this does not mean that he has learned nothing, nor that work, in the sense in which parents may think of 'work', has not been done.

Piaget (1924) suggests that for the young child under seven years of age there is no real difference between play and reality, because play for the child is a particular kind of reality, though it is clear (Garvey, 1977) that even young children under five years of age do understand when they are 'pretending' to do something and when they are 'really' doing it. Garvey (1977) has called play a 'non-literal' activity, and she suggests that the infant learns early in life that some activities are of the non-literal, that is, playful kind, and some are not. An infant's mother will show purpose in feeding, dressing and changing him, but he will also be played with, and Garvey suggests that the small baby early in life is made aware of these two different modes of behaving towards him. She suggests that play probably emerges spontaneously for most children if, as she puts it, 'the very young child experiences some basic model of non-literal treatment of resources' (Garvey, *ibid*., page 117).

Possibly a major defining feature is that play is an activity which is freely entered into, ostensibly as an end in itself, and, as Isaacs (1933) suggested long ago, it is the attitude of mind of the player which defines it as play and not as work, or reality, or whatever is 'non-play'.

It is difficult to over-exaggerate the importance of play activity for the young child; indeed, playing and taking part in games are even for the older child of great value, though Piaget (1951) thinks of games as an activity different in kind from playing. Many of the young child's experiences of the world, of people, and of things, come to him during an impressionable period of his life through play activity.

Philosophers have been interested in elaborating theories of play, for it seemed necessary to account for the apparently purposeless behaviour of both young animals and young humans. Today we know that play is for the young child a proving ground for the serious experiences of life which come later, and we know that it has many important functions in the development of the child. Indeed, it is difficult to name any part of the developmental process which is not helped by play activities. 'Practically every form of psychological activity is initially enacted in play' (Piaget, 1968b). Experimental work with animals and observational work with children who have been prevented for whatever reasons from playing with other infants and/or with materials of various kinds, show that such children and animals have difficulties in their social relationships and are also usually retarded intellectually. However, one has to remember, particularly in relation to grossly deprived children, that so many factors in their lives may add to the total picture of retardation that the absence of play facilities may be only one of these.

The exact function of play varies, of course, with the age of the child. The baby feeling a wooden cube with hands and mouth; the toddler building a small tower with three or four cubes; the older child trying to get as many cubes as possible on top of one another; these are all apparently merely playing with cubes, but the exploration in which they are engaged is different for each child. The baby is finding out about shapes, learning to co-ordinate what he sees with what he feels; the toddler is exploring how cubes can be used and so learning to manipulate objects in his environment; and the older child may be attempting to build something which is his own height, and in this way using the cubes to see what his own height looks like — he is learning something about measurement and something about himself. Again, the fantasies which are worked out through imaginative play will vary according to the needs of the child at a particular age; the small child may be establishing his relationship within the family, and through fantasy play he may be learning to cope with his fears and jealousies; the older child, in taking on adult roles, is testing one aspect of reality which he has observed or has had fantasies about, but which he cannot yet know in actuality. From the development of the senses in infancy and during emotional, intellectual, moral and social growth in childhood, play activities aid the processes of psychological development. In addition, as we see on page 196, playing has great therapeutic value. Erikson (1950) has written that he considers play to be the most self-healing activity engaged in by children.

Play not only serves many functions, but it also, clearly, changes in nature with the child's increasing age. Most aspects of play can be observed at most childhood ages, though some kinds of play are more prevalent at some ages. It is possible to classify the purposes of play into two fundamental classes: one has to do with the development of skills, whether these are physical, social, cognitive, linguistic or manipulative; the other concerns the child's inner fantasy world, which, inter alia, involves linking together the child's inner and outer worlds, and is also concerned with the reduction of anxieties of various kinds.

Although theories of play are not in themselves of special interest today, they do provide a framework within which to discuss the purposes which play fulfils in the child's life. These theories will here be discussed within the context of modern observational and experimental work.

One can say that Bühler and Piaget and modern observers of the child at play have been largely, though by no means wholly, concerned with play which comes within the first category described, that is, with the many and varied skills which the child exhibits and develops while playing; and observers from the psychoanalytic school, with ideas stemming primarily from Freud's work, such as Isaacs, Winnicott and Erikson, have been interested in defining the role which play has in relation to the child's inner fantasy life; however, as described on page 188, most kinds of play activity serve more than one purpose.

Bühler divided play periods during childhood into:

(1) functional,
(2) imaginative and
(3) constructive play.

As in most theories of child development the particular divisions made are used for convenience and indicate a *predominance* during particular periods of childhood of an activity or a mode of functioning (page viii). Such classifications do not mean that the influence of a particularly predominant period ceases altogether when the child enters the next period. Thus, although Bühler's 'functional' play is predominant from birth to eighteen months, children continue to engage in such play long after this period. During this period children learn about objects and about people, and each child learns too about his own bodily movements. 'Imaginative' play is at its height between eighteen months and about four-and-a-half years of age, though it continues to be an important aspect of activity at least until the seventh or eighth year. During this period children use objects and people to 'stand for' something else; between four and seven years of age imaginative play loses some of its symbolic characteristics and becomes more realistic, and after four-and-a-half years of age Bühler's 'constructive' play period proper begins. Constructive play is much more purposive and more related to the real world rather than to the child's inner world.

Piaget's close observation of children playing has led him to propose that the two processes of assimilation* and accommodation* which together he has termed adaptation* (page 62) are applicable to play as they are to all other childhood activities. By 'assimilation' Piaget means that the child uses some new experience or objects in his environment for an activity which is already part of his behavioural repertoire — that is, a new situation evokes a particular pattern of behaviour because it resembles other similar situations in the past which have evoked such behaviour. By 'accommodation' Piaget means the addition of *new* activities to a child's behavioural repertoire (page 62). Piaget suggests that whenever a child in early years *imitates*, the accommodatory process is operating, and whenever a child *plays*, the process of assimilation is being used. Piaget relates the development of play to the child's general growth of intelligence and to his experiences in childhood. The play equivalent of the sensori-motor* period Piaget terms *jeu d'exercice* or 'functional' play; play during the two to four age period he has termed *jeu symbolique*, and for the period four to seven years of age he has given the name *jeu de règles* — that is, play with rules. It can thus be seen that Piaget and Bühler both place emphasis on the same aspects of play during the infancy and early childhood periods, but whereas Bühler considers that play in the four to seven age period has the major function of helping the child realistically to learn how to use objects in his environment, Piaget for this age period places the emphasis on the child's relationship with others in regard to his appreciation of the rules of games and consequently how rules relate also to social life.

More recent work by Smith and Connolly (Smith, 1975) interestingly relates Bühler's and Piaget's ideas about play. They describe two ways of playing engaged in by children: one kind is fairly quiet and sedentary, involves objects and is concerned with, for example, playing at shops or having a tea party; the other kind is noisy and active, and involves fast motor activity and rough-and-tumble play, such as playing at being cowboys and Indians, or monsters. Smith and Connolly from their observations of children say that with the latter sort of playing one can often see up to six children playing together, and the playing is of shorter duration than in the former kind of playing, and involves a lot of changing of roles without many overt changes in behaviour. This kind of playing also develops certain kinds of social skills. The quieter type of playing seems to foster language and creative skills more. As one can imagine, more boys engage in the latter, more girls in the former, kind of playing; and adults prefer the quieter games of the girls!

Piaget suggests that the pleasure of causing something to happen is the beginning of enjoying play: a baby of under six or eight months will manipulate things for the sheer pleasure of doing this, though since much activity in infancy and childhood seems to arise from a need to explore, one suspects that the pleasure experienced is not the aim of play but is incidental to the activity.

In the next play stage, one activity, according to Piaget, is linked to another, and ritualization often emerges: Piaget gives examples of a child lying down and sucking his thumb as if preparing to go to sleep, but the activity only lasts about half a minute, and it is not followed by sleep itself. This seems to be the beginning of symbolic play. By the beginning of the second year this symbolic activity often includes imaginary objects. The child at first uses himself as the object of his imaginary play, and then he uses other people and objects: he may pretend to drink from something which looks like a cup, or get someone else to do so. Thus the objects and people he encounters are 'assimilated' to the needs of his symbolic play.

Symbolism is of great importance, for once a child begins to understand language, he realizes that one thing, a sound, represents something which is not a sound. Piaget says that symbolic play is not, however, like the symbolism of language, because symbolic play remains, as Piaget puts it, 'an egocentric assimilation'. Whereas language uses symbols in order to communicate the expression of needs, symbolic play is a private activity. Thus for Piaget symbolic play is relatively late in developing, and early infant play is, in his view, without any fantasy content. Piaget suggests that the imaginary people who populate the child's fantasy world at this stage may have an important role in his inner life. Piaget says that fantasy play involving imaginary people is a prolongation of reality, and that the imaginary symbol is used as a means of expressing and extending reality, and not as an end in itself. The psychoanalytic view, that fantasy activity is present from early infancy, is not directly observable in the infant's activities and has thus not found general favour with experimental psychologists. However, this discounting of early fantasy life seems to have had the effect of lessening interest in studying children's fantasies even as far as such studies are possible, and the importance which these creative imaginings may have in life has not been adequately assessed. Frank (1965) considers that psychopathology may not be caused so much by a child's experience of life as by his tendency to distort reality by fantasy; and it is not improbable that we are affected not only by our interpretation of experiences, but also by the fantasy creations of our minds. Indeed Piaget believes that for the child at this age the division between play and reality is not at all clear, and it is not, therefore, inconceivable that real experiences and fantasy creations become fused, so that the development of the child's personality may be affected as much by the one as by the other.

Colomb and Cornelius (1977) have suggested that in symbolic play the child engages in a kind of duality which allows both for the real and the imaginative to be present simultaneously: a piece of plasticine is a cake while still remaining plasticine, and a child who is a train driver will still speak to his mother as the child he is while driving his train. The child has to engage in reversible thought operations for this kind of playing, just as he has to do when he is asked to engage in a conversation task (chapters 2 and 4) in a Piagetian experiment; and Colomb and Cornelius' work seems to show that children under five years of age who have had experience of symbolic play are better at such conservation tasks than children who have not had this experience. This work also supports Donaldson's findings (page 67) that young children are often able to bear two concepts in mind simultaneously, in this case the continuing real nature of an object and its 'pretend' nature, if the situation is one which comes within their realm of experience.

Fantasy play forms a link between the child's inner world, which is at first inexpressible, and the outer world of experience: the two are joined by investing reality with some of the attributes of the inexpressible inner world, and play of this kind at this age stage enables the child to restructure the environment to fit his ego. Here Piaget and Freud's views coincide, for it is suggested by them both that the child restructures his environment, partly because by doing so he can cope with experiences which he might otherwise find too painful or threatening, and partly because by such reinterpretation of reality the child is able vicariously to indulge in forbidden desires. A fuller consideration of this function of play will be given later when psychoanalytic views of play are discussed.

For Piaget the main purpose of symbolic play is that it allows the child to relive his experiences in some degree to his own satisfaction; he can exteriorize his thoughts, and through such play his inner speech — that is, thinking in words rather than in actions — can begin. This kind of play continues after four years of age, but due to the effects of socialization Piaget considers that it becomes progressively rooted in reality. Role taking, dressing up, behaving like adults, are all forms of imaginative play indulged in by children after this age, but it is *reproductive* of reality, rather than *symbolic* of it.

Bruner and Sherwood (1976) report Garvey as saying that 'one of the objectives of play in general is to give the child opportunity to explore the boundary between the "real" and the "make believe"' (page 284). In the game of 'Peekaboo' Bruner and Sherwood comment that none of the babies who played this game with their mothers in Bruner and Sherwood's experimental set-up showed the anxiety in playing which they showed when their mothers really left the room. They also say that the pattern of the game established between a mother and her baby is used in new ways as the baby's skills increase, when, for example, he learns to crawl and then to walk. So playing ritualistic games of this kind and adapting them to new skills is, for the child, similar to the way he uses language in which, according to Slobin (1972) new ideas are expressed in the child's existing language structure. Also, through such infant–mother games the baby learns about the rules which govern such games, and this introduction to rule-governed behaviour is the forerunner of an understanding that rules also govern language production and social behaviour (chapters 4 and 5).

Social play

Very young babies cannot play with one another although, as we discuss on page 163, even young babies are more interested in strange children than they are in strange adults. However, quite early in life the baby responds to *adults* playing with him, and by seven months he can participate, even if in a rather one-sided manner, in games with adults. He will take objects offered to him, but not until he is between about nine to ten months of age will he regularly give back an object as part of a game (Bruner, 1978). By thirteen months he seems more interested in the game of exchanging objects than in the objects themselves, and he is entering into a 'round of exchange involving two other persons' (Bruner, 1978, page 78). The relationship of playing to language growth is discussed variously throughout this book (but see page 123), and Bruner (1978, and elsewhere) has shown that, as he puts it, 'a stunning number of linguistic prerequisites is being mastered' (page 78) in the role shifting, turn taking, signalling and acting which underlie the games which babies and mothers play; but these early mother–infant play activities have another function, and that is that the baby learns to *trust* another human being because she adapts to, and meets his needs (Winnicott, 1971). In playing with his mother the infant is sharing a non-literal activity with another person; this means that not only is he learning about the possibility of engaging in shared activities, but he is also forging a link both between his inner world and the inner world of *another person*, and also between his inner world and the *outer world* in the shape of the person with whom he is playing.

As far as playing with other children is concerned, Schaffer (1978) reports the work of Mueller and Lucas, who suggest three progressive stages of interaction between children, starting at the beginning of their second year: in the first stage each child is so interested in a play object that he does not notice the effects of his own actions with the object on the other child; in the second stage he notices the other child's behaviour, perhaps even laughing at him, but he cannot act socially in relation to the other child; at the third stage two children can enter into reciprocal activity, giving to each other, and receiving, a toy, or playing jointly with a ball. Each child's action at this stage involves being aware of what the other child is doing and gearing his own behaviour to suit the actions of the other. Schaffer comments that reciprocity and timing are basic to behaviour at this age stage; the younger child cannot himself act while also watching another, but the older child can do this. However, such interaction for children of under three years of age is usually of very short duration. Real co-operative playing, particularly with other children, comes about much later. Two- to three-year-olds engage in parallel play in which they independently use the same plaything; after three years of age associative play is possible in which children can involve one another in what they do. They take ideas from one another and borrow toys, but each is still concerned with his own interests. Children, particularly boys, of this age fight over play objects and they engage in rough-and-tumble playing which often becomes 'formalized into games like "tag" and "cowboys and Indians"' (Blurton-Jones, 1976, page 356). Co-operative play does not usually begin until children are at least four years of age: Piaget (1951) indeed gives the much later age of seven years. If by the term 'co-operative' one assumes that meaningful conversation is taking place between children so that they can effectively combine in an activity, then such playing is not really possible until a much later age than four. A child has to be able to see another's point of view and to communicate effectively before he can engage in true co-operative play. Often children of five and under, who are relatively strange to one another, can be seen to play together apparently with co-operation, but closer observation will indicate that usually one child is using the others as part of his own private play activity. Frequently one dominant child will in this way incorporate other children into *his* play.

Isaacs (1933) says that in apparently co-operative play at five years of age a child will note other children but not their personalities, nor will he see that they have a purpose independent of himself. She says that the egocentric situation is marked by fantasy influencing the aim and style of the play, and other children are given roles in the play set-up; reality enters into such play in this form. Thus Isaacs gives as example children playing at 'shops' where one child is sent to the shop to wait and ask for things to buy.

Children who know one another well, particularly siblings near in age, and other children raised together such as children who are members of the same kibbutz, are able to play co-operatively much earlier. Constant propinquity probably enables them to understand non-verbal communications which they receive from each other and which aid co-operation, whereas children less familiar with one another have to rely on speech with which to communicate.

Co-operation between children can be helped by keeping the play groups small; three-year-olds cannot attend to more than one person at a time, and their power of concentration is limited, so that these factors, in addition to language problems, make it unlikely that small children can co-operate in any meaningful sense.

Co-operative play among the children of junior age leads inevitably to co-operation in the playing of games, which Piaget thinks, however, is different from just 'playing'. Playing games implies following rules, and rule-following means that the player is accepting certain obligations. Piaget (1932) has closely observed how children play marbles, and what they believe and understand about rules in playing. The importance of understanding rules in relation to both moral and social development is discussed in chapter 5. It is clear that social and moral growth imply learning both to appreciate the rights of others, and also that to an extent these rights can be safeguarded by everyone observing rules.

So, when children begin to play with other children they first use them as stimuli for their own activities; later, when co-operation is possible, they are able to extend their own activities by working with others, and they also thereby help others to develop their own skills and abilities. Later again, when rules have to be adhered to in games playing, they learn about the need for regularity in social life. Through playing with others language use is also developed, though this is not so important as having opportunities of talking to and listening to adults who present a good speech model (chapter 4). Also through play, and the verbal interaction with other children which this brings, a child will learn what others think of him and he will begin to form a self-concept.

Psychoanalytic view of play

Day-dreaming and night dreams, art, and the experiences of the mentally disturbed are all aspects of fantasy life. However, they all serve a purpose; indeed, that no human activity is without meaning was one of Freud's most important discoveries. He considered that play, which seems purposeless and is apparently unrelated to reality, is part of fantasy life. Like other aspects of fantasy, however, it is certainly not without purpose, and, again like dreaming, its form and content are, according to the psychoanalytic viewpoint, dominated by wishes. Freud's views about the relationship of reality and fantasy in children's play are not dissimilar from those of Piaget, for both consider that a child when playing re-orders events and uses objects and people in ways which please him, or at least in ways which are less worrying than they are in actuality. Whenever a child reproduces in a play situation events which are similar to, but in many respects different from, a frightening or threatening experience, he is 'abreacting'* his anxieties — that is, he is reliving in his imagination the actual event he experienced. 'Children repeat in their play everything that has made a great impression on them in their actual life . . . and so to speak make themselves masters of the situation' (Freud, 1920). Thus Freud thought of play as a 'repetition–compulsion' mechanism, which enables a child to work out his anxieties. By re-enacting on several occasions something which has been anxiety-producing, the anxiety is slowly dissipated. This theory seems to account for the curious observation that children will repeat in a play situation experiences which, according to a common-sense viewpoint, one might expect them to wish to forget.

Isaacs has developed Freud's ideas from her extensive experience with children. Though not all her ideas about the origin of behaviour are wholly acceptable, her observations on the nature and purpose of play, considered partly in terms of psychoanalytic theory, add to our understanding of the dynamics of child development. Isaacs suggests that there are three main varieties of play activity:

(1) imaginative or make-believe play,
(2) play which involves movement and bodily skills and
(3) play with physical objects.

Part of the purpose of imaginative play is to ease the anxieties and fears which all children feel to a greater or lesser extent throughout childhood. These anxieties arise from a number of causes: there are first the anxieties which spring from recollected experiences, and the abreacting of these through play has already been discussed. Then there are, according to Isaacs, those anxieties which are generated by the child's own fantasy life, such as fear of the damage which destructive feelings and thoughts might inflict on people with whom the child is emotionally involved. By imaginative play these fantasies can be projected outwards, or externalized, and they thus lose part of their force — destructive impulses can be assigned to witches or other imaginary, wicked persons! Aggressive feelings, which spring from jealousy, can be vented on inanimate objects rather than on live persons who have occasioned such feelings; dolls, rather than the child, can be made to be naughty. Thirdly, fantasies can be amended to fit reality. One can say that, in Freudian terms, this view of the function of play assigns to play the role of mediator between the 'primary'* and 'secondary'* processes. Through play activity the child is helped to come to terms with reality and there is, according to Isaacs, constant interaction between fantasy life and reality. This interaction is of the greatest importance in child development. She considers that the child's make-believe play is part fantasy and part thought, that progressively throughout childhood experiences of life penetrate feelings and fantasy, and that for this reason make-believe play becomes more reproductive of reality as the child gets older. A fourth purpose of imaginative play is that it enables the child to explore and test in safety new experiences, and to make the familiar ones even better known. For young children there is a constant approach–avoidance conflict in operation between being attracted to new experiences and seeking to avoid them because of their potentially dangerous unfamiliarity. In play such situations can be postulated and tried out without any danger.

Isaacs, unlike Piaget, ascribes fantasies to the early infancy period and she gives the infant more emotional and symbolic life than Piaget would allow; indeed, she considers that imaginative play derives its energy from repressed infantile wishes and fantasies. There are, of course, no means by which such a theory can be verified by observation. Indeed, there seems to be no need to postulate what the origin of the energy needed for imaginative play might be in order to discuss the purposes of such play.

As the child gets older imaginative play becomes more closely linked to the real world and soon the child begins to explore adult roles. In psychoanalytic theory role-taking has a deeper significance than merely trying out what it feels like to be adult; it is linked to identification, which is discussed in some detail in chapters 2 and 5. This is bound up with the taking on of sex roles; with overcoming jealousies experienced for the parent of the same sex; and with working through the Oedipal situation.

Play involving movement, play with objects and exploratory play

Play which involves movement is predominant in the first eighteen months of life, but the toddler is for ever 'on the go'; later children enjoy planned movements, such as games of skipping or 'hopscotch', which involve bodily expertise and skills. Almost all children, except the most severely deprived, have opportunities for this kind of play. In contrast, play with objects does depend on the provision of the objects. When the child is very young he has to learn to co-ordinate hand and eye, and in his earliest days his mouth probably tells him more about the nature of an object than his eyes! Later he learns that objects do not change their shape though they look different from different viewpoints. The world has to be experienced in order to be understood, and in order that actions involving objects can be internalized. White (1960) has written that 'exploratory play, even in the first years of life, shows it to have the characteristics of directedness, selectivity and persistence'. The child is attempting to learn about his world, and the more opportunities he has in early life to experience the world the more competent his handling of his environment will be. It is probably no exaggeration to state that the three factors most potently affecting the development of intellectual capacity in the young child are:

(1) the opportunities for listening to and conversing with an understanding adult who has good linguistic ability and an extensive vocabulary,

(2) the provision of conditions in which he can play with objects and materials which vary greatly from one another in shape, colour, size and texture and

(3) the opportunity to explore with new materials and in new situations within a secure framework. Although there is no adequate proof to justify the statement, it is not unlikely that the young child who has been allowed to explore his surroundings while knowing that he has a security-giving familiar adult to return to whenever he feels threatened by an unknown situation, is more ready to enjoy the exploration of new knowledge at school and later in life.

Continuing opportunities to handle a variety of objects and a variety of materials during the nursery and primary school periods, and generally to explore the world, will enable a child to move away from his somewhat percept-centred view towards an evaluation of the world through reasoning and deduction. This is one of the reasons why play with objects and materials, and the granting of a reasonable degree of freedom to choose the activities he wishes to be engaged in, is not a waste of time for the child in the infant school, but an integral part of learning.

Individual, familial and cultural differences

Sex differences in play are very evident. Blurton-Jones (1976) in his description of rough-and-tumble play mentions, as one might expect, that small boys engage in such play more than small girls. The difference between boys' preference for active and noisy games and girls' interest in quieter games involving the use of objects is discussed on page 190. To what extent children of both sexes are indoctrinated into their sex roles by the type of playing permitted, the kinds of toys offered, and the sorts of games encouraged, is difficult to decide. There is little doubt that cultural norms and sexual stereotypes influence parents in the toys they give children, but when varieties of toys are available for children of both sexes, one does find girls choosing different kinds of toys, and engaging in different kinds of play, from boys.

Reference is made on page 192 to the relationship between symbolic play and cognitive functioning. Hutt and Bhavnani (1972) found that the ability of 48 three- to five-year-old boys and girls who were observed by her during play to invent imaginative ways of using a new toy was related to these children's 'divergent' thinking abilities when these children were tested later for such abilities between seven and ten years of age, and this relationship applied more directly to the boys than to the girls. Hutt also found that boys played in an exploratory manner for longer in their lives than girls. She was particularly interested in seeing to what extent children were 'explorers' (they actively investigated a toy); or 'non-explorers' (they looked at a toy but did nothing further with it); or 'inventive explorers' (who, after investigating a toy's possibilities, used it in a number of imaginative ways). Hutt found more girls than boys were non-explorers and more boys than girls inventive explorers.

Singer (1975) found that there were individual differences between children who have a disposition to engage in fantasy play, and those who do not engage much in such play. The former were found by Singer to be more self-controlled, to be divergent thinkers and more creative in their playing; they were also able to concentrate better, they enjoyed their play more, and they differed from other children, too, in such measures as colour preferences. Singer's sample of high-fantasy North American children also had fewer older siblings than the low-fantasy children, though Smith (1975) could not replicate this latter finding with British children.

Children who come from deprived backgrounds do appear to engage in fantasy play less than other children, and as there seems reasonable evidence to show that the ability to play in this way has a number of developmental advantages, such play should be encouraged in play groups.

As far as cultural differences are concerned, it seems that in those societies, particularly societies living at subsistence level, where children are early in life pressed to help with food gathering and domestic work, there is much less fantasy play, but in societies where, for example, among the bushmen of Botswana, as in our society, young children are not usually expected to help adults with their work, make-believe play in children can be observed (Smith, *ibid.*).

Further reading

GARVEY, C.: *Play* (Fontana, 1977)
BRUNER, J. S., J. JOLLY and K. SYLVA: *Play* (Penguin Books, 1976)

SECTION THREE

The role of the influential adult

CHAPTER SEVEN
Observing and understanding children

In chapter 1 it was stressed that experts today no longer give advice about how to treat children. They are reticent about advocating specific child-rearing practices, partly because they are more aware than writers of a previous generation of how much is still to be learned about the development of the human personality and the factors which influence human behaviour, but also because we now know that what is helpful behaviour towards one child may not be helpful when applied to another. The emphasis is, therefore, on trying to understand each individual child and adjusting adult behaviour accordingly. Teachers who are 'good with children' do this quite automatically when they behave differently towards different children in their class. Often they feel guilty and unfair because of this, and often too they are justified in having these feelings, for behaviour towards children is dictated as much by the degree particular children appeal to adults as it is by considerations of what ought to be done; but this does not mean that differential treatment is wrong in itself. What is important is that adults should try to adjust their behaviour according to an understanding assessment of the temperament, anxieties, desires, motivations and other characteristics of children.

The National Children's Bureau has been able, through a large research project which was initiated as the Child Development Study in March 1958, to analyse the development of children who can be classified as falling into many different kinds of categories. These categories include, *inter alia*, 'only' children, children who come from large families, children from one-parent families, and children who have been bereaved, adopted or are handicapped.

In a chapter on observing and understanding children it would have been of interest and value to have referred to the many findings of the NCB and other investigators which in recent years have become available about the psychological effects, long-term consequences and practical problems which arise when children suffer different kinds of disadvantages, difficulties or family circumstances, as well as looking at the advantaged, highly-gifted children. Clearly a detailed description of all such findings is not possible here, but the reader interested can consult the various publications issued by the NCB, whose address is given at the end of this chapter, and also the publications referred to there.

Observation of children

Good observation of each child is important if an evaluation of his characteristics is to be valid. Such observation includes not only noting his own behaviour, but also developing a skill in interpreting parental attitudes during teacher–parent interviews. It is important also to be aware of possible anxieties caused by, perhaps, the illness of a parent, the arrival of a new baby or other domestic disturbances, such as the possible or actual break-up of the family. It goes without saying that a child who is already somewhat anxious about life when all is going well may be overwhelmed by the mere threat of such disturbances at home, so that a knowledge of a child's physical and emotional environment is important for the teacher. In addition, however, it is also useful to make an assessment of a child's traits and characteristics in response to daily handling.

Such an assessment can be made by several means, including: observing his behaviour when by himself and when with others; getting to know the parents' attitude to work, discipline and other matters affecting their children, as well as being familiar with the child's family environment generally; noting the kind of work the child does in school and how he does it; and by applying formal tests.

Responsibility for behaviour

As far as behaviour and responsibility for behaviour is concerned, society's attitude towards adults and children alike appears to be based on an assumption that humans are entirely in control of their behaviour, and that when such behaviour conflicts with the needs of society, or, in the case of children, with the demands of parents and teachers, then the offending person is considered to be culpable. To what extent humans are controlled by the genetic and environmental influences which contribute to their shaping, and how much control in the last resort is a matter of a free exercise of will, is, in part at least, a complex philosophical problem.

In chapter 3 we examine studies which seek to investigate the factors which influence the way the human personality develops. These include studies which relate body build and temperament and observational work starting at two months of age which notes the persistence over at least ten years of behavioural factors such as activity levels, distractibility, adaptability, etc. These factors are, of course, all affected by the environment, since all behaviour is to a greater or lesser extent determined by an interaction between innately determined and environmental influences. So far as the teacher is concerned, it is of value to note here the findings of studies which indicate the significance of influences apparently present from very early in life, since these findings will help her in her understanding of the children in her care.

Sex differences

Without always being consciously aware that they do so, most adults respond in subtly different ways to boys than they do to girls, even though in these sexually egalitarian times a conscious effort is probably made by many adults to minimize any tendency they may suspect they have to do this.

We discuss in chapter 5 the various ways in which boys and girls differ from one another and how these differences affect their social development. The differences discussed on page 102 which relate, *inter alia,* to girls' greater verbal abilities and boys' greater spatial and mechanical abilities, must be allowed for when teaching children of both sexes. In addition, we know that boys even from pre-school age generally manifest greater behavioural disturbances than girls (Davie, 1972); many more older boys than girls are involved in delinquent acts, but when questioned girls admit to more delinquent behaviour than is recorded (Smart, 1977). There has, however, in recent times been a rise in the number of violent crimes committed by girls and detected (Criminal Statistics, HMSO, 1975). Until recently at least boys and girls were treated differently by the law, the girls being offered more psychiatric help than the boys. Delinquent behaviour is discussed on page 226.

Understanding a child's temperament

It is important for the teacher to understand the child's temperament and to realize that his behaviour is often a spontaneous expression of inner drives and needs and not something which the child can easily change. The studies of Thomas and Chess (1977) indicate that when the home or the school make demands which are in gross conflict with a child's temperamental characteristics then the child is put under heavy stress. What can reasonably be expected of one child is an unreasonable expectation when demanded of another. A young child with a high activity level should not be expected to sit still for long; a persistent child can be forgiven if he doesn't come quickly when called while he is engaged on a task; a child who finds all manner of approach-making difficult, whether to new people, objects or jobs, should not be chided for attempting to avoid such approaches. Similarly the highly extraverted child will need the stimulation which the presence of other people provides, and to be left alone could be a particularly severe trial for him which might not trouble a more introverted child. The friendly, pleasant child who enters into everything with joy and who is obviously likeable is no more responsible for his sunny nature than the child who, from birth it seems, has found everything done to him, or which he has had to do, a trouble and a pain. It is obvious, too, that such naturally disadvantaged children often have had matters made worse for them by the way they are handled by non-understanding adults, who find them difficult to deal with and often quite unlovable. It is with such children particularly that the teacher can be of especial help, not only in her attitude to the child in class, but at times also in helping parents towards a better understanding of their child.

It is obvious that a child's temperamental characteristics not only affect his interaction with other people, but also influence his learning ability. A child with a basically good learning capacity may find learning difficult if he is easily distracted, and insufficient allowance is made for his having to learn in distracting surroundings. Again some children find it much more difficult than others to respond to external stimulation, while some others have a short attention span and cannot be expected to persist with an activity for as long as children who are not subject to this difficulty. Much emphasis has hitherto been laid on the relationship between a child's measurable IQ and how he should, therefore, be expected to perform in learning tasks, and too little attention has been given to temperamental factors which affect learning ability. Hamilton (1970) has shown that personality variables, as well as 'A' level results and IQ scores, differentiate the successful university student from the unsuccessful one. It is known, for instance (Eysenck, 1960), that highly extraverted adults find learning more difficult than introverted persons. Work (Eysenck and Cookson, 1970) with 4,000 eleven-year-olds seems to indicate that introverts are more frequently 'late developers' than extroverts. Generally one finds that the more stable child does better in school subjects than the anxious child, but results of a number of studies are somewhat contradictory, particularly as the sex factor — whether one is dealing with boys or girls — appears to enter into the relationship between extraversion, stability and scholastic achievement.

Understanding children's language use

Another factor worth bearing in mind when observing and listening to children is that when they speak they do not always mean what adults think they mean, nor are they always fully able to understand what adults say despite the fact that children use language so fluently from quite an early age. Reference is made in chapter 4 to language learning and to the difficulties experienced by young children in particular, and to studies by Donaldson and Balfour (1968) and by Cromer (1970). The lesson to be learned from these studies is that when children appear to misunderstand adults they are not necessarily inattentive or dull, but that a particular turn of phrase, even when quite ordinary words are used, may not be within their range of comprehension.

Understanding the child's view of the world

Practical use can be made of the many studies which have supported much of Piaget's work (chapters 2 and 4) which indicate how relatively egocentric and percept-centred the young child is. It is also important to remember that children do not interpret the behaviour of others nor understand motives for behaviour in the same way as adults do (chapter 5), and that their ideas of morality also change with age (chapter 5). By constantly reminding themselves of the inevitable difference between the young child's view of the world and the adult view, and also trying to see with the child's eyes, teachers may help themselves, to some extent at least, to understand the children they teach.

The working-class child and school

When the child from a middle-class home enters school he enters an atmosphere which is only an extension or a variation of home, but the child from a lower-working-class home enters a community which from a social-class point of view is quite alien to him. Children go to school to learn, and the value which is placed on education is a middle-class value. Implicit in a belief in the value of education is a belief in the value of taking a long-term view of life; but such a view is alien to many people who, as Vernon (1969) has suggested, have little economic control over their future and who see little point in planning for it. In chapter 4 we see how profound is the influence of the different use of language by the two social classes on moral development, thought processes, and parent–child relationship. The child from a lower-working-class home coming to a primary school enters a community where language is used as it is used in a middle-class home. When under the 1944 Education Act bright children from linguistically deprived and socially different homes went to a grammar school the pressures which they experienced were great, despite their earlier partial familarization with middle-class values through having attended primary school. The problems they encountered have been outlined by Jackson and Marsden (1962), and by Stevens (1970), who reports actual testimonies of pupils in her book. The strains under which such children had to work, and the conflicts and confused feelings which were engendered, are, apparently, no less when they are put into the top stream of a comprehensive school.

The fundamental cleavage which exists in our society cannot easily be overcome by equal educational opportunities from five years of age onward, though it might be reduced if more nursery-school facilities existed. Teachers will have to recognize that at present children from certain types of under-privileged homes will inevitably find it much harder to take advantage of what the school offers than children who are more fortunate.

The problem is not confined to difficulties with school work; in matters of behaviour children who are used to quick orders being given them, and who have as yet developed little internal control but rely on the physical strength and greater size of the teacher to exercise control over them, find the middle-class approach to discipline strange and possibly consider it a rather weak way for adults to behave. The idea that learning is a preparation for life and work, and that it is an example of taking a long-term view of living, is a difficult one for children whose training at home is so largely directed to the present.

Although teachers themselves now come from a variety of social classes and some may personally have experienced the difficulties which have been described, they have, through their training and by their association at work with persons from other classes, largely adopted middle-class speech forms and most middle-class values. It may, indeed, be more difficult for some teachers who have come from a linguistically deprived background to show understanding for children from a similar background, for they may quite unconsciously tend to reject such children because they are a reminder to them of associations which they have discarded.

It has been suggested that probably these language differences and their associated problems are slowly declining in society, and we can presumably look forward to a society where the present divisions will not be so pronounced, though the recently (1979) published findings of Nuffield College researchers do not lend support to this hope.

Knowing parents

Knowing the parents of children in her care is a help to the teacher in trying to understand the children's behaviour. This is often difficult, because for many parents schools and teachers reawaken unhappy childhood feelings and memories, and this makes them reluctant to establish any but the most necessary contacts with their children's school. For working-class parents too the educated teacher is often seen as a middle-class authority figure. In addition many parents are simply not interested in their children's scholastic progress or emotional development. Unfortunately also it is the parents with whom contact is most desirable who are usually the least ready to come. However, most good schools can find some way of seeing parents occasionally. If a child does appear to have some kind of difficulty it is well worth while trying to see in what way, if at all, the home environment may be contributing to the child's problems. If the problem is severe it is, of course, vital for the parents to be seen. This need to obtain parental co-operation is further discussed when children who require special help are considered (page 224).

Obviously parents vary greatly in their attitudes to such matters as discipline, work, progress at school and other factors affecting their children's behaviour. Evidence exists from a number of sources (chapter 8) to show that parents of disturbed children are more directive and restricting; they diminish their children's individuality, have little empathy and are lacking in imagination, when compared with parents of non-disturbed children (Adams *et al.*, 1965). What was particularly noticed in the Adams study was such parents' *puzzlement* when the experimenters asked: 'How do you think the child sees that?' or 'Do you, in addition to trying to discipline and teach your child, also try to stop occasionally and see things the way he sees them?' It is very difficult to influence such parental attitudes, but by knowing that a particular child has parents who are unable to understand their child the teacher can both allow for this in the child's behaviour and attempt to show understanding towards the child.

Extremes of body build and associated temperamental characteristics

Before discussing children who appear to suffer from more than the usual amount of stress and who can be termed 'emotionally disturbed', it is worth considering children whose body build is extreme in one of three directions. There is a certain amount of evidence which indicates that children who are in build *predominantly* 'muscular', 'round' and 'linear' respectively vary in temperament from one another (chapter 3). (By 'linear' is meant a body build of relatively greater height and lesser weight, and 'round' means 'roundness of physique and ability to grow fat'.) Vernon (1964) has said that work relating bodily characteristics and temperament shows sufficiently high correlations to justify the assumption that persons with *marked* 'round', 'linear' or 'muscular' physiques differ from one another in a number of important characteristics. In a sample of 50 boys and 50 girls of seven years of age who were classified in this way, Davidson, McInnes and Parnell (1957) found 'linear' children to be far the best readers of the three groups of children. A 'linear' child often seems to have a shy, protective shell and his inner world tends to be more important to him than what is happening outside. Although he is usually superior in academic performance to his peers, he is often less able to use his intelligence when confronted with non-academic situations. He is shy, not very responsive, has high standards and may lack confidence. He is also likely to be anxious, and this anxiety often expresses itself in emotional unrest of various kinds — thumb-sucking, nailbiting, temper tantrums, bedwetting, etc. However, it seems that more than a third of all supposedly healthy children display one or other of these habits, so that only if the habit is very intense or persistent, or if three or more such habits are in evidence, would one consider such a child to suffer from emotional unrest.

The extremely muscular child has, as one might suspect, much more practical ability than children of the other two body build types. In the study under consideration it was found that in school examinations at eleven such children did less well in reading than the other children and they obtained fewer grammar school places than children of the other types of body build. The muscular child is not so prone to be anxious and he is least likely to be submissive. He is usually also a good communicator and is more likely to be aggressive.

The more than usually 'round' child is the great 'allrounder'. He is neither especially anxious nor aggressive. He comes out well on intelligence tests; he is emotionally responsive to his environment, so that he is more lively, socially well adjusted and better able to cope with new situations than the other types of children. He has more confidence and his energies are often well directed.

It would, of course, be unwise to categorize even those children who are extreme in body build *exclusively* according to their physique. However, it would also be unwise to ignore such findings, since a child's bodily build is the most immediate, obviously noticeable feature about him. Knowing the strengths and weakness of children who are extreme in body build can give teachers an indication of the kind of child with whom they are dealing; in particular, it can warn them what they should expect and what they should not expect from such children.

Stress in normal childhood

It is difficult for most adults to reflect on the distress and anxieties they experienced in childhood, and beyond a certain age it is in any case not possible to recollect thoughts and emotions. Moore (1970) suggests that most adults and children experience three major forms of stress: one form is due to the ordinary strains of living. The second occurs whenever a child, or an adult, has to take a new step forward in life; in a child's life such steps occur at specific 'critical' periods when a new phase of development starts. The third cause for stress lies in special occurrences, such as separation from home and parents, loss of a parent, illness, the arrival of a new baby and so on. Moore says that one must assume that small children learn about human behaviour at least in part through the reactions of parents and siblings to stressful situations. However, we are only just beginning to understand rather inadequately what form this learning can take and what the effects of such experiences are on different kinds of children. We do not know what factors both in the environment and in the child himself can pinpoint either the damage that may be done by stress, or, alternatively, establish a resilience which may be helpful in later life. Yet, says Moore (1970), daily decisions are made about children, such as whether to send a child to nursery or boarding school, whether to provide him with a sibling this year or next, etc. Until we know much more about the way specific children react to particular factors in their environment we cannot make such decisions with any degree of certainty about their beneficial or damaging effects.

In an earlier paper Moore (1966) states that about 80 per cent of children experience difficulties in the infant school, of which surprisingly and unfortunately nearly half seem to be of moderate or marked severity. In a longitudinal study of 164 boys and girls aged from six to eleven years, Moore found that the greatest difficulty in adjusting to school occurred among only boys. The most common difficulty was a general reluctance to go to school; but children also seemed to have difficulties with teachers and with work, and they reported disliking school dinners and the lavatories! Less frequently reported were difficulties with other children. From this investigation it seems that many children in the infant school are daily afflicted with the anxiety of having to do something they do not wish to do, and of having to face conditions and experiences which potentially or actually trouble them. It is perhaps difficult for most adults to appreciate the many fears which small children experience in their first days and weeks at school, and the teacher of the reception class should be particularly sensitive to these fears.

In a more recent study of 260 children and their difficulties in starting school, Hughes, Pinkerton and Plewis (1979) found that 13 per cent had general difficulties of a social–emotional nature after half a term at school, and about 25 per cent had difficulties with language and persistence at school activities. The researchers say that these difficulties were significantly affected by sex, age, class size, and term of entry to school, and that the general pattern and extent of difficulties were similar four terms later. It will be appreciated that the child who goes to a nursery school for the first time at three or even four years of age is likely to suffer fears and other social–emotional difficulties to an even greater extent.

The problems and difficulties encountered by children

It is clear when one considers the problems and difficulties which may be encountered by children, one is discussing three factors:

    (1) what a child may be suffering emotionally, though there may not be any overt sign of this in his behaviour,

    (2) very adverse social and/or familial conditions in a child's life which may or may not produce an effect on the child's feelings or his behaviour and

    (3) behaviour which may be anti-social, neurotic or out of character, whose cause may, at least in the first instance, not be known or understood.

We consider on the following pages a number of different factors which can be classified under (2) and (3) above.

Throughout this book emphasis has been laid on the importance of studying the individual child. Descriptions of how children develop will also have given the reader an insight into the difficulty of identifying possible causes of 'good' and 'bad' development. The reader will also be aware by now that to describe behaviour is not to explain it. Thus one may say that a child is 'for ever wanting my attention', as if one had thus explained something about this child when, in fact, one has done no more than to *describe* his behaviour. Perhaps it is apt, therefore, before beginning a section on children with various kinds of difficulties and maladjustments, to emphasize what Charlotte Bühler has written (Webb, 1967):

    (1) 'Never assume that a problem can be explained by one specified cause.'

    (2) 'Never believe that explanation can be given without study of the individual situation.'

    (3) 'Do not accept descriptions of a child's behaviour as explanation.'

Webb has listed eleven different kinds of behaviour which worry teachers in infant schools in some way or another, and consideration will be given to the most important of these. The author has, indeed, incorporated many ideas expressed by Webb in the author's account of the aggressive, thieving, anxious and withdrawn child. Other aspects of infant and older children's behaviour, which new teachers in particular may find worrying or puzzling, are also considered.

Because the teacher is in daily contact with the children in her class she is in a unique position to notice difficulties which may arise with any particular child, or, if she is aware of adversely changed circumstances in a child's life, she is in a position to make life easier for such a child at school. A teacher must be particularly aware of the occasions when a child is suffering a stress which appears to be too great for the child to bear. Unsupported intense anxieties in childhood can be re-awakened by similar circumstances later in life, and create problems for the then adult person.

When we consider children's maladaptive behaviour we have to remember that our society must present conflicting norms to the developing child: at times he is told to be gentle, at others that he must stand up for himself. He must not be aggressive, but he notices aggression daily displayed on television, and he can see that the more aggressive an actor is the more likely he is to defeat his adversary and win approval. He is expected 'not to be a baby' and to control his feelings, but he not infrequently sees adults both angry and upset. He may not take other people's possessions, but in the supermarket he will see his mother pick up goods which do not belong to her!

Familial or social circumstances which may cause suffering or produce unusual behaviour in the child

The social and familial disadvantages and disturbances from which children may suffer can be classified into

(1) those which are part of their daily living conditions, for example, being a member of a very large family, or being parentally deprived, being a member of a one-parent family, or living in poor housing conditions;

(2) those which are of a temporary nature but nevertheless can be disturbing to the child, such as the birth of a sibling or when a child himself or a parent or sibling has to go into hospital, or when the family move house; and

(3) those which mostly are highly disturbing to a child, and often, though not necessarily always, long term in their effects, such as the departure from home, or the death, of a parent.

So-called maternal deprivation and temporary separation

We discuss variously throughout the book (see chapters 3 and 5) the value to the developing infant of a bonded relationship with at least one person. Some children suffer the experience of a broken bond between themselves and their caretaker, usually the mother, due to a temporary or even permanent separation after early childhood; but some other children have never had the opportunity to form a bond with anyone during their early childhood if, for example, they have lived all their life in an institution with its constantly changing staff. It

is important when discussing the effects on emotional developm
so-called maternal deprivation experiences to differentiate the ei
of the experiences suffered by the child who has been *separated* from ...is
mother, whether for a long or short period, from those of the child who
has *never formed a secure bond* with any other person, or who has had that
bond severely disrupted and who has never thereafter been able to
form another such bond in childhood. Rutter (1978) has written that
'circumstantial evidence suggests that these early [during infancy]
selective bonds provide the basis for sound later social development
. . . [and] that the nature and quality of these early relationships is
probably crucial' (page 3); and, Rutter adds, after the age of three or
four years it may be increasingly difficult to make stable attachments
for the first time, though a child who has made such attachments early
in life can transfer them to other people later. The Rutter statement,
and many similar statements by Bowlby and others, raise two important questions of relevance: one is whether there is, indeed, a 'critical'
period for the formation of bonding relationships, and the other is
whether, if there is such a period, the lack of opportunity to form such
a bond during this period means that it is not possible, except for the
most unusual child, unless very special remedial action is taken, for
the child to grow up to be an emotionally mature adult, that is, a fully
balanced, stable, sensitive and loving person, who can make happy
relationships with others.

The evidence which can be produced to show that lasting deleterious effects on the personality of the child who has lived in a residential
home all his life, with a changing staff, so that he has not been able to
form a lasting relationship from infancy onwards with any adult person, is impressive. There seems little doubt that most children who
experience such and similar inadequate care for all their lives will in
nearly all cases become damaged personalities. There are adults who
have overcome the most appalling deprivation experiences in childhood, but these are undoubtedly very much the exception. However,
how will a child who is removed from such surroundings before four
years of age fare? Tizard (1977) has reported the results of her recent
study of 65 children who had lived in an institution from under four
months to between two and four years of age, when 24 of them were
adopted, 15 restored to their own mothers and 26 remained in the
institution. All these children were studied again at the ages of four-
and-a-half and eight years. Tizard found that the majority of the
children who had remained in the institution were, at the age of four-
and-a-half years, found to be detached or they had formed only superficial relationships with adults, and also had bad relationships with
peers. However, the children who had been adopted at an average age
of three-and-a-half years were said by their adoptive mothers to have
formed a deep attachment to them. By eight years of age the children

seemed to behave at home as if they had not had an institutional experience, although their behaviour at school still showed the marks of their early life by their attention-seeking from other adults, and only partially successful relationships with peers. The children who were restored to their own parents did not develop so well as the adopted children. Tizard reports that at eight years of age about half the adopted children and three-quarters of the 'restored' children still showed the effects of their early life in some form or another; but it was also evident that the children who were still so affected at eight years of age had already been seen to be the more difficult children when in the institution.

It seems from this study, and from others reported by Clarke and Clarke (1976), that, as Rutter puts it in his preface to Tizard's book 'the die had not been cast by age three years (as some people have claimed)'. However, as we have seen, for many children the early experiences had left their mark. Also, several of the children were adopted *before* three years of age. Again, the sample size of this study was relatively small (20 adopted children were followed up at eight years of age). Nor do we know how these children will develop still later in life: it is possible that the improvement reported will continue. However, what is of special interest is that the adoptive parents, who had spent much time and effort in fostering a relationship with their child, and who were able to accept the child's dependence on them, had been able to form a good relationship between themselves and the child, though some children were not so successful with other adults nor in their peer relationships. It is reported by Tizard that half the children were not, apparently, liked by other children. The statement made by Rutter and Bowlby and many others, that the early mother–child relationship forms the basis for later social relationships, does seem to be borne out by this study despite its more optimistic general findings.

As far as the effects of temporary separation are concerned, we have seen how the very young infant is usually unconcerned at the absence of his mother, whereas the baby after the second half of his first year can become acutely distressed when left with strangers. Many small children will either protest immediately they are left with strangers, or protest if too much time passes before mother returns. If the period is very extended many children follow their protest with withdrawal from activity and with apathy; and they may reject their mother when she does return. If, in addition, the child himself is subjected to frightening experiences, such as being in hospital, and his care has to be undertaken by several different strange people, the fear and distress he suffers can be very acute. Rutter (1978) reports that the single hospital visit does not usually have serious after-effects, but recurrent admissions (and probably also other kinds of recurrent stressful separations) 'are associated with an increased risk of psychiatric disorder in later childhood and adolescence' (page 47). When a child in hospital reaches the apathetic stage, unobservant adults often comment on the 'wisdom' of not allowing mothers into hospital with their children because, they say, children 'settle down' quite well without fuss after a time; but Bowlby and Robertson (1952) have referred to this stage as 'mourning'. Whether such an experience has a long-term effect will depend a great deal on the age of the child, the length of the separation and the quality of the mother–child relationship before separation. If this has been good the child's immediate reactions to separation are more severe, but the long-term effects are not so bad as they are when the mother–child relationship was poor prior to separation. Robertson's work with children in hospital has shown — and he has vividly illustrated his findings by filming children as they go into hospital and during their stay in hospital, some being unaccompanied and others accompanied by their mother — how strongly unaccompanied children react to separation both immediately after separation, and on their return home.

There is interesting corroborative evidence from animal studies, particularly of rhesus monkeys (Harlow, 1962), where separation experiences and other variables can be artificially controlled, showing how necessary it is for infants and young children to experience continuing attachment to a mother figure, and how distressing and also harmful separation can be for the development of normal social, sexual and maternal behaviour, particularly if such separation takes place at certain ages, and if continued for long. In more recent years Hinde has studied the mother–infant relationship of rhesus monkeys in the context also of the mother and the baby's social interaction with others (Hinde, 1978).

It is clear that when a child is separated from his mother other factors, such as illness or death, or a disturbed marital relationship, or some other distressing circumstance, are almost invariably also present (page 216). It seems important, therefore, when it is possible to avoid separation, such as when it is necessary for a child to go to hospital, that this burden additional to his illness should not be placed on him. Sufficient is also known about how a child can be *distressed* by certain kinds of separation from his mother early in life. If separation has to occur and can be foreseen, then it greatly helps the child if sensitive alternative arrangements can be made for his care.

However, to date we still understand far too little about the various factors which determine what kinds of psycho-social experiences are likely to be harmful to any particular child. Hinde (*ibid.*) has attempted to describe the kinds of characteristics which should be studied in detail in order to enable us better to understand the 'dynamics of interpersonal relationships' (page 26). And when these have been fully grasped we will be in a better position to understand why various kinds of separation experiences appear both harmful and hurtful to the child. In addition, Rutter (1972) quotes Caldwell as writing that research is needed

(1) into the relationship between individual constitutional factors, and the susceptibility to certain environmental conditions (not all children are equally susceptible to all conditions);

(2) into what exactly the factors are in the environment which affect human behaviour; and

(3) into finding better ways of discovering in detail the constituents of the psycho-social environment. Meanwhile it is safe to assume that for *optimal* development most children need continuity of care by not too many, more-or-less consistently present adults, with whom affectional bonds can be formed. It does appear, however, that unfortunate and irreversible effects on a child's personality development are only likely if separation is early and prolonged, coupled with inadequate alternative arrangements, or a child has not been able to form a bond with an adult fairly early in life. However, in saying this the author has no desire to appear to suggest that the impact which separation can have on many children may not be unfortunate, particularly on sensitive children, nor to diminish the very real suffering which such separation can entail.

Family discord, divorce or parental separation, one-parent families and bereavement

Today, when one marriage in four founders, very many children suffer from the parental discord which mostly precedes the break-up of a marriage, and subsequently the difficulties which are encountered when each parent tries to maintain some contact with their child.

Rutter *et al.* (1975) in a study of ten-year-old children isolated six factors which were associated with psychiatric disorders in children. These factors were: severe marital discord; low social status; criminal father; child taken into care; psychiatric disorders in the mother, and overcrowding. In families with marital discord but where none of the other factors were present, the children were not especially at risk psychiatrically; however, whenever any two of the factors mentioned above were present together the risk to the child was four times as great as it would be if only one were present. Rutter *et al.* conclude that marital disharmony on its own is no more a risk factor as far as likelihood of the child becoming psychiatrically ill is concerned than any one of the other five factors, but that any two together increase this risk very greatly. However, one has to remember that disturbed family relationships are very often present together with at least one of the other five factors listed above, and there is evidence from several studies that children who behave in an anti-social manner often suffer a background of disturbed family relationships. If and when such children later experience more harmonious relationships the risk of their engaging in anti-social behaviour or suffering psychiatric disorders is likely to be significantly diminished. Rutter, Quinton and Yule (1978) also found that some schools were very much better at helping children from discordant homes than other schools; and that those children who had a good relationship with one parent were also less at risk. It is, therefore, possible to help such children by showing an understanding of their difficulties and allowing them to talk about their problems should they feel able to do so.

When parents separate and/or divorce, many children, even though they may have greatly disliked the discordant domestic atmosphere prior to separation, suffer very acutely. The National Children's Bureau (1975) in a summary of the research findings on the effects of parental divorce on children comment on the paucity of direct research within this field. They refer, however, to the emotional disturbance which such separation is known to produce in children, for many children have a sense of guilt in relation to it. (We discuss on page 218 the effects of parental death on children, and the seemingly illogical sense of responsibility felt by children for the death or self-removal of a parent.)

It is difficult to know how much the separation itself, or the discord prior to separation, contributes to the clinical depression and behavioural disorders of children from divorced parents. Brown (1968) quoted by the NCB (*ibid.*) 'found a significantly higher incidence of disturbed behaviour in children of divorced parents. The children may become accident-prone, apathetic, withdrawn or hostile, with outbursts of aggression. Boys are more vulnerable.'

Children from divorced or separated parents, in addition to the emotional pain of having a second parent but not being able to interact with him/her daily, very often suffer the social disadvantages which other kinds of one-parent families also sufer, such as lower income, an overworked parent, and often a diminished social life for the family.

Children do not suffer bereavement by death as often today as they did even in Edwardian times, and death is not discussed much in our society. The apparent finality of death must be infinitely shocking to children, but it is important to give an honest explanation if a person close to them, or even a pet animal, has died. Apart from other considerations, children must be allowed to express their feelings, though it is understandably a very difficult task for adults who are themselves in a state of grief to help children with their own grief; this is particularly so when young children do not show their grief overtly, nor discuss what they are feeling and thinking. Wolff (1973) writes that 'only at about nine years of age do children accept death realistically as a biological fact. Even at that age, not all children consider that death is irrevocable' (page 97). After this age children react to the death of a loved person in the often fluctuating and seemingly irrational manner which characterizes some adult grieving, at times sorrowing very much, at other times being angry or apathetic. Children often have intense feelings of guilt when a parent dies or leaves home; such feelings of guilt are in part produced because the young child especially cannot understand why a parent should leave *them* unless the child himself had, by his naughtiness, driven the parent away. In addition, many young children indulge in magical thinking, and if, in a fit of resentment against a parent they had at one time in the past wished for his or her death or absence they may feel that they had in fact caused this to come about just through wishing it! This can cause additional distress, and the child may become temporarily 'unnaturally' obedient. Pre-school children are often very puzzled by what has happened, and at times behave as if nothing had happened, at other times showing deep grief. Rutter (1975) found psychiatric disturbance most marked when the death of a parent occurred during the child's third and fourth year, and 'the risk is increased if the death involves the parent of the same sex as the child' (page 163). Apart from the emotional problem, the long term consequences can be similar to those suffered by children from other types of one-parent families discussed on page 217.

It is of interest to know that the likelihood of a child developing a personality disturbance following the death of a parent is not as great as that following parental divorce or separation, even though following a break-up of the family both parents are still living. It is possible, as Rutter has suggested in a number of papers, that it is the discord rather than the effects of parental separation which is most damaging, and this discord is usually absent prior to the death of a parent.

If a sibling dies this can also have very unhappy consequences, not only directly on the child himself but on the parents, which in turn affects the child.

In recent years it has become apparent that the relationship between a mother and a baby born to her *following* a stillbirth can be deleteriously affected if the mother was not able adequately to mourn the stillbirth (Lewis and Page, 1978). The importance of allowing everyone in the family to mourn the death of another family member, however young the deceased or the mourner, helps to prevent the suppression of powerful feelings which may, if unexpressed through socially accepted mourning, cause emotional disturbances.

Non-accidental injuries

Nearly 5,000 children in Great Britain are treated annually in hospital for non-accidental injuries. Although it is nearly always the child of under-school age who is abused, the effects of such behaviour on the pre-verbal infant can appear very much later, and this is one of the sadly interesting proofs of the relationship which exists between the quality of early experiences and later behaviour. Maltreated infants often become very aggressive to other children and animals later in childhood. Kempe and Kempe (1978) describe how potentially abusing parents can be predicted within 24 hours after childbirth, and how a high proportion of such parents can be helped in such a way as to enable them to form a loving relationship with their children. The concentration by the law on punishing parents has proved to be worse than useless, and does nothing to help the child. Children who have been abused must be treated very promptly, but this must be done not only with the co-operation of the parents but also by giving the parents treatment too. The authors discuss causes, treatment and prognosis, as well as the kind of research work which is still required to be done so that this problem can be fully understood. The treatment of children and parents is particularly important if only because abused children so often become abusing parents.

It seems that infants who, for whatever reason, have not become securely bonded to their mother are particularly prone to be abused (Lynch, 1975). It can be seen that bonding, as referred to on page 171, is a two-way process, tying the mother to the baby as well as the baby to the mother. Such bonding, when it has been securely established, enables the mother to accept trying behaviour not only from the infant, but later also from the older child and from the adolescent, without resorting to physical violence or rejection.

Individual differences

We refer earlier in this chapter to Moore's suggestion that most adults and children can experience during life three major forms of stress. We have referred here to some of the more acute stresses, but there are many occasions when, due to fantasy and 'magical' thinking, events which are for responsible adults either ordinary or even welcome, such as the birth of a new baby, may appear highly threatening to a young child. We also comment on page 191 on the possible effects of fantasy on the way a child *perceives* his environment; and we refer on pages 130 and 205 to the fact that quite simple words are not always understood by children in the way adults want them to be understood. Such misunderstandings can cause disturbance and anxiety to a child. In addition, we refer to the difficulty of knowing when a particular experience for a particular child might be stressful but bearable, with no deleterious consequences in fact, or when such an experience may, indeed, for a particular child, be beneficial, helping him to develop resilience to meet life's inevitable difficulties; or when an experience may overwhelm a particular child.

There are great differences between the way individual children are able to withstand difficulties which come their way, and the differences in temperament described by Thomas and Chess (1977) referred to on page 204, as well as the quality of early relationships which a child has experienced, underlie the degree of resilience with which some children, but not others, can meet the experiences of life. It would be possible to list many different kinds of experiences which *can* be traumatic for some children though possibly only slightly disturbing for others, but little purpose would be served by this. The most important point, to which reference is also made on page 204, is that adults should not expect any one child to react to experiences in the manner in which another child reacts; in addition, one has to remember that the strengths and weaknesses of each individual child should be valued and acknowledged, respectively, and that all children should be safeguarded, as far as this is possible, against the long-term effects of experiences which for nearly all children are likely to have serious and deleterious consequences. It is important also always to comfort a child when either the child himself displays his unhappiness, when it is easy to comfort, or when he hides his suffering, when this is much more difficult to do. Because children do not always display what they suffer it is important for the teacher to be aware of any circumstances in a child's life which may be making him acutely unhappy.

Personality disorders, anti-social behaviour and psychiatric symptoms

It is important to be able to put behavioural disorders of one kind or another into perspective. It would appear that during the course of a year between 5 and 15 per cent of all children suffer behavioural difficulties, which to a not inconsiderable extent are either a trouble to themselves or a nuisance to other people, or both. The difficulties we are discussing are not diseases, such as autism, which would render them *qualitatively* different from normal behaviour, but they are mostly conditions which differ *quantitatively* from normal behaviour. For this reason it is often very difficult to decide when such quantitatively different behaviour manifests itself whether the child is just passing through a phase, or whether the behaviour is a sign of probably greater problems to come. In order to do this it is helpful to take into account

(1) the child's age and sex,
(2) whether this behaviour is specific to one situation, or to a number of situations, or more general,
(3) the extent of the behaviour, i.e. is it an isolated symptom or are there several symptoms present,
(4) the persistence of the disturbance,
(5) the child's life circumstances, e.g. has a new baby arrived in the family, has he just changed schools, or been separated from a parent,
(6) the severity of the symptom, and also, finally, whether
(7) there has been a change in the child's behaviour which does not seem congruent with his style of development (Rutter, Tizard and Whitmore, 1970). It is, of course, also necessary to know the child's socio-cultural background in order to make a valid assessment of the extent of his difficulties.

At times a child's behaviour may be peculiar but it may not be necessary to do anything about it. It is helpful to ask oneself how much the child himself seems to be suffering, whether because of his behaviour he is experiencing social restrictions, whether the behaviour (or symptoms) he displays affect other people, and also the extent to which his behaviour is interfering with his development. It is only when one looks at the extent of the symptoms or behaviour, coupled with their effect on the child and on those who interact with him, and one also makes an analysis in detail of the circumstances relating to the child's behaviour, that it is possible to say whether the child should be referred for help. (These questions are discussed in greater detail in Rutter, 1975.)

The limited number of anti-social behaviours discussed in this chapter are those with which a teacher, particularly a teacher of nursery- and primary-school children, is likely to meet. We will discuss later the aggressive child, the truanting child, and the over-anxious child, as well as commenting briefly on attention-seeking, hyperactive and withdrawn children.

The child of nursery school age with behaviour problems

Although we discuss below specific behaviour problems exhibited occasionally by children in the primary school, it is worth commenting briefly in a general way on the behavioural difficulties nursery-school children at times exhibit, and on the extent children who exhibit such behaviour can be helped. Many remedial schemes which have been attempted have been research orientated, and so they could not, even if successful, always be replicated by nursery teachers, either because special training and the extra money required might not be available or because by the nature of such schemes they were not always acceptable by teachers for their own use. In an exploratory study on the assessment and treatment of difficult and aggressive children of nursery school age, Manning (1978) initially made observations of 60 'troublesome' children, who, it was observed, 'neither interacted well nor played well with most other children', (page 1). They tended to attract attention by various unsocial means, and were often noisy and disruptive. Manning, in advocating play-tutoring as the major means of treatment, states that it is necessary not only for adults to initiate the children into new games, but actively to take part in such games, or in some other way interact with the children. She advocates the spending of ten to fifteen minutes two or three times a week by one teacher with one child in, preferably, role-playing type games; also that the teacher should engage the child in friendly conversation about his life and activities. This is also recommended by Holmes (1978); and Manning advocates an *avoidance*, whenever possible, of confrontations and control by reprimanding, and instead the use of diverting techniques. Laishley and Coleman (1977–8) also advocate for the treatment of disadvantaged children with behavioural difficulties that nursery-school staff should 'look for behaviours to reward rather than spend all their energy in preventing problem behaviour' (page 221).

Manning refers to the fact that because in most previous research work which has made use of play-tutors the emphasis of such work has been on effecting *cognitive* improvements, the results of such intervention on social behaviour have mostly not been examined. Play-tutoring of the type advocated was tried with a limited number of children for a period of seven to eight weeks and the changes then assessed. Manning carefully defines what is meant by 'improvement', and the results of the intervention appear to have been that in all but one of the eight children treated there were 'a number of improvements in behaviour following treatment' (page 12). Manning stresses that such play-tutoring intervention cannot be regarded as a substitute for also improving, if possible, the disadvantageous social and familial conditions from which the child may be suffering, but constitutes an 'addition to such efforts' (page 4) and she considers that the nursery school can be of especial help to such troubled children in the manner she advocates.

The aggressive child

Psychologists are not agreed whether aggression is initiated by an inner drive, which has to express itself in some form, or whether it is always a response to an external stimulus; this stimulus can be positive, such as threatening behaviour, or negative, in the form of frustration. Some psychologists say that, in the last analysis, all aggression is a response to frustration of some kind. One can, though, support the view that, whatever the ultimate origin of aggressive behaviour, the energies which might be used for such behaviour are normally channelled into activities of which society approves.

A certain amount of positive, forceful behaviour, or a naturally angry reaction to the annoying actions of another person, cannot be termed 'aggressive'. Teachers, however, vary in the amount of aggressive or assertive behaviour they can tolerate, and indeed in whether they call certain behaviour 'aggressive' or 'assertive'. It is salutary for the teacher to examine her own feelings when she is faced with forceful behaviour which she finds disturbing and to consider why she is so worried by it. We are here, however, chiefly concerned with the over-aggressive child, who is usually so obviously a nuisance or worse, that no subtleties are needed to interpret his activities.

Sometimes, though, aggression may be covert, presenting a trouble and a threat only to the child's peers; other children are normally good sources of information about such aggressive behaviour, and their tales can usually be relied upon if reports of such aggression come from more than one child (Williams, Meyersson, Eron and Semler, 1967).

Most small children are unable to tolerate frustration if it continues too long or comes their way too often. The younger the child the shorter the time he can bear to be frustrated or restricted, and obviously the less control he can be expected to employ. If, in addition, he comes from a home where his aggressive behaviour is met by inconsistent behaviour on the part of his parents, he will become confused and even less able to control the expression of his feelings. For instance, in some homes parents punish aggression when it is directed towards themselves, while at the same time positively encouraging their children to be aggressive outside the home. Parental behaviour of this type produces children who are either excessively aggressive or very anxious (Bandura, 1963). Over-indulgence by parents of children's aggressive acts also tends to increase such behaviour.

It seems that some aggressive children learn from their parents that aggression, at least outside the home, is not disapproved of; for other children aggressive behaviour is a form of attention-seeking which expresses a need to feel wanted or admired, and possibly also shows a lack of self-esteem. The need for admiration seems most obvious in children who lead aggressive gangs; such children at least relate to others, and express their need to be assertive in a social, even if not socially-approved, manner. By contrast the lonely aggressor is often the more disturbed child, possibly feeling rejected, and expressing his feelings and his surplus energy in destructive and hurtful activities. If such behaviour is very severe and the child appears to treat other children in his attacks as if they were mere objects he may be potentially psychopathic, and in such cases psychiatric help is urgent. It is obvious too that such a child can present a real danger to other children in the school and in the neighbourhood.

The method of dealing with children who display this kind of disturbance will depend on the exact nature of the aggression, the age of the child, and what is known of the parents. If the teacher discovers that the parents in fact encourage the child to 'stand up for himself' outside the home in a manner which he interprets as licence to attack, it may help to discuss the matter with the parents and explain the problem their child's attitude is creating in school. A child who is known to come from a home where he is likely to feel unwanted or rejected can be helped by being given work to do where he can organize and assist others, particularly if it involves working in a friendly relationship with a sympathetic adult. Being allowed to take mechanical objects or puzzles to pieces sometimes helps the child who is destructive of material things rather than aggressive towards people, though this by itself will not be much use without a personal interest in the child. One might postulate that it is the child with a great deal of surplus energy whose feelings of unhappiness, anxiety or rejection will express themselves in aggressive behaviour rather than in some other kind of symptom; and it would seem important, therefore, to find him activities where he can expend his energy as well as enhance his self-esteem. It also helps such a child if he can learn through association with a helpful adult that he can often obtain by legitimate and socially acceptable means the things he needs so badly, such as attention, assurance and an enhanced view of himself, even if he does not consciously recognize his needs.

Sometimes older children, who were severely punished for aggression when they were young, express their aggressive feelings covertly and in time become adults who are strict law-enforcers, who desire severely to punish law-breakers, and who tend to persecute minorities (Berkowitz, 1964). It would seem that for aggression, as for most other apparent misdemeanours, punishment for styles of behaviour, as opposed to isolated acts, serves only to drive the undesirable behaviour underground (chapter 8).

It is important when dealing with the over-aggressive child to handle him firmly and with consistency, and to let him see that all the adults in his world are acting together.

Thieving in the classroom

Stealing in a classroom is often more upsetting to some teachers than any other form of misdemeanour. Because we live in a property-owning society our sense of security depends to an extent on the assurance that in most normal circumstances we can trust others not to take our possessions away. We often feel very angry with people who take our goods, not only because they threaten our security, but because our possessions become an extension of ourselves and we invest them with certain emotions. In a classroom there are additional complications; the teacher feels she must protect the other children from the pilferer, and yet the thief is often for a time unknown. Some teachers are driven in their anxiety to asking the culprit to own up, and acute tension can be created in the class which not infrequently ends in a sensitive child confessing to an act he did not commit. Often too such sensitive children, without actually confessing guilt, will blush and show every sign of guilt (page 155). When she discovers that pilfering is taking place it is as well for the teacher to remind herself that the intensity of the emotions possibly engendered in her is probably greater than is justified by the situation.

In an infant school there will be many children who have not learned fully to respect other people's possessions. Even in homes where it is made clear that one must not take other people's things it is difficult for the young child to differentiate between those things at home which belong to everyone, and those which are personal possessions; so at school he may not understand the difference between using materials in school and taking them home, or between what belongs to the classroom and what belongs to another child. We know well how very tenuous are children's concepts of morality (chapter 6) and in a society where mother picks up goods from a supermarket and is permitted to put them into one kind of basket (the shop basket) but not into another kind, it takes time to learn the rules.

In many homes too personal possessions are not valued, and the child comes to school with little idea that to take things which have not been specifically given to him is not approved.

Punishment for pilfering is mostly found to be ineffective, and long verbal explanations given to young children are usually worse than useless, for young children cannot cope with abstract concepts (chapter 4), and ideas about morality are abstract concepts. With many younger children free giving of the kind of goods, often small colourful objects, which they previously stole can be effective. Webb (1967) suggests that small children can be helped to learn about the private nature of personal possessions by the teacher making it her practice daily to empty her desk, tidy her pockets and generally make it clear that in tidying up she is returning various items both to the *people* to whom they belong, as well as to the *places* where they belong. It also helps to allow children to borrow things on the understanding that these are returned in due course to their owner. They must learn what can and what cannot be taken.

However, we know that children who are older and who have learned the importance in our society of personal possessions also sometimes begin to pilfer. It has already been suggested (page 229) that this is one form of drawing attention to themselves, and the teacher will either already know something about the child's background which will give her a clue about his behaviour, or she will be wise to try to find out. When children come from homes where there is disturbance of some kind the pilfering can be seen as a cry for help, or a compensation for feelings of rejection. It happens, though, that children from good and intact homes suddenly begin to show signs of disturbance, which may include thieving, and as domestic situations, particularly in young families, are seldom static, it is nearly always worthwhile trying to discover what changes may have taken place in the family set-up which may account for the child's behaviour.

More serious delinquent behaviours

Other, or additional, delinquent behaviour of a more serious nature can be associated with both personal factors relating to the child's personality, such as an ineffectual self-concept, lower than average intelligence and aggressive tendencies, as well as with social factors, such as poverty, poor housing, being a member of a large family, and the absence of the father for long periods.

In addition, there is often a belief in local communities that delinquency is 'natural, and that the child will grow out of it'. These differences, where they exist, between home and school in the kinds of behaviour expected and tolerated make it difficult for the child to know what is appropriate behaviour. West and Farrington (1973) report that the school in the face of such difficulties cannot have a *major* effect on the delinquent behaviour of its pupils. However, it is of interest to know that the differences between middle- and working-class delinquent behaviour appear not to be so great as the official figures indicate when children themselves are asked to report on their, often undetected, delinquent behaviour (Rutter and Madge, 1976).

Unhappily, the frequent resort by sentencing bodies to the use of detention centres to effect correction of adolescents' behaviour is at best merely unsuccessful. The new scheme of 'short, sharp' periods of detention now (1979) being promulgated will, for reasons well understood by psychologists, do little if anything to correct such aberrant behaviour. A variety of non-custodial schemes have been tried in recent years, and the fostering of young delinquents seems to show some promise of success (Pugh, 1977).

Non-attendance at school

Rutter (1975) has interestingly shown both how varied and complex may be the reasons for a child's non-attendance at school, and also how analysis of the different reasons why a child might be absent from school can act as a model for analysing why children behave in non-approved ways in relation to other modes of behaviour. (Rutter uses the same model of analysis for attempting to understand why a child indulges in faecal soiling.) As far as non-attendance at school is concerned, one wishes to know whether the child is truanting, that is, is he both away from home and school, or is he at home; whether he has refused to go to school or is being kept at home, and whether, if he is refusing to go to school, this is due to one or a number of fears and anxieties. (See diagram 5.)

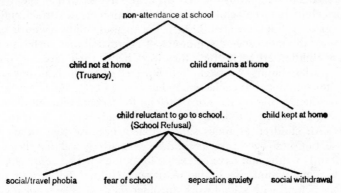

Diagram 5: *Different mechanisms which may contribute to a school refusal*

Reproduced from Rutter, M.: *Helping troubled children* (Penguin Education, 1975), by kind permission of the publishers

It is clear that no one cause can exist which is the reason for all non-attendance phenomena, so no one 'cure' can be prescribed for dealing with non-attenders; but it is essential in relation to each individually absent child to arrive at the major reasons for non-attendance.

The over-anxious child

Most children have what adults would term 'irrational' fears of some kind, but over-anxiety, which is much more serious, can show itself in a number of ways, not infrequently in the crying of the five-year-old when his mother leaves him at school. 'Anxiety is the expectation of something as yet unknown' (Rycroft, 1968), but it also is a fear which

227

springs from unease. To be separated from his mother in a building probably never entered before, and to be left alone among strange adults and many children, can be a terrifying experience for the young child, particularly for the only child who has not previously mixed a great deal with other children. However, some five-year-old children's anxiety at separation continues for much longer than is usual. If the child appears too attached to his mother then the teacher should take suitable action with the head's approval. If by the end of the first term in the infant school a child will still not separate happily from his mother, then it would be wise to refer the child to the child guidance clinic. Apart from help which the child can be given, a social worker can also work with the mother. Action taken at this stage may prevent school refusal later.

It seems to be established that the aggressive as well as the withdrawn child, in fact all children who are emotionally disturbed, suffer from anxiety, but there are other types of anxious children who do not evidence the more severe symptoms of aggression and withdrawal. These children are ineffectual; they work below their capacity; they have restless habits. More is often expected of them than they can give, for parents and teachers may know them to be intelligent and accuse them of not trying. For these children school remains often a perpetual worry, for it seems to make demands which they cannot meet. All children at times suffer anxiety because they desire to please, but these over-anxious children particularly feel that they are constantly failing and have no excuse for doing so. This sense of failure becomes cumulative so that many such children fall further and further behind with school work the older they get. The teacher can do a great deal to help such children by giving them tasks well within their capabilities and by not making unnecessary demands. Jersild (as reported by Webb, 1967) has mentioned that 'the school dispenses failure on a colossal scale . . .!'

Parents too often make excessive and unrealistic demands in relation to their child's success at school, and some children are used by their parents in order to compensate for the parents' sense of failure or lack of opportunities. There is also little doubt that some adults use their power over a child to diminish the child's sense of self-esteem (chapter 8), which further increases the child's sense of failure. Sometimes a child may become acutely anxious due to the marital problems of his parents, but in such circumstances a teacher may be able to do little more than give him support.

Attention-seeking, withdrawn and 'rigid' children

Attention-seeking is nearly always a symptom of emotional disturbance, and some children constantly seek attention, either overtly and consciously, or covertly and possibly unconsciously. A particular example of the latter kind of attention-seeking is that of girls who have frequent accidents (Mannheimer and Mellinger, 1967). There are many other ways in which children of varying ages will seek to gain the teacher's attention: they make demands on the teacher, or they have always to be in the forefront; often they have to be the leader and cannot tolerate being a follower, and sometimes petty thieving and story-spreading are used as means. It is possible for this thieving to be seen as a symbolic form of 'stealing' love, though such pilfering can spring from a number of causes which are considered elsewhere in this chapter. Attention-seeking is a well-known symptom of the maternally deprived child (chapter 8), though the opposite symptom of withdrawal is also noted in such children.

In several ways withdrawn children present the teacher with especially difficult problems; they do not readily come to the teacher's notice, yet they may need the teacher's attention more than the attention-seeking child. Unlike the hyperactive or aggressive child the withdrawn child gives few clues about his troubles because he does not express himself. One may, of course, notice the lonely child in the playground, or realize that a particular boy or girl appears never to make contact with other children or use apparatus or materials in the classroom; but there is a danger that, because he is neither noisy nor a nuisance, he will be thought of as 'shy' and consequently ignored. It is only when the teacher finds that she can remember nothing about the child, and has few records of his work, that she should begin to watch him more, and she may then notice how he keeps himself apart from human contact.

It is usually wise to find first the cause of attention-seeking or withdrawn behaviour rather than to attack the symptoms of either; it is possible that the origin of both kinds of behaviour may lie in a feeling of being rejected at home.

The terms 'maternally deprived' and 'rejected' indicate a culpability on the part of parents, particularly the mother, which they should not imply, for rejection of a child or children may be quite an inevitable act for some parents, and may often be unconsciously determined. Sometimes a bad birth experience for the mother, or a depression following the birth, will not enable her to feel as warmly towards a particular child in her family as she does towards the other children. Again some children are themselves unable to respond to affection, and persistent attempts by parents to evoke a response may end in their giving up the effort. However, this does not mean that the child itself is not in need of the affection it cannot demonstrably reciprocate. Sometimes mothers are unaware consciously that they feel rejection towards a child, yet they suffer a sense of guilt because they cannot respond as they feel they should respond, and this makes them over-anxious and over-protective. Evidence that such over-protection can cause emotional disturbance, which shows itself not infrequently in a child's difficulty in getting on with its peers, comes not only from clinical studies, but also from experimental work with animals (Harlow, 1962). The child who stands by himself in the playground may well have problems because of over-protection. This need not, of course, be due basically to rejection, but could indicate a severe anxiety on the part of his mother which it might help the teacher to know about.

The kind of family problems which tend to produce withdrawal often seem to be problems which, if investigated, appear to infringe the parents' privacy; the possibly hyperanxious mother of the over-protected child may not readily wish to discuss her feelings with a teacher. In addition, since a child's withdrawal is not infrequently his response to severe mental illness in a parent, and this kind of illness is often, even today, considered a shame on the family, the remaining parent may not wish the teacher to ask questions and will probably refuse to come to the school.

Sometimes a child will withdraw from human contact after being bereaved, as a defence from having other potentially warm relationships broken; the fear of being hurt once more by making an emotional tie which may have to be severed is too great; so no contact is made in order to prevent the possibility of further hurt being experienced.

Such children are obviously in very great need of help, and if the situation is not too acute the teacher can do a great deal by keeping close to the child and showing him that she is interested in him. However, children who have been deprived of a warm and close personal relationship with a parent or a parent-substitute may suddenly form an intense attachment to a teacher, and the teacher should be most careful not to allow this attachment to develop too far, for undoubtedly such a relationship cannot continue indefinitely and the child might then experience a feeling of rejection. For this reason it is wiser usually to encourage other children to establish contacts with the withdrawn child, while at the same time displaying an interest in him without giving him too much special attention. If a child is obviously acutely withdrawn psychiatric help must be sought.

The 'rigid' child has experienced difficulties at home usually very different from the attention-seeking or withdrawn child. Teachers will occasionally have to deal with a child who appears to be living in a kind of psychological straitjacket. The first sign may be an extreme reluctance to get his hands or clothes messy with paint, clay or plasticine. Then the teacher may notice that the child has difficulty in thinking except in a very narrow way. Most children of eleven can classify objects in a number of ways (chapter 4) according to their function, colour, material, etc., but very rigid children cannot do this.

Often they cannot even recognize a classification made by someone else, when this is not the way they think about the objects thus ordered. Leach (1964), who has interested herself in such children, has described how she grouped together a red apple, a red ball of knitting wool and a red tin. The very rigid children she tested said that these objects do not go together as 'the knitting wool must go with mother's things. The apple is for eating.'

The moral judgements of such children too will be more limited than those of other children of the same age. We know that young children's moral judgements are dictated by effects and not by intentions (chapter 5), but the rigid child is even more restricted in his judgements than other children. Children of eleven years of age usually know it is a rule not to speak to strangers in the street. Leach showed both very rigid children and non-rigid children a picture of an old lady who had dropped her shopping in the street, and she asked them if it were all right to break the rule in order to help the lady. The non-rigid children said that in such circumstances the rule could be broken, but the rigid children tended to say that it would be wrong to stop as it was a rule that one should not speak to strangers.

It is possible that parents of very rigid children have, from the beginning of their children's lives, set standards of behaviour which are too high for their children to achieve. We have discussed anxiety in children (page 227) and how the fear of not pleasing is a potent source of worry for certain children. If a parent makes demands which a child cannot understand, he cannot meet these demands, and he becomes perplexed and highly anxious, for he cannot hope to please his parents however hard he tries. We will consider in chapter 8 the effects on children of authoritarian behaviour. Suffice it to say here that excessively high parental expectations can cause a child to adopt a rigid way of behaving in order to try to make sure that his behaviour will meet with approval.

Research seems to indicate (Leach, 1964) that, although the effects of such early upbringing can be very influential in forming rigidity in behaviour and thinking, a non-authoritarian liberal school atmosphere can modify such rigidity. Authoritarian parents usually lay great stress on scholastic success; even a liberal school will be seen by such parents as 'good' — as an organization representing authority and power, which they admire. If, therefore, a child can be persuaded to accept the norms of such a school his parents will usually support him if he does well, and the rigid bounds of his behaviour and thinking may be weakened.

It is important for the teacher to recognize a real emotional problem in the child who seems afraid of messing up his clothes and hands, and not to deal brusquely with such a child; often the fear of mess and untidiness is sufficiently strong to be labelled obsessional, and then the child will require additional help. Knowledge of the parents will usually shed light on the origins of the child's behaviour, and will give some clues about possible ways of overcoming the difficulty.

In older children and in adolescents the rebel may well be the boy or girl who has thrown away completely the rigidity of his upbringing. It is a pity that such behaviour, which often results in lawlessness, has to be met by society with the very forces of authority against which the young person is rebelling.

Physical defects

The teacher in an infant or junior school is often the first person to detect a minor though important physical defect from which a young child may be suffering. Such children can be viewed as 'bridge' children between those with severe physical handicap, such as frequent illness or an obviously discernible disability, and those with emotional or educational problems and no *apparent* physical disabilities.

In many education authority areas there are now no longer any routine medical checks in school, except for tests carried out on entry at five years of age, and later the occasional 'sweep' test for hearing and sight. Poor sight is unusual in small children, and so the onset of myopia can easily be missed without regular eye tests. Teachers in both junior and secondary schools should be on the look-out for the child who screws up his eyes when trying to see the blackboard, or who complains of headaches.

Other children have been called 'brain damaged', and this term is used in at least three different ways (Furneaux, 1969):

(1) for the obviously severe disorders, such as cerebral palsy;
(2) to describe the possible origin of certain kinds of child *behaviour*; and
(3) to describe a number of disorders which have a common origin in damage to, or *dysfunction of*, the brain.

Wortis (1957) has said that there is no 'brain-injured' child, only a variety of brain-injured children, whose problems are quite varied, and whose condition calls for a more refined analysis than some of the current generalizations. However, Silver (1957) has specified three areas which brain damage influences:

(1) it causes *interruption of maturation*, and this means a retention of old behaviour patterns and difficulty in forming new ones;
(2) it makes it difficult for the child to *control impulsive actions*; and
(3) it makes it likely that such children are *anxious*.

A perceptive teacher will note the child who shows an unusual degree of anxiety, who has learning difficulties and who presents certain behavioural problems, such as either emotional lability*, sensitivity to frustration, a distorted body image and a controlling bossiness on the one hand, or a withdrawn, defensive and possibly compulsive kind of behaviour on the other hand. However, it by no means follows that children with some of these problems are brain-injured, but a combination of such difficulties should cause a teacher to observe the child more closely and to ask for specialized help for the child. Such children often have marked spelling and reading problems since they may suffer from poor auditory or poor visual discrimination. On the other hand a child with such spelling and reading difficulties may be suffering from high-frequency deafness, or temporary, but frequent, mild deafness due to a head cold.

Reading and reading difficulties

A discussion of subtle physical deficiencies which may affect scholastic performance leads naturally to a consideration of reading problems, and what has been called 'dyslexia' or 'word blindness'. It has been suggested that this term has been used to cover so many different kinds of reading difficulty that it is of little value for the purposes of classification. There is no real agreement on diagnostic criteria, nor does one know how many children are at risk, nor whether there is one cause or several.

In recent years the very great problems which illiteracy presents in the adult and adolescent population have begun to receive some attention. We will be concerned here to examine briefly the extent of the prevalence of illiteracy and its possible causes, so that teachers may know what measures can be taken early in a child's life to prevent him becoming illiterate, and in what ways, if any, (other than not being able to read) the incompetent reader differs from the competent reader. It is also helpful to know whether the potentially backward or retarded reader can be predicted before he actually falls behind his peers in reading ability, and what remedies can be applied to help him if he should fail to reach the standard normal for his age.

We refer in chapter 4 to Donaldson's remarks that learning to read *early* in life is an invaluable aid to learning about language and learning to think. Wells (1979b) quotes Olson, 1977 when he writes that 'the faculty of language stands at the centre of our conception of mankind; speech makes us human and literacy makes us civilized' (page 1). We also comment on page 118 on the fact that some methods of teaching children to read are more helpful than other methods. We will return to both these topics later in this chapter.

Being able to read is not an 'all-or-none' activity: there is a minority of adults who are completely illiterate, but for very many more reading is difficult, and the terms 'semi-literate', or 'backward' or 'retarded' in reading are better used in order to describe the very many who have difficulty in making sense of the written word, even if some rudimentary knowledge of letters and words is present.

Various estimates of adult illiteracy have been given at various times but a conservative estimate of adults in Great Britain who have great difficulty in reading appears to be about 2 million. As far as children are concerned, the retarded reader differs from other children in respect of either accuracy or comprehension by having a reading age some two years four months or more below the level predicted on the basis of his chronological age and a short WISC (Wechsler Intelligence Scale for Children) IQ test. Such retarded readers have a relatively high IQ when compared with backward readers, whose reading difficulties are probably associated at least in part with their lower intelligence. M. D. Vernon (1971) quotes Pringle, Butler and Davie (1966) as reporting that 18 per cent of children entering the junior school were 'poor' readers and 9.8 per cent non-readers at the time their (1966) report was prepared. Data published in 1973 by HMSO show that at eleven years of age 30 per cent of all children had a low reading score. Having a relatively low reading score is very strongly related to the social class of a child's parents: HMSO figures show that a child whose father's occupation falls within the lowest social class category has only an even chance of not having a low reading score at eleven years of age, whereas only 12 per cent of children from the highest social class have low reading scores. Similarly Wedge and Prosser (1973) state that 'socially disadvantaged' children (page 93) in their study 'were some 3½ years behind ordinary children in their reading scores', though they add that 'this does not mean that all of them [i.e. the socially disadvantaged children] did worse than all the ordinary children' (page 53). Backwardness or retardation in reading is, therefore, associated with being socially disadvantaged, but clearly the social conditions do not in themselves cause a child to have a low reading score.

The term 'dyslexia' has been widely used to indicate 'word blindness', and it is often used synonymously with retardation or backwardness in reading. Although there is no real agreement on diagnostic criteria for dyslexia, it is suggested by M. D. Vernon (1971) that the basic dyslexic syndrome seems to be failure to grasp the "sequential spatial relationships of printed letters and the temporal sequential relationships of phonemes [units of significant sounds in a given language] in words", (page 176), and an ability to relate these together to form meaningful words. The cause for this is unknown, and there may, indeed, be several causes. Children who do not have such specific difficulties may nevertheless have problems which cause them to be backward or retarded in reading without being actually 'word-blind'.

We do not yet know what precisely contributes to success or failure in reading. Wells and Raban (1977) have explored in detail in relation to children's reading abilities the interaction, in individual children, between certain variables, such as their oral language ability, their motivation to read, their pre-school experiences and also other factors, including the school's teaching strategies, and the characteristics of the home. Although the number of children subjected to detailed investigation was small, the findings of the study are corroborated by a larger sample for whom less detailed information was available. 'The most significant and general finding of the investigation is that, of all the factors considered, level of attainment in literacy at age 7 years is most powerfully predicted by the child's academic readiness for school, and specifically by his knowledge about the activities of reading and writing' (page 114). As the authors themselves write, this is not a new finding, but their specific contribution has been to throw additional light on the separate contributions of home and school, and on the interaction between them. Children who at home are treated as autonomous beings, are allowed to explore in safety, who become confident about the world, who share experiences with their parents, and who find being read to and looking at books with their parents an enjoyable experience are, as Wells and Raban put it, 'ready, both motivationally and intellectually, to develop in the more formal context of the classroom' (page 115).

The authors of this research report state that children should be introduced to 'real books and the activity of reading as soon as they enter the infant school if they are to reach a satisfactory level of attainment before they move on to the junior school' (page 117). Wells and Raban also say that the written material to which children are introduced in the infant school should be of 'immediate interest' and, as far as this is appropriate for the written language, should capitalize 'on the patterns of speech'. Donaldson (1978) also has written that the 'grammatical structure of the text must not be too alien to the grammatical forms of the child's speech' (page 98). She also considers it of great importance that all children, but particularly those who are not usually read to at home, should be read to at school, and that what is read should be chosen for the quality of the language as well as the merits of the story (*ibid.*, page 99). It also seems desirable when teaching children to read to stress not at all to the child the necessity of responding with speed, because it is very helpful to the child to 'enhance the child's reflective awareness' (*ibid.*, page 99). Donaldson stresses how important it is for the adult teaching children herself to 'decentre' (page 111) and put herself into the frame of mind of the child, as far as the child's understanding of words is concerned. She also reminds us that young children seldom spontaneously ask for further information when they are unsure what an adult has meant, but if they are encouraged to ask they will often do so. Also in teaching to read, as in teaching other subjects, a teacher's major aim should be to find out precisely what it is that any one child appears to find difficult. Donaldson describes how Siegler (1976) analysed precisely how two groups of children, aged five and eight years of age respectively, represented to themselves a problem which they had been asked to solve, and which the five-year-olds did not seem able to solve; when he had established why they had difficulties he was able to tailor his teaching so as to make it possible for them to learn how to solve the problem.

Further, with regard to reading, Donaldson says that at one extreme children must learn to understand in general that there is a correspondence between marks on paper and the words we speak; at the other extreme they must learn precisely what the relationship is between specific marks and specific sounds. One of the problems here, especially as far as the English language is concerned, is that such a relationship is not of a strict one-to-one kind. (For example, 'c' can sound like an 's' or like a 'k'.) Donaldson considers that children must be disabused of the belief that there is an exact correspondence which, she says, many teachers actually encourage; such disabusing does not confuse them, for children are able to accept that there can be such options, and it is easier in the long run to have this knowledge at the beginning of learning to read than to be given wrong information which has subsequently to be changed, and which can then lead to confusion.

Wells (1979a) suggests that children should be encouraged to compose before they are fluent readers. Such 'compositions' can be given aloud by the child, that is, the teacher does the actual writing, but the child composes the matter to be written.

However, learning to read is very much an individual matter. Some children 'catch' reading, hardly being able to recollect later in life how they learnt. Other children have specifically to be taught, but in doing this the strategies individual children adopt to help themselves must be understood. Raban, Wells and Nash (1976) have observed some of these strategies. Similar observations carried out by teachers in their own classrooms can be of great help in showing them how individual children actually experience the classroom situation, and how this influences their learning progress. Such observations will indicate what may be the specific difficulty experienced by an individual child who is not progressing well. It is not necessarily ideal that all children should be fluent readers in their third year at school, that is, when they are between seven and eight years of age, but it has been observed that beyond the age of eight children who have difficulties seldom overcome these without extra help. Nor can one assume that the relatively bright child with reading problems will inevitably catch up. For such a child the lack of reading ability is particularly tragic, since it may cut him off from academic pursuits which he would otherwise be capable of following. M. Newton of Aston, Birmingham, advocates for such children a strategy of 'overteaching', that is, teaching by old-fashioned rules, and teaching spelling, and doing all this with interest. In addition, it is important to pay *individual* attention to such a child's specific reading problems.

There seems little doubt that teachers in training are, by and large, not adequately taught what is important in helping children to learn to read, nor, for that matter, in helping children to understand what the teacher is trying to teach them, whether it is reading or arithmetic. The emphasis has been too much on seeing teaching as an operation from the point of view of the adult and not from the point of view of the child, and too much time has been given by researchers to finding 'new' methods of teaching. It is far more relevant for teachers themselves to learn to understand how the learning situation in school looks from a particular individual child's point of view, and also to learn how she, the teacher, can best help a child's parents to make it easier for the child to take advantage of what the school can offer.

Mental subnormality

In chapter 3 we discuss the meaning of 'IQ' and also how it is measured. Diagram 2 on page 83 shows the near-normal distribution of IQ scores in the population of this country. The intelligence quotient of 95 per cent of the population falls within the range of 70 to 130 points, and it is usually considered that scores both above and below these points indicate departures from normality. Both the number of children with an IQ above 160 points and the number of children with an IQ of between 20 and 50 points are, however, greater than one would predict if intelligence were exactly normally distributed. To the extent that genetic factors affect the degree of intelligence which any one person can display, it is assumed that within the normal range the genetic contribution is due to a large number of genes each having a small effect; but very low scores are almost certainly due to either rare, single, recessive, or mutant, genes, which can strongly affect the degree of intelligence. Brain damage at birth, or intra-uterine damage can also have a marked, unfortunate effect.

Different terms are used in Britain and the USA to indicate different degrees of intellectual retardation. Apart from the fact that these terms now seem to have a pejorative meaning in relation to the total personality, and should for this reason alone be avoided, the use of such terms to indicate levels of mental ability is not very helpful. The IQ score obtained by any one particular child indicates very much better what this particular child may be capable of. However, as discussed on page 234 in relation to reading abilities, a child may well have a normal, or near-normal IQ and still be two years or more late in reading ability when compared with other normal children. In Great Britain since the 1964 Education Act a child who has only 80 per cent of the ability of the average child of his age, even if his measured IQ is in the normal range, is classified as educationally subnormal (ESN). Again, the use of even this classifying term to indicate a less-than-normal ability is best avoided, though it is important not to fail children who are in need of special help because in seeking not to differentiate them from others we fall into the trap of ignoring that they are in this special condition.

ESN children can be referred to special schools; otherwise they should be taught in special classes in ordinary schools. Their problems are often not dissimilar from those children who are on the IQ 'borderline', that is, children with scores of between 70 and 84 IQ points, who are sometimes referred to as 'dull'. The reasons for such 'dullness' may be various, and we have already discussed the relative lack of scholastic attainment of children who suffer social disadvantages (pages 94 and 234), or whose hearing may be slightly impaired. There is no reason to assume that with proper individual teaching, which takes into account an individual child's particular difficulties, such children cannot be helped to a considerable extent to overcome at least some of the problems they encounter.

Stones (1966) describes the problems inherent in an adequate diagnosis of the nature of a child's backwardness, which is essential before individual remedial help can be given; and he also discusses the treatments available.

He makes the interesting and valuable point that whereas young teachers may have had little experience, if any, of this type of educational failure, and so 'probably have difficulty in understanding the problems of backward children' (page 318), backward children themselves will have experienced little else but such failure. Again, as suggested earlier in this chapter, the adult must attempt to decentre* from his own viewpoint in order to be able to understand what the child he is seeking to help may be feeling and thinking.

The gifted child

Relatively recently society has become interested in children whose only problem appears to be that they are more gifted than the average child; however, being unusual can in itself create difficulties for gifted children. It is important for teachers to know how best to educate such children; for example, if special arrangements are to be made for them, is it better to educate them with others of similar gifts separately from average children?

The gifted child has been variously defined, but one can say that he either has outstanding general intellectual ability and/or he shows in excess some specific ability, such as in mathematics, or in a particular artistic skill, or he is highly creative. A number of studies have shown that these children, contrary to common belief, are usually outstanding in such personality characteristics as common sense, a sense of humour, conscientiousness, self-confidence, truthfulness and other similar admirable characteristics (Terman, 1926; Parkyn, 1949).

The gifted child also usually has an extensive vocabulary for his age, together with good powers of comprehension, observation, reasoning, memory and relational thinking (Shields, 1968). Although there appears to be some contradiction in the evidence from a number of studies regarding the relationship between intellectual gifts and creative gifts, it appears that most highly intelligent children have usually obtained high ratings on so-called creativity tests. However, psychologists are not yet sure exactly what they are measuring when they appear to measure 'creativity', and it may be that creativity is not a unitary factor at all; it is possible, as Burt has suggested (1962), that creative ability is highly specific and usually related to a particular field of interest. It is also possible that creative ability is related more to personality factors, such as intellectual independence, less acceptance of authority and lack of emotional inhibition, than to *extremely* high intellectual gifts. Again, as we discuss in chapter 3, so-called creativity tests may only be tapping the least representative aspects of the quality one is interested in identifying. However, Vernon, Adamson and Vernon (1977) suggest that giving individual, as opposed to group, IQ tests to potentially gifted children does enable the tester to observe aspects of a child's performance which can give the tester good clues about a child's creative gifts.

In relation to other aspects of identifying highly gifted children, Vernon, Adamson and Vernon are concerned to stress that the identification of the gifted child is 'not a single once-and-for-all assessment. Rather it should be regarded as an ongoing process' (page 116). They quote De Haan and Havighurst (1957) as saying that the most frequently 'missed' children are those from deprived minorities, children from rural areas and (a big and surprising group) girls! They consider that a keen and knowledgeable headteacher with a good staff can pick out most of his gifted and talented pupils, but that it is more satisfactory if a trained psychologist is asked for help.

Regarding the education of the gifted child, there are a number of possibilities, and which of these is chosen for any one child will depend not only on whether he has high general intellectual gifts or is unusually gifted with artistic or other special abilities, but also on what is educationally available in the district where he lives, and on the degree of choice which his parents otherwise have. It will also depend on the willingness of the education authorities to co-operate with his parents in order to provide him with what he needs. Vernon, Adamson and Vernon list areas of special talents, and they concentrate in their description on those talents for which, as they say 'schools should, if possible, assume some responsibility' (page 51). These are: mathematics, science, engineering, visual arts, music, language, drama, sport, social leadership and creativity. However, they state that creativity presumably enters into all the previous categories; and the child gifted with leadership abilities can usually, by definition, make his own way; also children who are highly gifted in an area of sport can normally get the help and recognition they deserve.

If it is possible it may be advisable to send the gifted child to a special school, or to give him an individually accelerated and/or enriched teaching programme or for him to be 'streamed' or 'set' in the local school. The advantages and disadvantages of these methods of education, where they are available, are fully discussed in Vernon, Adamson and Vernon (*ibid.*). It is more usual for children with special artistic gifts to attend special schools whose purpose it is to develop these gifts, but it is not usual for such attendance to start before the secondary-school stage. Arrangements which can be made for such children in Great Britain are described by Gold (1965) in *The Year Book of Education*, 1961, and *The Year Book of Education*, 1962. The Schools Council in Great Britain has recently (1979) developed so-called 'packs' for gifted children of junior age who are being educated in ordinary schools. These packs relate to work in mathematics, the sciences, the humanities and the arts, and are designed to be used by the individual gifted child working on his own, but under the guidance of his teacher.

It is important for the teacher to be as fully aware of the sensitivities and abilities of gifted children in her class as it is for her to be aware of the difficulties which less fortunate children experience. Because gifted children have these special abilities they should be given opportunities in the ordinary school of exercising these abilities as widely as possible; it is also important for these children, as indeed it is important for all children, to be provided with a curriculum which encourages flexibility and originality of thought. The Plowden Report has suggested that special arrangements might be made to give junior children 'interest' teaching, by obtaining help from local persons who have specialist knowledge or specialist abilities which reflect a child's interests. It is not unusual for a gifted child to have developed an expertise, or a range of knowledge, in a subject which surpasses that of many adults, and the interests of such children can be greatly fostered by their being able to discuss their subject with knowledgeable adults.

Groth and Holbert (1969) found that the emotional needs of gifted children showed more concern with self-actualization than those shown by normal children in their control group, and the ten- to fourteen-year-old children in this study expressed a continuing desire for love and for belonging. It would seem then that there is a definite need for such children to express their high gifts and find them to be appreciated. Wallach and Kogan (1965) have found that the child who is highly creative but of *relatively* low intelligence finds life at home and at school more difficult than other creative children. They suggest that such children should have an environment which is as free from stress as possible.

Pringle (1970) has identified what she calls the 'able misfit', the child with high ability who is unable to make full use of his ability. She stresses early identification of such a child, in the hope, not always realizable, that the provision of a more helpful environment may enable such a child to develop his gifts. She suggests that when a child is performing badly in school but can still learn easily and quickly, has a good memory and a thirst for knowledge, then the teacher should investigate further.

The administration of tests

Reference has been made throughout this chapter to a number of methods by which a good teacher can evaluate and assess a child's capabilities and needs. We have not, however, so far considered the actual administering of formal tests. Most teachers give group intelligence tests to their class from time to time, and although there are some disadvantages attached to the giving of such tests, these are most probably counterbalanced by the teacher's personal knowledge of the children in her care. It is inevitable that when a test is administered to a number of children simultaneously, not all factors of influence and importance are under control, and there will inevitably be a margin of error which is not so great when an individual test is given. A low score in a group test is not very significant if the teacher knows the child to be capable, but a high score from a child who has not done well in school is significant. A test of this kind may first indicate to the teacher that she has an 'able misfit' (see above) in her class; indeed, the main function of the school group IQ test is to pick out the under-functioning child; it is useful also to assist in the making of broad categorizations if these are required for a special purpose.

Teachers are sometimes concerned when an educational psychologist, whose help may be sought in special circumstances, appears to duplicate the teacher's work by administering an individual IQ test. This is done not because the psychologist doubts the teacher's findings, but because a great deal more information can be obtained from individually administered tests than from group tests. An individual test enables the psychologist to detect relevant factors other than cognitive functioning, such as the child's attitude to work and interest in work, whether he is capable of sustained effort, and whether he is emotionally disturbed. The trained and experienced educational psychologist can from this information get a fairly comprehensive picture of a child's emotional attitude to life, as well as being able to measure intellectual functioning with more important factors under control than when a group test is given. In addition, the educational psychologist can bring his clinical knowledge to bear on the interpretation of various additional projective tests which can also be administered by him.

If the psychologist's test result should differ somewhat from the teacher's findings then this need not mean that the teacher has administered her test badly; it is difficult to cross-compare IQ test results without knowing which particular areas of cognitive functioning are being tested, whether verbal or non-verbal reasoning abilities, spatial or number ability, etc.

Apart from administering and interpreting a variety of tests in accordance with his special training, the educational psychologist may at times be asked to give assistance when the school has difficulty in getting parents to co-operate. The educational psychologist has also been trained in an interview situation with adults to find the vital areas of trouble more quickly than a teacher can and the fact that he is someone outside the school may result in some parents being less reluctant to discuss matters of difficulty with him than they would be with someone from within the school.

When a child exhibits deeply disturbed behaviour in one of the several ways we have considered, or when he is obviously grossly underfunctioning, then the educational psychologist's assessments may result in the child being referred to a clinic and in the assignment of a specially trained social worker to help him and his family.

Further reading

DONALDSON, M.: *Children's minds* (Fontana, 1978)

THOMAS, A. and S. CHESS: *Temperament and development* (Bruner/Mazel, New York, 1977)

VERNON, M. D.: *Reading and its difficulties* (Cambridge University Press, 1971)

WOLFF, S.: *Children under stress* (Pelican, 1973)

VERNON, P. E., G. ADAMSON and D. VERNON: *The psychology and*
  of gifted children (Methuen, 1977)
RUTTER, M.: *Helping troubled children* (Penguin Education, 1975)
WEBB, L.: *Children with special needs in the infants' school* (Smythe, 1967)

Much helpful information about children is obtainable from the
National Children's Bureau, 8 Wakley Street, London EC1V 7QE.

ЧIGHT

n interaction with the child

Chil... methods and personality formation

Loevinger, in an amusing article called 'Patterns of parenthood as theories of learning' (1959), makes the point that child-rearing patterns only work if one can be sure that the child is aware what effect the parent (or teacher) intends to produce with the particular child-rearing pattern which has been adopted. It is unlikely, though, that the child will be aware of this intention, and, she says, since children generally seek the gratification of their own impulses, they will in any case mostly find ways of circumventing the social learning methods which their parents have adopted. 'A shift in parentmanship is countered by a shift in childmanship.' Loevinger suggests that there are three different kinds of social learning theories available to parents:

Parent one will use a reinforcement theory, whereby a child is punished for wrong-doing, probably by physical means, and rewarded for right-doing, though the latter is mostly overlooked and children are seldom rewarded as conspicuously as they are punished.

Parent two believes in learning by insight. Parents (and teachers) explain why certain acts are wrong and persuade children to behave differently another time.

Parent three is sure that children learn mostly by identification; that is, he believes that children model themselves on adult behaviour (chapter 2) and that the way children are controlled should never be by means which in themselves set a bad example.

However, whatever the intentions of adults, the children may see the matter quite differently; reinforcement theory, particularly when physical punishment is used, may be interpreted by a child as if he were being reared by identification theory; and children of parents *two* and *three* may not understand about insight and identification, and merely enjoy the lack of serious consequences following a particular misdemeanour!

This somewhat frivolous approach to a serious problem — which, as indicated in chapter 1, has troubled and is still troubling most conscientious people who want to act in the best way in relation to the children in their care — emphasizes the very real difficulty experienced by so-called experts when asked by parents and teachers how they should treat children. Loevinger herself suggests that the main value of a parental (and teacher) social-learning theory for behaviour (chapter 2) lies in demonstrating to a child the ability of adults to curb their own impulses simply because it is better for the future welfare of another person, the child, that they should do so. This is, of course, adopting basically a theory of identification. However, although consistency in behaviour is important, it may also be possible, by understanding the level of development which a particular child has reached, to use successively a number of learning theories, each appropriate both to the particular misdemeanour it is intended to correct and also to the child's developmental stage.

We refer on a number of occasions throughout this book to the fact that there seems to be no direct relationship between parental actions and child behaviour, and also to the difficulty of making predictions about later personality development based on known early, or even later, experiences in childhood. There are two major reasons why this is so. One reason relates to the methodological difficulties which have beset investigators in this area of psychology, and the other reason is that at present our knowledge about the many possible influential factors which go to form the human personality is still very incomplete. It is, indeed, likely that it will never be possible to establish a direct relationship between certain childhood experiences which fall within the normal range of experiences and later, apparently corresponding aspects, of personality development.

The detailed reasons why it has not been possible, and may not ever prove possible, to relate specific child-rearing methods, and also the more general experiences which a person has during his childhood, to later personality characteristics are many and various. They include the following:

(1) We do not yet know enough about what contributes either to stability or to change in human behaviour (Clarke, 1978).

(2) We also know far too little about the relationship between a child's constitutional factors and his susceptibility to certain environmental conditions (Rutter, 1972).

(3) Again, our knowledge is incomplete about what aspects of the psycho-social environment actually affect human behaviour to a discernible degree. It is possible that those aspects which were at one time considered important influences may prove to be of lesser importance than other, hitherto unsuspected, influences (Sameroff, 1975).

(4) We discuss in chapter 5 how difficult it is to delineate the reasons for a person engaging in so-called moral behaviour because, outside certain limits, his behaviour may well be highly dependent on the particular role he is occupying as well as the situation in which he finds himself. Similarly, Danzinger (1971) has stated that there is no point in looking for 'general antecedents of personality traits in the social background of the child'

245

(page 23) if we are unclear whether the traits we are studying are, indeed, general traits, that is, that they are not very strongly related to particular situations rather than residing, as it were 'in' a person (chapter 3). Extreme experiences, as Danzinger also points out, often lead to extreme behaviour, but though this knowledge may help us to try to avoid such extreme experiences for our own children, it does not help us in our understanding of normal behaviour and its antecedents.

(5) Psychologists are also now aware that parents are not consistent in their behaviour, so that it is difficult to relate behavioural outcome in a child to parental behaviour if the latter has in fact been inconsistent (Bayley and Schaefer, 1960).

(6) It is known, too, that different children in the same family interpret parental rearing differently one from another (Stott, 1941). This may well be because different kinds of personalities of children in the same family call forth different responses from parents, but it could also be due to the fact that different children interpret the same behaviour in parents in different ways. Kelly (1955) has remarked that we are not so much the victims of our history (again, within the bounds of *normal* experience) as of our construction of that history. This means that the way a child interprets his life-experiences may well be an influentially contributory factor in the formation of his personality. Frank (1965) concluded that as far as child psychopathology is concerned this may be determined as much by a child's proclivity towards fantasy-distortion of reality, as by his actual experiences of life.

(7) The assumption has also been made in the past that socialization influences have been uni-directional (Bell, 1968), that is, from parent to child only, but we discuss in chapter 5 the now recognized fact that children also influence parents.

(8) Again, it has been assumed that the mother's rearing methods have the major influence on her children, and so her methods have been almost exclusively studied. Although there is some justification for this view, since the mother normally spends much more time with a child than the father does, and consequently her influence may be greater, there is evidence to show that where actual delinquency or other problem behaviour is exhibited in a child, his father's contribution to causing such behaviour appears to be by no means negligible (Grygier, Chesley and Tuters, 1969).

Many more examples could be given of the problems and difficulties inherent in the study of the causes of behaviour.

In seeking to find the antecedents of behaviour and of the specific factors which affect the development of the growing personality, psychologists have until relatively recent years understandably been concerned to find main influential causes. It seemed important to discover these in order that prescriptions might be given which could help parents, teachers, social workers and society in general to make wise decisions about the upbringing of children. However, as we discuss on page 246, the hope that we can, in relation to *ordinary* levels of behaviour, as opposed to extreme kinds of behaviour, find *the main* causes of the development of certain personality characteristics which give rise to behaviour has proved unfulfilled. We also discuss in chapter 3 and later in this chapter the fact that the adoption of a 'transactional' model which allows for the continuously interacting effects of temperament and environment is the only realistic manner in which to seek to understand the complexities involved in the formation of a new personality. Such a model also enables the psychologist to focus attention on, for example, highly specific aspects of a child's or a parent's temperament in detailed interaction with various aspects of the environment, such as described by Sameroff (1975) quoting his own and Zax's work in 1973. They describe a sequence of transactions which starts with a mentally-ill pregnant woman whose anxiety causes her obstetrician to expedite her birth experience through the use of extra medication and instruments. These interferences result in the production of a hyperactive and unresponsive infant, whose behaviour in turn makes the mother more anxious and even hostile to the baby. The mother's preoccupation with herself means that she is less able to adapt her behaviour to her child's temperament, and a 'vicious circle can then be produced in which the mother becomes increasingly maladaptive in her caretaking, resulting in emotional disturbance for the child' (page 284). A 'main-effects' model, says Sameroff, would cause one to see the child's emotional disturbance as *either* due to his delivery *or* to his constitution *or* to his anxious mother. It is the 'complex interweaving' of these factors which is the cause of the outcome, and this knowledge can enable intervention in the process to produce better results than if a more simple, main-effects model had been adopted.

It can readily be seen that the value of such a model lies in relevant persons being able to delineate appropriate intervention points in highly specific, individually applicable situations, but it can give little help to parents and others in the way of providing generally applicable methods of child rearing. However, as discussed in chapter 5, certain types of informed behaviour exhibited by adults are *more likely* to be helpful than others in aiding children to develop characteristics which will help them towards an eventual realization of their full innate potential abilities, and also enable them to become 'caring, sharing, and helping' members of society. It is appropriate here to summarize some of the findings of Mussen and Eisenberg-Berg (1977) in relation to the treatment of children and the *likely* outcome of such treatment. However, in citing their findings it is necessary to say that we do not yet know for certain what is the eventual outcome of long-term exposure to parental behaviour of the type advocated below. We also do not yet know 'what are the motivational factors underlying pro-social activities', in order that one can capitalize on these motivational factors, nor do we know what are the properties and the strengths of socializing factors outside the home, including the effects of the school and of the peer group.

We have referred on a number of occasions to the advantages which a 'bonded' child experiences, and also to research work, which indicates that such a child's social behaviour in later years appears to be favourably affected by the emotional attachment he was able to make early in life to one, or a few, adults consistently involved in his care and well-being. Mussen and Eisenberg-Berg suggest that children who are in this manner securely attached are not 'preoccupied with their own desires and can pay attention to the needs and feelings of others' (page 170). It is probably unnecessary to stress yet again the seeming importance of good social–emotional experiences early in life.

Mussen and Eisenberg-Berg report that children who will give some of their possessions away to more needy children, or who will help their peers when these are distressed, appear to be children who are self-confident and active, 'advanced in moral reasoning as well as in role-taking skills and empathy' (page 159). Altruistic children are also likely to be under the influence of parents who have encouraged their children early in life to take responsibility, who are nurturant, who themselves set a good example, in relation to helping behaviour, and who insist on high standards. They also discipline by reasoning with their children. (We discuss disciplining techniques on page 249.) However, whether children always behave in altruistic and helping ways will depend on other factors, such as whether they are also happy and successful; whether they are given specific responsibilities; and whether they have been 'exposed to preaching that stresses reasons for helping' (page 159). It is also suggested that children are more likely to engage in pro-social behaviour if they receive rewards for helping. This later condition causes one to question whether such helping behaviour is merely temporarily pro-social or whether children who are treated in the ways described above in due course develop altruistic personality characteristics. Mussen and Eisenberg-Berg state, however, that parents who wish to raise 'pro-social children' should also encourage their children to reflect on their own and other people's feelings, emotions and expectations; but the writers also say that 'we know almost nothing about parental re-inforcement of pro-social conduct and their effects on pro-social *dispositions*' (page 161). We return to this question later in this chapter.

On page 246 we refer to the fact that different children in the same family call forth different responses from the same parents. Rutter, Quinton and Yule (reported in Rutter, 1978), using the classification made by Thomas, Chess and Birch (1968) of temperamental characteristics observed in small infants, found that children who had at least two of the four classified 'negative' characteristics — low malleability, low fastidiousness, negative mood and low regularity — 'were three times as likely as other children to develop psychiatric problems' (page 51) during the four-year follow-up period of this investigation. This outcome, the observers consider, was in part due to the parental criticism which such children attracted; and they found that these children were twice as likely as other children to be criticized by their parents. Criticism, especially when seen by the child as unjust, can be highly destructive of self-esteem. This study does remind us that whatever prescriptions may be recommended for the treatment of children, parents will, as suggested earlier, be affected in their behaviour towards any particular child by the temperament of the child in question.

The effects of various disciplining techniques, including rewards and punishments

Parents and teachers are not only concerned with the establishing of pro-social behaviour and the correction of disapproved behaviour, but also, as inferred above, with such education of children in their care that they may become adults who have a *desire* to act altruistically, and whose behaviour is governed by an informed conscience. Ideally, disciplining techniques should enable parents and teachers both to aid the production, as it were, of good behaviour, as well as establish in the child deeper, internal forces which positively guide approved behaviour and restrain disapproved behaviour. To this end it is necessary to consider the role of punishment in the disciplining of children.

The whole question of whether to punish children, and if so, when and how, and the place of rewards and punishment in child-rearing methods is a complex one. A number of studies indicate that while it is important always to reward or punish particular acts (if one punishes at all), so that the child is informed what is approved, and what is not approved, behaviour, it is better not to make any kind of reward or punishment which will be administered predictable. It is important also to give the child verbal explanations of approved and disapproved behaviour, so that he can understand how he should act another time in a similar situation but in a different place (Burton, 1968). Because this kind of cognitive support for approved and disapproved behaviour is mostly lacking in a linguistically deprived home, a child from such a home is relatively handicapped in the internalization of authority, i.e. in the formation of a conscience, and also in the ability to generalize behaviour from one specific act to other similar acts (chapter 4).

It might appear that to rely on rewards for approved acts and punishments for disapproved acts is a fairly straightforward way of teaching social behaviour, particularly if one were not concerned with problems of identification. Indeed, early learning theorists were of the 'common-sense' opinion that responses which are rewarded are 'stamped in', and responses which are punished are 'stamped out' (Thorndike, 1911). However, Logan and Wagner (1965) pinpoint something sophisticated learning theorises have known for a considerable time, which is that the terms 'reward' and 'punishment' cover complex happenings in widely varying situations, so that behaviour arising from such situations depends on the timing, quantity and quality of reward or punishment, together with the probability of receiving or not receiving such appropriate treatment, and that all these factors, as well as extraneous situational cues, have to be controlled if the would-be modifier of a child's behaviour wishes to be successful in the kind of behaviour he seeks to inculcate. The problem of when, how, and how often to give rewards and punishments is a complex one when the experimental animal is a rat; how much more complex is such an endeavour when the animal is a human child! It is probably because the problems associated particularly with punishing children have been viewed in too simple a fashion that this method of controlling a child is still used so extensively, but also often so unsuccessfully.

Effects of punishment

It is now well established that administering certain kinds of physical punishment is negatively associated with the development of a strong conscience. It has been found that punishment produces anxiety, and it is possible, though by no means inevitable, that the extremely anxious child is also a heavily punished child (chapter 7). Punishment also encourages the production of techniques for avoiding punishment rather than producing desirable behaviour; it also has other complex effects. It is possibly quite effective in momentarily stopping some disapproved act, but physical punishment may generate hostility; it may drive the act underground; also it may provide an example of punitiveness and possibly aggressiveness; the child may very likely identify with the punisher, seeing him as an aggressor. There is a good deal of experimental and observational evidence to show that punishment produces fear of being found out, rather than the establishment of an internal control. Sluckin (1970) has also suggested that the effects of punishment 'over-generalize' (to use learning-theory terminology) — that is, the effects spread to activities which are associated by the child, probably unconsciously, with the punished activity, but of which it is not the intention of the adult to disapprove. Punishment may, therefore, be more extensive in its effects than the punisher intended it should be. An example of this is illustrated when parents punish children for playing with their genitals, and this for the child generalizes to feelings of guilt later associated with all sexual activities.

Support for the findings that physical punishments are probably not effective as a normal means of inculcating desirable behaviour and eradicating undesirable behaviour, particularly with older children, comes from work reported by Minturn and Hess (1969). Minturn and Hess designed a cross-cultural study involving 600 children aged ten to fourteen years of age, from six countries, 50 per cent boys and 50 per cent girls, with half the children from lower-class homes and half from middle-class homes. All the children supported the hypothesis that it was more wrong for a child to hit an adult than for a child to hit another child, and that it was less wrong for an adult to hit a child. The children also confirmed the hypothesis that an aggressor using physical aggression will be judged as being more wrong than an aggressor using verbal aggression; but the children did not assume that a child who was being hit must necessarily have been naughtier than a child who was merely being told off. The children in this cross-cultural study were virtually unanimous that hitting was very wrong, and Minturn considers that this finding has important relevance for parents and teachers, in relation to the use of physical punishment.

However, in this discussion we are primarily interested in the *total* parent–child relationship, including the use of punishment by parents within that relationship. It is necessary for children to learn to discriminate between approved and disapproved behaviour, and the occasional punishment applied immediately following a misdemeanour can be appropriate. Such punishment may well have an 'informative' effect and its use is very different from the application of frequent punishment which will produce a generally punitive atmosphere in home or school. It is suggested on page 244 that social teaching by identification is probably the most suitable rearing method for adults to adopt. There is a danger, however, that this could be confused with the giving of 'unconditional love' in all circumstances. Whiting and Child (1953) say that if the giving of unconditional love were, in fact, consistently applied in principle, a child could not learn to discriminate, and that such a method would produce children whose behaviour would be directionless, asocial and completely unpredictable.

However, the use of physical control is not, by and large, very effective, at least not in the way it is normally used by adults in their dealings with children. The works of Sears, Maccoby and Levin (1957) and others contrasted only two kinds of rearing methods — what have been termed the 'physical control' method, and the 'love withdrawal' method, whereby parents and teachers indicate their disapproval by coldness of manner and other non-physical ways of indicating anger. However, Hoffman and Saltzstein (1967) have described a study which investigated the use of *three* different kinds of control methods, the two methods mentioned above and what they call 'induction', that is, a method whereby adults indicate to the child the consequences to others of his acts. In a later article (1975a) Hoffman writes that induction also directs the child's attention away from the possibly punitive consequences to himself and towards the 'logical demands of the situation' (page 234). In this way he is also provided 'with cognitive understanding of the ramifications of his actions, and [this allows] him sufficient autonomy to process this information and use it as a basis for controlling his behaviour'. The children in the original (1967) study were thirteen- to fourteen-year-olds, and the experimenters were concerned to 'tap' different aspects of conscience, such as guilt-intensity feelings and the use of moral judgements about other people based on internal rather than external considerations. They were also interested in seeing how far the child confessed his misdeeds and accepted responsibility for them and what consideration he showed for other people. They found that the use of the induction method by *middle-class mothers* was consistently associated with advanced moral development, but the findings regarding the use of different methods of control by the *fathers* did not fit any apparent pattern, though there is substantial evidence that where children are maladapted the father's behaviour is usually a contributory factor. Curiously, the 'love-withdrawal' method was negatively associated with strong moral development. With the *lower-class* sample of children there appeared no particular relationship between the child's moral development and the mother's disciplining methods, and the writers conclude that for a child from a lower social class the mother's method of disciplining her child may be less crucial and singular a factor in such a child's developing moral standards than it is for the child from a middle-class home. Hoffman and Saltzstein write that the effects of different disciplining methods used by parents from different social classes may mean that the basis for internalizing authority and acquiring moral values may be quite different for children from the two major social classes, and that different *kinds* of morality develop in consequence. It certainly seems important for teachers to bear this in mind when dealing with children from different social backgrou. (chapter 7).

Parents and teachers cannot, however, use explanations of consequences of behaviour when children's moral knowledge (chapter 5) or their knowledge of causality (chapter 4) is too limited to make such explanations comprehensible to them. Scott, Burton and Yarrow (1967) report work with nursery-school children which will appeal to tender-minded parents and teachers. They achieved success in changing the behaviour of small children from undesirable to desirable acts by ignoring in every way undesirable behaviour and responding immediately with affectionate attention to desirable behaviour.

If one looks at the literature which compares observational work on children's moral development with parental child-rearing practices one can make a few tentative generalizations, though it is too early to draw definite conclusions about the relationship between parental behaviour and child morality. It does seem that physical coercion is more conducive to establishing *fear* of detection and *fear* of external punishment as inhibitors, rather than contributing to the establishment of internal controls. A frequent expression of warmth and affection towards a child helps identification with the parent. Explanations about why a child should not behave in a certain way appear to help the formation of a strong conscience, though when children are very small, or the situation very complex, ignoring (where possible!) an undesirable act and quickly rewarding with affection a desirable act, helps to stamp out the former and encourage the latter. There is experimental evidence too that clearly labelling behaviour — that is, giving cognitive support — helps a child to discriminate between approved and disapproved behaviour, and to transfer this learning to other situations.

Parental personality traits and child personality development

It is, of course, obvious that the method a parent chooses by which to rear his children will be closely related to his own personality characteristics. It is also clear that, even if a parent's personality characteristics, and hence his child-rearing methods, are influential in affecting a child's personality, such influence may nevertheless not be the only, or even the prime, influence. We return to this question later. It is helpful here to repeat what Thomas and Chess (1977) write as a final comment in their book *Temperament and development*. Although this comment refers to behavioural disturbance in children, it is equally applicable to the formation of normal personality traits. They write that 'the recognition that a child's behavioural disturbance is not

irect result of maternal pathology should do much to
) feelings of guilt and inadequacy with which innum-
have been unjustly burdened as a result of being held
ics] responsible for their children's problems'. And
iy that it is their conviction 'that the difficulties of child
significantly lightened by advocating an approach of
which the average mother is capable — the recognition of her child's
specific qualities of individuality, and the adoption of those child-care
practices that are most appropriate to them' (page 192).

Studies of the effects of parental personality traits on child
behaviour have produced some generally clear-cut findings, but also
some contradictory evidence. The contradictions have related especially to whether in a good and loving home it is better, by and large,
for parents to be permissive rather than firm and demanding. It
appears, however, that whether parents are permissive or firm may
not be as relevant as the presence of other qualities in their relationship with their children, as, for example, love; understanding; valuing
the child as a person to be respected; and being non-punitive and
being rewarding. Again, it may be that some children work more
happily in a structured atmosphere and others in greater freedom,
providing always that the other, positive qualities are also present.
Burton (1968) indeed has suggested that a number of what *he* calls
'positive' parental characteristics usually cluster together, such as
using the disciplinary techniques of rewarding, praising and reasoning; providing a warm home environment; developing the children's
talents and showing an interest in their happiness; and he suggests
that such a 'cluster' seems to produce children who show such characteristics as: low aggression, feelings of responsibility, high level of conscience, low undesirable dependency and high sociability. Conversely
parents who display the so-called 'negative' qualities of scolding,
derogating, threatening and punishing by physical methods, who are
unloving or only moderately loving and who show little interest in
their children, appear to produce children who display in their
behaviour traits which are the reverse of those of children who have
parents with 'positive' characteristics. There is no mention in Burton's list of either permissiveness or firmness; but reference is made to
the disciplinary techniques of rewarding, praising and reasoning.

It would seem reasonable, then, to suppose that the display of what
we have called 'positive' characteristics by parents and teachers,
rather than punitive or permissive behaviour, will provide a home
and school atmosphere which is more conducive to the growth of
qualities which make for a happy and responsible relationship with
other people and for effective functioning in life generally.

Some parents, and perhaps some teachers too, are, however,
unable to display the kind of behaviour which aids good personality

growth in children when they are in the company of children, because they themselves have personality problems which often make their relationship with other people difficult, and which in some kinds of disturbed persons are particularly evoked when they deal with children. Thus it has been suggested that one of the reasons why some adults use physical methods of punishing is that for them punishing can be a satisfying activity; when such adults are frustrated and anger builds up which cannot be dissipated, the use of physical power over a child can be excused as being good for the child. In effect such a display of power will usually be good only for the adult who is releasing his pent-up emotion! Similarly it has been shown that people who are self-rejecting tend also to reject their children more than parents who have a reasonable degree of self-esteem (Medinnus and Curtis, 1963); and when one considers how important self-acceptance is in the development of a child's healthy personality, and how self-acceptance is related to acceptance of the self by important other people (Rogers, 1951), one can see how a parent with a low self-acceptance can influence the development of his child's personality in unhappy directions. Because, also, children are so powerless in relation to adults — indeed the only freedom they have is the freedom adults permit them to have — it is too great a temptation for some persons not to refrain from exercising their power over helpless children by making sarcastic comments and by belittling them. Teachers may indeed from time to time encounter a colleague who seems to be using one, or even several, of the children in her class as a scapegoat for her own inadequacies. It is a tragedy for all concerned when a teacher manages to pass through the various necessary selection and training procedures but whose own personality difficulties make it hard for her both to treat children as individuals and to open up lines of communication with them.

The influence of the school and of teachers on the developing child

What do children themselves think about teachers, and what is known about the most effective teachers? A number of studies have investigated children's views. Eleven-year-old children in a study by Taylor (1962) considered that the following are a teacher's most important qualities: ability to help, explain and encourage; knowledge of subject; firmness in keeping order; fairness; good manners, patience and kindly understanding. Jersild (1940) found that children mentioned sympathy, cheerfulness and good temper as desirable qualities in a teacher, as well as the ability to be a good disciplinarian. She must be fair, consistent, able to explain well, and permit an expression of opinion. Wood (1968) found that children within a wide age range often commented on helpfulness and ability to discipline as desirable qualities in a teacher. Bad temper and roughness were disliked characteristics, and children of all ages disliked being shouted at. A sense of humour was also appreciated by children. Older children thought that the ability to produce a good atmosphere in class was important, and being able to get children to work was also referred to as an admirable trait! Indeed, Biber and Lewis (1949) say that the children they interviewed in their studies saw teachers as authority figures who were expected to exercise their authority even if the atmosphere in the school or the classroom is non-authoritarian, and it appears from more recent work that the views of children have not changed fundamentally in the last twenty years. It does seem that children see the teacher mainly as someone who should be helpful; who should enable them to learn; and who must be able to keep control. As Moore (1966) has put it: '[Teachers should display] teaching ability plus a combination of firmness and respect for the child as an individual.' In his study of the difficulties which the ordinary child has to face when adjusting to primary school, Moore comments that the lack of these qualities in a teacher can mar a child's happiness and progress at school. Although he is very sympathetic with the teacher who has to work with large numbers of children, he nevertheless comments that children cannot learn if they are frightened, angry, bewildered or bored; and he found that the sensitivities of small children to their own appearance, to the state of the school lavatories, to the enforced eating of food which may be strange and unpalatable to them — these sensitivities, if unappreciated by adults in the school, make it difficult for the child to use all his gifts.

A teacher's character and personality is thus of particular importance when young children are being taught, as Moore's findings emphasize. How a child is able to meet the inevitable anxieties of his first few weeks at school may powerfully affect his continuing attitude to school and to learning. The teacher's role, especially in the junior school, is in many respects not very different from that of a parent of a large family. In a classroom jealousies can arise, as they arise in families, and a class may react to the return after a temporary absence of a form teacher by 'trying her out' rather as children test a parent's love. The teacher who has empathy for children is likely to be a good teacher, largely because of her powers of understanding and her ability to be firm. Burt (1970b), quoting Ballard, an 'erstwhile and renowned' inspector of schools, says that it is the twin abilities of being able to keep order and being sympathetic which distinguish the good teacher from the bad; and seemingly children of all ages agree with Ballard's views.

It is, of course, largely the individual personality of the majority of the teachers in any particular school which sets the values and the norms of behaviour of the school in which such teachers teach. Rutter *et al.* (1979) reporting on the research project carried out in twelve inner London secondary schools (chapter 3) describes how the academic expectations which the teachers have of the children and the behavioural standards they expect from them, also the types of models which the teachers themselves present to the pupils, and the degree and quality of feedback the children receive both in relation to approved and disapproved behaviour and the standard of their academic performance, all contribute to the quality and type of social group which each school represents. If children are given the confidence to do good work, and are expected to produce good work, many of the children in a school which gives such confidence and shows such expectations will do better in national examinations than if these expectations are not present. If children are given responsibility for looking after the school's possessions, then they will behave responsibly. The kind of model which a teacher provides in relation to his own behaviour, particularly in relation to his helpfulness towards his pupils, and his behaviour in class, such as being punctual and conducting his lessons well, affects pupil behaviour. In addition, children should be informed, directly and immediately, what is acceptable and what is unacceptable behaviour. Although, as has been said elsewhere in this book (page 251) certain kinds of punishment have their place within an otherwise warm environment, it is important, as Rutter *et al.* write, that 'there should be the right balance between reward and punishment' (page 191). The writers also say that praise and appreciation for really well-done work are stimulations to further good work; but reward also comes to the child from the satisfaction of having worked well, and so it is important to arrange work in such a way that each child can be successful in what he does most of the time, while at the same time finding the work he has to do a challenge. The writers consider that their research project has shown that the quality of a school can have an appreciable effect both on the attainment and on the behaviour of the pupils who attend it.

Retrospect

The reader who has perused the major part of this book will be aware by now that many traditional ideas about children, their development and their upbringing, have neither been supported by controlled observational or experimental work, nor have they invariably been derived from valid interpretations of clinical data. A number of such ideas have in themselves been contradictory, for example, the idea that both punishment for misdeeds and a permissive type of rearing will produce moral and responsible adults. Again, the notion that children are miniature adults who differ only from grown-up people because they know less and lack experience of life, is an idea which was held almost universally, with one or two exceptions, until comparatively recent times. The impetus which Piaget's work has given research in attempting to discover how children think, and the results from the work of current researchers who have been influenced by Piaget's work, and who are concerned, as he is, to understand children's minds, should in due course have important pedagogic implications.

The influence of the environment on child development, and the importance of a 'good' environment for healthy functioning, have been stressed in baby- and child-care books for decades. It is clear from material presented in this book that the definition of what is a 'good' environment is not as simple as it may have seemed at one time. Nevertheless, although our knowledge is still far from complete, we are, for example, a little nearer to understanding the needs of the infant, and the possible relevance for the child's later behaviour of having these needs met. It is now also realized that important though good environmental conditions are, the mind of a child is not a *tabula rasa*, a blank sheet on which the experiences of life are written and thus form the personality, but that children may differ as much from one another in innate *psychological* characteristics, such as temperament and ability, as they do in such physical characteristics as height, facial and bodily features, and eye colour. We are far from understanding how great such innate differences are, or how far an enriched environment can compensate for a poor hereditary endowment, but it is certainly clearer now than it has been in the past that man's personality and abilities cannot be fashioned entirely by providing good environmental conditions. This is not to decry the importance of such conditions, but it does enable us better to understand the wide range of ability and temperamental differences which exist naturally in a human population.

We have noted that children born into homes belonging to the lowest social classes are handicapped in many ways when compared with other children. It would seem that neither an egalitarian scholastic system, nor indeed the provision of nursery-school education, can *in themselves* compensate for such handicaps. The disadvantages apparently suffered affect such children almost from the beginning of life. In addition to involving parents in the education of their children from an early age it seems important to interest adolescents at school in the factors which affect the physical and psychological development of children, so that they may know, as potential parents, how to maximize their children's abilities, and *how to understand their emotional needs*.

This might be the best way in which to help potentially disadvantaged children to overcome the handicaps from which they might otherwise suffer.

One of the major concerns of parents and of many teachers in bringing up children is that the children in their care should develop into moral and responsible adults, using the word 'moral' in its widest sense, and many parents suffer acute anxiety when quite young children display apparent immorality by telling lies or by seemingly behaving unkindly towards other children. From the results of careful observational and experimental work with young children it is clear that they do not have the same ideas about moral behaviour as mature adults have, and that the development of moral behaviour progresses through a variety of stages as the child grows up. Thus one cannot expect young children to understand adult concepts of morality, and in our handling of children their different ways of viewing so-called moral behaviour must at all times be borne in mind. It is also worth reminding ourselves that children cannot be *made* to do anything unless they are under compulsion, but that their willing co-operation can usually be enlisted. Fortunately most children do want to please other people most of the time!

We have seen that previous generations had clear ideas about the kind of human being they sought to produce through the adoption of specific child-rearing methods. Today it is realized that the universal application of a specific rearing method, regardless of the abilities and temperamental characteristics of the child with whom the adult is interacting, is of little value, and that in any case the indiscriminate application of such methods to all children denigrates the unique individuality of each child. Nevertheless, there are probably some common aims which all thoughtful adults in our society have when bringing up the children in their care. Two of these seem to be paramount: one is that to be able to live happily in the company of other people children must learn to get on well with them, respecting their rights and wishes; the other is that the adult–child relationship should be such that children can grow up able to use their natural abilities to the full. How far these aims can be fulfilled will depend to an extent on the child's own temperament and the ease with which he can respond to other people; on parental characteristics and the general environment in which parents and child find themselves; and on the extent to which the child's fundamental needs can be met. Pringle (1972) has suggested that all children have four basic needs: a need for love and security, for praise and recognition, for responsibility, and for new experiences. She goes on to imply that the provision of these basic needs remains the ultimate responsibility not only of parents but of the whole of society through its health, housing, social and educational institutions.

Further reading

RUTTER, M., B. MAUGHAN, P. MORTIMORE and J. OUSTON: *Fifteen thousand hours* (Open Books, 1979)

PUGH, G. (ed.): *Preparation for parenthood* (National Children's Bureau, 1980)

McGURK, H. (ed.): *Issues in childhood social development* (Methuen, 1978)

MUSSEN, P. and N. EISENBERG-BERG: *Roots of caring, sharing and helping* (W. H. Freeman and Co., San Francisco, 1977)

Glossary

NOTE: Words in bold face type are themselves to be found in the glossary.

Abreaction:　Term employed by psychoanalysts; the process of releasing a repressed emotion by reliving in imagination the original experience (Drever, 1964).

Accommodation:　In Piagetian developmental psychology, 'modification of behaviour as a result of experience' (Piaget, 1968).

Adaptation:　In Piagetian developmental psychology, the combined effect of **assimilation** and **accommodation.**

Affect:　Feeling or emotion.

Anal Stage:　In psychoanalytic theory, the second of the psychosexual stages of development.

Assimilation:　In Piagetian developmental psychology, 'the incorporation of an object into the activity of the subject' (Piaget, 1968).

Authoritarian and Authoritative:　In developmental psychology authoritarian rearing refers to a manner of relating to children in which the adult's wishes and demands are imposed on the child. This is not to be confused with authoritative rearing, in which the adult exerts a competent authority but is highly mindful of the child's individuality and specific needs. Both are often contrasted with *laissez-faire* or permissive upbringing, where authoritative control is not exercised.

Conation:　Will or drive, striving.

Consanguinity:　Blood relationship (Concise Oxford Dictionary, 1964).

Conscience:　An individual's system of accepted moral principles (Drever, 1964). In Freudian psychology, the restraining part of the **superego.**

Critical Period:　A stage in development during which the organism is optimally ready to learn certain response patterns. It is closely related to the concept of maturational readiness (Hilgard and Atkinson, 1967).

Decentre:　Refers particularly to the concept in Piagetian psychology which suggests that the young child cannot move away from his own (and only) viewpoint to view the world from other viewpoints.

Defence Mechanism:　In psychoanalytic theory, unconsciously adopted methods of behaviour which alleviate anxiety by distorting, denying or falsifying reality.

Dendrite: Process of a **neuron** usually, though not always, short and branching, but defined scientifically as a process traversed by nerve impulses in the direction of the cell body (Drever, 1964).

Dendrogenesis: The formation of a **dendrite.**

Displacement: In psychoanalytic theory, the process by which energy is channelled from one object to another object (Hall, 1954).

Dyzygotic Twins: Twins developed from two ova; also called fraternal or non-identical. Can be of either sex or both. See **monozygotic.**

Ego: In Freud's tripartite division of the personality, that part corresponding most nearly to the perceived self, the controlling self, which holds back the impulsiveness of the id in the effort to delay gratification until it can be found in socially approved ways (Hilgard and Atkinson, 1967).

Ego-Ideal: In psychoanalytic theory, that part of the superego which sets a standard for behaviour.

Enactive Stage of Cognitive Growth: Term used by Bruner to denote the first stage of the child's representation to himself of the world, which depends on motor responses rather than visual–spatial imagery (**iconic** stage) or **symbolic** representation (second and third stages respectively).

Genotype: In genetics, the characteristics that an individual has inherited and will transmit to his descendants, whether or not he manifests these characteristics; (contrast with **phenotype**) (Hilgard and Atkinson, 1967).

Holophrases: Early child utterances which consist of one word only, such as 'Mummy', 'There', 'Up' (Lee, 1979).

Homeorhesis: The maintenance by a dynamic organism of a steady progressive development while interacting with its environment.

Homeostatic: Term borrowed from physiology, employed by some psychologists for compensatory adjustments to meet any threat to the personality (Drever, 1964).

Iconic Stage of Cognitive Growth: Term used by Bruner to denote the second stage of the child's representation to himself of the world, which depends on visual–spatial imagery, rather than on motor responses (**enactive**) or **symbolic** representations (first and third stages respectively).

Id: In psychoanalytic theory, part of Freud's hypothesized tripartite personality system. The id is present from birth, represents the biological aspects of the personality, is the repository of all psychic energy and operates on an unconscious level.

Identify: A process by which an individual, unconsciously or partially so, as a result of an emotional tie, behaves, or imagines himself behaving, as if he were the person with whom the tie exists (Drever, 1964).

Idiographic: The aim of idiographic personality research is to understand and describe as fully as possible the unique nature of an individual in the totality of his forms of expression and at the same time in the unity of his determining forces. See also **nomothetic.** (Eysenck, Arnold and Meili, 1975.)

Internalization: In developmental psychology the taking into himself by the child of the norms, values and attitudes of others, especially those with whom he has an emotional relationship. It is implied that through the process of internalization the presence of an external authority is no longer required to enforce moral behaviour.

Introject: Psychoanalytically, taking into oneself the characteristics of another person.

Labile: Unstable, liable to displacement or change (Concise Oxford Dictionary, 1964). In psychological contexts usually meaning emotionally unstable.

Latency Period: In psychoanalytic theory, that period of a child's life, approximately between five and puberty, when, according to Freudian theory, sexual drives are latent.

Mechanisms of Defence: See **Defence mechanisms.**

Monozygotic Twins: Twins developed from one divided ovum, also called identical. Can only be of the same sex. See also **dyzygotic.**

Morphology: Study of the structure or form of organisms.

Neo-Freudians: Meaning 'new Freudians', those persons who have helped to develop Freudian psychoanalytic theories and ideas since Freud's death.

Neuron: The body of a cell, together with its processes.

Nomothetic: The aims of nomothetic personality research are (a) to describe individual behaviour in terms of general personality dimensions present in all individuals in the same way, though in different degrees; (b) to explain individual behaviour with the aid of general laws. See also **idiographic.** (Eysenck, Arnold and Meili, 1975.)

Object: In psychoanalytic theory, any thing or person on whom psychic energy is expended to satisfy an instinct.

Oedipus Complex: In psychoanalytic theory, the largely unconscious complex, developed in a son from attachment (sexual in character, according to analysts) to the mother and jealousy of the father, with the resulting feeling of guilt and emotional conflict on the part of the son, held to be normal in some form or other in any family circle (Drever, 1964).

Oedipal Stage: In psychoanalytic theory, the stage of development during the phallic period of psycho-sexual development when the Oedipal complex is resolved.

Ontogenesis: The evolution and development of the individual (contrast with **phylogenesis**) (Drever, 1964).

Oral Stage: In psychoanalytic theory, the first of the psycho-sexual stages of development.

Orexis: The conative and affective aspects of experience — impulse, appetite, desire, emotion (Drever, 1964).

Phallic Stage: In psychoanalytic theory, the third period of psycho-sexual development.

Phenotype: In genetics, the characteristics that are displayed by the individual organism — e.g. eye colour, intelligence, as distinct from those traits which he may carry genetically but not display (contrast with **Genotype**) (Hilgard and Atkinson, 1967).

Phoneme: A unit of significant sound in a given language (Concise Oxford Dictionary, 1964).

Phylogenesis: Origin and evolution of race or species (contrast with **ontogenesis**) (Drever, 1964).

Pleasure Principle: The tendency inherent in all natural impulses or 'wishes' to seek their own satisfaction independently of all other considerations; according to Freudian theory, the principle ruling the individual at the start, and remaining always as the guiding principle in the unconscious (Drever, 1964). Compare with **reality principle.**

Primary Process: In psychoanalytic theory, the process which produces a memory image of an object that is needed to reduce a tension (Hall, 1954). The primary process serves the pleasure principle; (contrast secondary process and reality principle).

Project: In psychoanalytic theory, the attributing unconsciously to other people, usually as a defence against unpleasant feelings — such as feelings of guilt, or of inferiority — of thoughts, feelings, and acts towards the individual, by means of which he justifies himself in his own eyes (Drever, 1964).

Psychopath: An unstable individual who has usually no marked mental disorders, but who has been defined as a 'moral imbecile'.

Psyche: Variously defined, but often used as a substitute for 'mind' or 'soul'.

Reality Principle: In psychoanalytic theory, the postponement of energy discharge until the object which will satisfy a need to reduce tension is found (contrast with **pleasure principle**).

Reinforcement: In learning theory, a process akin to, but not necessarily synonymous with, a reward, which seeks to ensure the repetition of a response in a learning (conditioning) set-up.

Secondary Process: In psychoanalytic theory, the process which aims at discovering in reality (as opposed to fantasy) objects or actions which bring satisfaction of needs and/or reduce tension. The secondary process serves the **reality principle**; (contrast **primary process** and **pleasure principle**).

Sensori-Motor: Term employed with reference to structures, processes, or phenomena involving both the sensory and the motor aspects, or parts, of the human organism. In Piagetian theory, the first stage of child development before about twenty-one months of age.

Superego: In psychoanalytic theory, part of Freud's hypothesized tripartite personality system. The superego, made up of the **conscience** and **ego-ideal**, is the moral part of the personality which both restrains the **ego** and strives to fulfil the demands of parents and society. It operates mostly at an unconscious level by producing conscious feelings of guilt and anxiety.

Symbolic Stage of Cognitive Growth: Bruner's final stage of cognitive development, when the child can 'translate his experience into symbol systems' (Osser, 1970).

Temperament: General nature of an individual, especially on the **orectic** side (Drever, 1964); that is, the **conative** (drive) and **affective** (emotional) aspects of the personality.

Trauma: Any injury, wound or shock, most frequently physical or structural, but also mental, in the form of an emotional shock, producing a disturbance, more or less enduring, of mental functions (Drever, 1964). More usually now used to refer to some kind of psychological shock.

Bibliography

ADAMS, B., M. GHODSIAN and K. RICHARDSON (1976): 'Evidence for a low upper limit of heritability of mental test performance in a national sample of twins' (*Nature*, vol. 263, 23 Sep.).

ADAMS, P. L., J. J. SCHWAB and J. F. APORTE (1965): 'Authoritarian parents and disturbed children' (*Am. J. Psychiat.*, 121).

AINSWORTH, M. D. S., S. M. BELL and D. J. STAYTON (1971): 'Individual differences in strange-situation and behaviour of one-year olds', in H. R. Schaffer (ed.): *The origins of human social relations* (Academic Press).

ALTMAN, J., G. D. DAS and W. J. ANDERSON (1968): 'Effects of infantile handling on morphological development of the rat brain: an exploratory study' (*Developmental Psychology*, I).

ARIES, P. (1962): *Centuries of childhood* (Jonathan Cape).

ARONFREED, J. (1968): *Conscience and conduct* (Academic Press).

BANDURA, A. (1962): 'Social learning and imitations', in M. R. Jones (ed.): *Nebraska symposium on motivation* (University of Nebraska Press).

BANDURA, A. (1963): 'The influence of rewarding and punishing consequences to the model on the acquisition and performance of imitative responses', in A. Bandura and R. H. Walters: *Social learning and personality development* (Holt, Rinehart and Winston).

BANDURA, A. (1968): 'A social learning theory of identificatory processes', D. A. Goslin (ed.): *Handbook of socialization theory and research* (Rand-McNally).

BANDURA, A. and R. H. WALTERS (1963): '*Aggression in child psychology: the sixty-second yearbook of the National Society for the Study of Education, part 1* (The National Society for the Study of Education).

BANNISTER, D. and F. FRANSELLA (1971): *Enquiring man* (Penguin Books).

BARTLETT, Sir F. C. (1932): *Remembering: a study in experimental and social psychology* (Cambridge University Press).

BAYLEY, N. and E. S. SCHAEFER (1960): 'Relationships between socio-economic variables and the behaviour of mothers towards young children' (*J. of Genet. Psychol.* 96).

BAYLEY, N. and E. S. SCHAEFER (1967): 'Maternal behaviour and personality development: data from the Berkeley growth study', in G. R. Medinnus (ed.): *Readings in the psychology of parent–child relations* (John Wiley and Sons).

BEARD, R. M. (1963): 'The order of concept development: studies in two fields' (*Educational Review* 15).

BEARD, R. M. (1968): 'An investigation into mathematical concepts among Ghanaian children' (*Teacher Education*).

BEARD, R. M. (1969): *An outline of Piaget's developmental psychology* (Routledge and Kegan Paul).

BELL, R. Q. (1968): 'A reinterpretation of the direction of effects in studies of socialization' (*Psychol. Rev.* 2, 75).

BENEDICT, R. (1955): 'Continuities and discontinuities in cultural conditioning', in M. Mead and M. Wolfenstein: *Childhood in contemporary culture* (University of Chicago Press).

BERKOWITZ, L. (1964): *The development of motives and values in the child* (Basic Books).

BERNSTEIN, B. (1958): 'Some sociological determinants of perception' (*Br. J. Sociol.*, 9).

BERNSTEIN, B. (1960): 'Language and social class' (*Br. J. Sociol.*, 11).

BERNSTEIN, B. (1961): 'Social class and linguistic development', in A. H. Halsey, J. Floud and C. A. Anderson: *Education, economy and society* (The Free Press).

BERNSTEIN, B. (ed.) (1973): *Class, codes and control* vol. 2 (Routledge and Kegan Paul).

BIBER, B. and C. LEWIS (1949): 'An experimental study of what young children expect from their teachers' (*Genet. Psychol. Monogr.* 40).

BLURTON-JONES, N. (1976): 'Rough-and-tumble play among nursery school children', in J. S. Bruner, A. Jolly and K. Sylva (eds): *Play — Its role in development and evolution* (Penguin Books).

BOWER, T. G. R. (1979): *Human development* (Freeman).

BOWLBY, J. (1944): 'Forty-four juvenile thieves' (*International Journal of Psycho-analysis* 25).

BOWLBY, J. (1979): *The making and breaking of affectional bonds* (Tavistock publications).

BOWLBY, J. and J. ROBERTSON (1952): 'Responses of young children to separation from their mothers' (*Courrier de la Centre Internationale de l'Enfance* 2).

BRADY-SMITH, J. E., A. F. NEWCOMB, and W. W. HARTRUP (1980): 'Friendship and incentive condition as determinants of children's social problem-solving'. Paper submitted to A.P.A. Convention and reported in H. C. Foot, J. R. Smith and A. J. Chapman (eds): *Friendship and social relations in children* (John Wiley).

BRITTON, J. (1970): *Language and learning* (Allen Lane, The Penguin Press).

BRONFENBRENNER, U. (1977): 'Towards an experimental ecology of human development' (*Am. Psychol.* 32).

BROWN, F. (1968): 'Bereavement', in J. Gould (ed.): *Prevention of damaging stress in children* (Churchill).

BROWN, R. (1973): *A first language* (Harvard University Press).

BROWN, R. W. (1965): *Social psychology* (The Free Press).

BRUNER, J. S. (1964): 'The course of cognitive growth' (*Am. Psychol.* 19).

BRUNER, J. (1975): 'The beginnings of intellectual skill: 2' (*New Behaviour* 3, 2).

BRUNER, J. (1978): 'Learning how to do things with words', in J. Bruner and A. Garton (eds): *Human growth and development* (Clarenson Press).

BRUNER, J. S. and V. SHERWOOD (1976): 'Peekaboo and the learning of rule structures', in J. S. Bruner, A. Jolly and K. Sylva (eds): *Play — Its role in development and evolution* (Penguin Books).

BÜHLER, C. (1935): *From birth to maturity: an outline of the psychological development of the child* (Routledge and Kegan Paul).

BURKE, K. (1966): *Language as symbolic action* (University of California Press).

BURT, C. (1962): 'General introduction: the gifted child', in G. F. Z. Bereday and J. A. Lauwerys (eds): *The world year-book of education* (Evans Bros).

BURT, C. (1970): 'Urgent issues in educational psychology' (Paper read to the British Psychological Society Annual Conference).

BURTON, R. V. (1968): 'Socialization: psychological aspects', in *International Encyclopedia of the Social Sciences* (Crowell, Collier, Macmillan).

BUTCHER, H. J. (1968): *Human intelligence: its nature and assessment* (Methuen).

CANTER, S. (1969): 'Personality traits in twins' (Unpublished paper read to the Annual Conference of the British Psychological Society).

CATTELL, R. B. (1965): *The scientific analysis of personality* (Penguin Books).

CATTELL, R. B. (1971): *Abilities: their structure, growth and action* (Houghton Mifflin).

CAZDEN, C. (1965): 'Environmental assistance to the child's acquisition of grammar'. Unpublished Ph.D. thesis, Harvard University, referred to in V. Lee (ed.) (1979): *Language development* (Croom Helm, in association with the Open University).

CECIL, D. (1973): *The Cecils of Hatfield House* (Constable and Co.).

CHARLESWORTH, R. and W. W. HARTRUP (1967): 'Positive reinforcement in the nursery school peer group' (*Child Dev.* 38, 4).

CHOMSKY, N. (1957): *Syntactic structures* (Mouton).

CLARK, E. (1978): 'From gesture to word: on the natural history of deixis in language acquisition', in J. Bruner and A. Garton (eds): *Human growth and development* (Clarendon Press).

CLARKE, A. D. B. (1978): 'Predicting human development: problems, evidence, implications' (*Bull. Br. psychol. Soc.* vol. 31).

CLARKE, A. M. and A. D. B. CLARKE (1976): *Early experience: myth and evidence* (Open Books).

COLLIS, G. M. and H. R. SCHAFFER (1975): 'Synchronization of visual attention in mother-infant pairs' (*J. Child Psychol. Psychiat.* 16).

COLOMB, C. and C. B. CORNELIUS, (1977): 'Symbolic play and its cognitive significance' (*Developmental Psychology* 13, 3).

CORTES, J. B. and F. M. GATTI (1965): 'Physique and self-description of temperament' (*J. Consult. Psychol.* 29).

CRIMINAL STATISTICS (H.M.S.O. 1975).

CROMER, R. F. (1970): 'Children are nice to understand: surface clues for the recovery of a deep structure' (*British J. psychol.* 61).

CROMER, R. F. (1974): 'The development of language and cognition: the cognition hypothesis', in Brian Foss (ed.): *New Perspectives in Child Development* (Penguin Books).

DANZINGER, K. (1971): *Socialization* (Penguin Books).

DARWIN, C. (1872): *The expression of emotions in man and animals* (Appleton and Co., reprinted University of Chicago Press 1965).

DAVIDSON, M. A., R. G. McINNES and R. W. PARNELL (1957): 'The distribution of personality traits in seven-year-old children: a combined psychological, psychiatric and somatotype study' (*Br. J. Educ. Psychol.* 27).

DAVIE, R., N. BUTLER and H. GOLDSTEIN (1972): *From birth to seven* (Longman in association with the National Children's Bureau).

DE HAAN, R. and R. J. HAVIGHURST (1957): *Educating gifted children* (University of Chicago Press).

DELAGUNA, G. (1927): *Speech: its function and development* (Yale University Press).

DE MONCHAUX, C. (1957): 'The contributions of psycho-analysis to the understanding of child development' (*Br. J. Med. Psychol.* 30).

DE MAUSE, L. L. (1974): *The history of childhood* (The Psychohistory Press).

DENENBERG, V. H. (1962): 'An attempt to isolate the critical periods of development in the rat' (*J. Comp. Physiol. Psychol.* 55).

DONALDSON, M. (1978): *Children's minds* (Fontana/Collins).

DONALDSON, M. and G. BALFOUR (1968): 'Less is more: a study of language comprehension in children' (*Br. J. Psychol.* 59).

DREVER, J. (1964): *A dictionary of psychology* (Penguin Books).

DUNN, J. (1977): *Distress and comfort* (Fontana Open Books Original).

DWIGHT, T. (1834): 'The father's book', in M. Mead and M. Wolfenstein (eds): *Childhood in contemporary cultures* (University of Chicago Press 1955).

ECKERMAN, C. O., J. L. WHATLEY, and S. L. KUTZ (1975): 'The growth of social play with peers during the second year of life' (*Developmental Psychology* 11).

Bibliography

ERIKSON, E. H. (1950): *Childhood and society* (Penguin Books, 1965).

ERLENMEYER-KIMLING, L. and L. F. JARVIK (1963): 'Genetics and intelligence: a review' (*Science* 142).

ERVIN-TRIPP, S. (1971): 'An overview of theories of grammatical development', in D. I. Slobin (ed.): *The ontogenesis of grammar: a theoretical symposium* (Academic Press).

EYSENCK, H. J. (1952): *The scientific study of personality* (Routledge and Kegan Paul).

EYSENCK, H. J. (1960): *The structure of human personality* (2nd ed.) (Methuen).

EYSENCK, H. J. (1972): 'The experimental study of Freudian concepts' (*Bull. Br. Psychol. Soc.* 89).

EYSENCK, H. J. (1976): *The measurement of personality* (M.T.P. Press Ltd).

EYSENCK, H. J. and D. COOKSON (1970): 'Personality in primary school children — family background' (*Br. J. Educ. Psychol.* 40).

EYSENCK, H. J. and D. PRELL (1951): 'The inheritance of neuroticism: an experimental study' (*J. Ment. Sci.* 97).

EYSENCK, H. J., W. J. ARNOLD and R. MEILI (eds) (1975): *Encyclopedia of psychology* (Fontana/Collins).

EYSENCK, H. J. and G. D. WILSON (1976): *A textbook of human psychology* (M.T.P. Press Ltd).

FARNHILL, D. (1974): 'The effects of social judgement situation on children's use of intent information' (*J. Personality* 42).

FARRELL, B. A. (1951): 'The scientific testing of psychoanalytic findings and theory' (*Br. J. Med. Psychol.* 24).

FESHBACH, N. D. (1977): 'Studies on the empathic behaviour of children', in B. A. Maher (ed.): *Progress in experimental personality research* vol. 8 (Academic Press).

FLAVELL, J. H. (1963): *The developmental psychology of Jean Piaget* (D. Van Nostrand).

FLAVELL, J. H. (1974): 'The development of inferences about others', in T. Mischel (ed.): *Understanding other persons* (Blackwell).

FLAVELL, J. H. and J. P. HILL (1969): 'Developmental psychology' (*Annual Review of Psychology* 20).

FOOT, H. C., J. R. SMITH and A. J. CHAPMAN (1977): 'Friendship and social responsiveness in boys and girls' (*J. Personality and Social Psychology* 35, 6).

FOOT, H. C., J. R. SMITH and A. J. CHAPMAN (1980): *Friendship and social relations in children* (John Wiley).

FRANK, G. H. (1965): 'The role of the family in the development of psychopathology' (*Psychol. Bull.* 64).

FREEDMAN, D. G., J. A. KING and O. ELLIOTT (1961): 'Critical period in the social development of dogs' (*Science* 133).

FREUD, S. (1910): *Two short accounts of psycho-analysis* (Penguin Books

1962).

FREUD, S. (1916): *Introductory lectures on psycho-analysis* J. Strachey (ed.) (The Hogarth Press and the Institute of Psycho-Analysis, 1963).

FREUD, S. (1920): *Beyond the pleasure principle* vol. 18 of the standard edition of the complete psychological works of Sigmund Freud (Hogarth Press and Institute of Psycho-Analysis).

FREUD, S. (1973): *New introductory lectures on psycho-analysis* (Penguin Freud Library).

FRY, D. (1979): 'How did we learn to do it?', in V. Lee (ed.): *Language and development* (Croom Helm in association with the Open University Press).

FURNEAUX, B. (1969): *The special child* (Penguin Books).

FURTH, H. G. (1964): 'Research with the deaf: implications for language and cognition' (*Psychol. Bull.* 62).

FURTH, H. G. (1966): *Thinking without language: psychological implications of deafness* (The Free Press).

FURTH, H. G. (1978): 'Young children's understanding of society', in H. McGurk (ed.): *Issues in childhood social development* (Methuen).

GALTON, SIR F. (1869): *Hereditary genius* (Watts and Co. 1950).

GARVEY, C. (1977): *Play* (Fontana Open Books).

GERIN, W. (1976): *Elizabeth Gaskell* (Oxford University Press).

GLUECK, S. and E. GLUECK (1950): *Unravelling juvenile delinquency* (Commonwealth Fund).

GOLD, M. J. (1965): *Education of the intellectually gifted* (Charles E. Merrill Books).

GOTTLIEB, D. E., S. E. TAYLOR and A. RUDERMAN (1977): 'Cognitive bases of children's moral judgements' (*Developmental Psychology* 13, 6).

GREENFIELD, P. M. (1975): 'The grammar of action in cognitive development', in D. Walter (ed.): *Human brain function* (Brain information service/Brain research institute, University of California).

GROTH, N. J. and P. HOLBERT (1969): 'Hierarchical needs of gifted boys and girls in the affective domain' (*Gifted Child Quarterly* 13).

GRYGIER, R., J. CHELSEY and E. W. TUTERS (1969): 'Parental deprivation: a study of delinquent children' (*Br. J. Crim.* 9).

GUILDFORD, J. P. (1967): *The nature of human intelligence* (McGraw-Hill).

HALL, C. S. (1954): *A primer of Freudian psychology* (Mentor Books).

HALSEY, A. H. (1972) (ed.): *Educational priority: EPA problems and policies* vol. 1 (H.M.S.O.).

HAMILTON, V. (1970): 'Non-cognitive factors in university students' examination performance' (*Br. J. Psychol.* 61).

HAMLYN, D. W. (1978): *Experience and the growth of understanding* (Routledge and Kegan Paul).

HARDING, A. C. (1979): *Moral values and their assessment: a personal construct theory approach* (Unpublished Ph.D. thesis, University of Hong Kong).

HARLOW, H. F. (1949): 'The formation of learning sets' (*Psychol. Rev.* 56).

HARLOW, H. F. (1962): 'The heterosexual affectional system in monkeys' (*Am. J. Psychol.* 16).

HARLOW, H. F. (1965): 'Sexual behaviour of the rhesus monkey', in F. A. Beech (ed.): *Sex and behaviour* (John Wiley and Sons).

HARRIS, B. (1977): 'Developmental differences in the attribution of responsibility' (*Developmental Psychology* 13, 3).

HARSH, C. M. and H. G. SCHRICKEL (1950): *Personality development and assessment* (John Wiley and Sons).

HARTLEY, E. L., M. ROSENBAUM, and S. SCHWARTZ (1948): 'Children's use of ethnic frames of reference: an exploratory study of children's conceptualization of multiple ethnic group membership' (*J. Psychol.* 26).

HARTRUP, W. W. (1978): 'Children and their friends', in H. McGurk (ed.): *Issues in Childhood Social Development* (Methuen).

HARTSHORNE, H., M. A. MAY, J. B. MALLER and F. K. SHUTTLEWORTH (1928–1930): *Studies in the nature of character* (3 vols) (Macmillan).

HEBB, D. O. (1949): *The organisation of behaviour* (John Wiley and Sons).

HEBER, R., and H. GARBER (1975): Report No. 2. 'An experiment in cultural-familiar retardation', in D. A. A. Primrose (ed.): *Proceedings of third conference of International Association for the Scientific Study of Mental Deficiency* (Polish Medical Publishers).

HECKHAUSEN, H. (1967): *The anatomy of achievement motivation* (Academic Press).

HEIDER, P. (1958): *The psychology of interpersonal relations* (Wiley).

HERRIOT, P. (1970): *An introduction to the psychology of language* (Methuen).

HILGARD, F. R. and R. C. ATKINSON (1967): *Introduction to psychology* (Harcourt, Brace, Jovanovich).

HINDE, R. A. (1962): 'Some aspects of the imprinting problem' (*Symposium of the Zoological Society of London* 8).

HINDE, R. A. (1978): 'Social development: a biological approach', in J. Bruner and A. Garton (eds): *Human growth and development* (Clarendon Press).

HINDLEY, C. B. (1957): 'Contributions of associative learning theories to an understanding of child development' (*Br. J. Med. Psychol.* 30).

HINDLEY, C. B. and C. F. OWEN (1978): 'Changes in IQ for ages between 6 months and 17 years' (*J. Child Psychol. Psychiat.* 19, 4).

HOFFMAN, M. L. (1975a): 'Moral internalization, parental power and the nature of parent–child interaction'(*Developmental Psychology*, 11, 2).

HOFFMAN, M. L. (1975b): 'Developmental synthesis of affect and cognition and its implications for altruistic motivation' (*Developmental Psychology*, 11, 5).

HOFFMAN, M. L. and H. D. SALTZSTEIN (1967): 'Parent discipline and the child's moral development'(*Journal of Personal and Social Psychology* 5).

HOLMES, E. (1978): 'Report on SSRC funded research on the St Margaret's/Parkhill pre-school unit for children in residential day care' (Unpublished interim report).

HORNEY, K. (1950): *Neurosis and human growth* (Norton).

HUGHES, M., H. PINKERTON and I. PLEWIS (1979): 'Children's difficulties in starting infant school' (*J. Child Psychol. Psychiat.*) (Accepted for publication).

HUTT, C. (1972): *Males and females* (Penguin Books).

HUTT, C. and R. BHAVNANI (1976): 'Predictions from Play', in J. S. Bruner, A. Jolly and K. Sylva (eds): *Play — its role in development and evolution* (Penguin Books).

HUTT, C. (1978): 'Sex-role differentiation in social development', in Harry McGurk (ed.): *Issues in Childhood Social Development* (Methuen).

INHELDER, B. (1978): 'New currents in genetic epistemology and developmental psychology', in J. Bruner and A. Garton (eds): *Human growth and development* (Clarendon Press).

ISAACS, S. (1929): *The nursery years* (Routledge and Kegan Paul).

ISAACS, S. (1933): *Social development in young children: a study of beginnings* (Routledge and Kegan Paul).

JACKSON, B. and D. MARSDEN (1962): *Education and the working class* (Routledge and Kegan Paul).

JAHODA, G. (1964): 'Social class differential in vocabulary expansion' (*Br. J. Educat. Psychol.* 34).

JENSEN, A. R. (1969): 'Environment, heredity and intelligence' (*Harvard Educational Review* 59).

JENSEN, A. R. (1978): 'The current status of the IQ controversy' (*Australian Psychologist* 13, 1).

JERSILD, A. (1940): 'Characteristics of teachers who are "liked best" and "disliked most"' (*J. of exp. Educ.* 9).

JERSILD, A. (1955): *Child psychology* (Staples Press).

KAY, W. (1969): *Moral development: a psychological study of moral growth from childhood to adolescence* (Allen and Unwin).

KELLY, G. A. (1955): *The psychology of personal constructs* vol. 2 (Norton).

KEMPE, R. S. and C. H. KEMPE, (1978): *Child abuse* (Fontana Open Books).

KING, F. T. (1937): *Feeding and care of baby* (Oxford University Press).

KLINE, P. (1972): *Fact and fantasy in Freudian theory* (Methuen).

KLINE, P. (1973): 'The experimental study of Freudian concepts: a reply to H. J. Eysenck' (*Bull. Br. psychol. Soc.* 26).

KOHLBERG, L. (1964): 'Development of moral character and ideology', in M. L. Hoffman, (ed.): *Review of child development research* vol. 1 (Russell Sage Foundation).

KOHLBERG, L. (1974): 'Education, moral development and faith' (*J. of Moral Education* 4, 1).

KOLUCHOVA, J. (1972): 'Severe deprivation in twins: a case study', (*J. Child Psychol. Psychiat.* 13).

LAISHLEY, J. and J. COLEMAN (1977/78): 'Intervention for disadvantaged preschool children: an action research programme to extend the skills of day nursery staff' (*Educational Research* 20, 3).

LASAREFF, V. (1938): 'Studies in the iconography of the Virgin' (*Art Bulletin* 20).

LEACH, P. J. (1964): 'Social and perceptual inflexibility in school children in relation to maternal child-rearing attitudes' (Unpublished Ph.D. thesis, London University).

LEE, L. C. (1973): 'Social encounters of infants: the beginnings of popularity'. Paper presented at the biennial meeting of the International Society for the Study of Behavioural Development, and reported in H. McGurk (ed.): *Issues in Childhood Social Development* 1978 (Methuen).

LEWIS, E. and A. PAGE (1978): 'Failure to mourn a stillbirth: an overlooked catastrophe' (*Br. J. Med. Psychol.* 51).

LEWIS, M. M. (1963): *Language, thought and personality in infancy and childhood* (Harrap).

LEWIS, M. and J. BROOKS (1975): 'Infants' social perception: a constructivist's view', in L. Cohen and P. Salapatek (eds): *Infant perception: from sensation to cognition*, vol. II (Academic Press).

LEWIS, M. and J. BROOKS-GUNN (1978): *Social cognition and the development of self* (in press, Plenum). Referred to in H. McGurk (ed.): *Issues in childhood social development* (Methuen).

LIEBERMAN, A. E. (1976): 'The social competence of pre-school children: its relation to quality of attachment and to amount of exposure to peers in different pre-school settings'. Unpublished doctoral dissertation, The John Hopkins University, referred to in H. McGurk (ed.): *Issues in childhood social development* (1978) (Methuen).

LIDZ, T. (1968): *The person* (Basic Books).

LINDENAUER, H. (1968): 'Importance of flexibility in parents' (Journal of Emotional Education 8).

LINDZEY, G., H. D. WINSTON and M. MANOSEVITZ (1963): 'Early experience, genotype, and temperament in Mus Musculus' (*Journal Comp. physiol. Psychol.* 56).

LOCK, A. (1978): 'The emergence of language', in A. Lock (ed.):

Action, Gesture and Symbol: the Emergence of Language (Academic Press).

LOEVINGER, J. (1959): 'Patterns of parenthood as theories of learning' (*J. abnorm. soc. Psychol.* 59).

LOGAN, F. A. and A. R. WAGNER (1965): *Reward and punishment* (Allyn and Bacon).

LORENZ, K. (1935): 'Der Kumpan in der Umwelt des Vogels; der Artgenosse als auslösendes Moment sozialer Verhaltungsweisen' (*Journal of Ornithology* 83).

LOUGHRAN, R. A. (1967): 'A pattern of development in moral judgements made by adolescents, derived from Piaget's scheme of development in childhood' (*Educational Review*).

LURIA, A. R. (1961): *The role of speech in the regulation of normal and abnormal behaviour* (Liveright).

LURIA, A. R. and F. I. YUDOVICH (1959): *Speech and development of mental processes in the child* (Staples Press).

LYNCH, M. (1975): 'Ill-health and child abuse' (*The Lancet* no. 7929).

MANNHEIMER, D. I. and G. D. MELLINGER (1967): 'Personality characteristics of the child accident repeater' (*Child Development* 38).

MANNING, M. (1978): Exploratory study on the assessment and treatment of difficult children in a nursery school (Project undertaken at Liberton Nursery, Edinburgh, unpublished).

MASON, H. (1979): 'Moral thinking: can it be taught?' (*Psychology Today*, Feb. 1979).

MCCARTHY, D. (1954): 'Language development in children', in L. Carmichael (ed.): *Manual of child psychology* 2nd ed. (John Wiley and Sons).

MCCLELLAND, D. C., J. W. ATKINSON *et al.* (1953): *The achievement motive* (Appleton-Century-Crofts).

MCNEILL, D. (1966): 'Developmental psycholinguistics', in F. Smith and G. A. Miller (eds): *The genesis of language* (M.I.T. Press).

MEAD, G. H. (1934): *Mind, self and society* (University of Chicago Press).

MEAD, M. (1928): *Coming of age in Samoa* (Pelican Books).

MEAD, M. (1932): 'An investigation of the thought of primitive children with special reference to animism' (*Journal of the Royal Anthropological Institute of Great Britain and Ireland* 62).

MEAD, M. (1935): *Sex and temperament in three primitive societies* (Mentor Books).

MEAD, M. (1955): 'Theoretical setting — 1954', in M. Mead and M. Wolfenstein (eds): *Childhood in contemporary cultures* (University of Chicago Press).

MEDINNUS, G. R. and E. J. CURTIS (1963): 'The relation between maternal self-acceptance and child acceptance' (*J. Consult. Psychol.* 27).

MELZOFF, A. N. and M. K. MOORE (1977): 'Imitation of facial and manual gestures' (*Science* 198).

MILLAR, S. (1968): *The psychology of play* (Penguin Books).

MINTURN, L. and R. D. HESS (1969): 'Authority, rules and aggression: a cross-national study of the socialization of children into compliance systems' (*International J. Psychol.* 4).

MISCHEL, T. (ed.) (1974): *Understanding other persons* (Blackwell).

MITTLER, P. (1971): *The study of twins* (Penguin Books).

MOORE, T. (1966): 'Difficulties of the ordinary child in adjusting to primary school' (*J. Child Psychol. Psychiat.* 7).

MOORE, T. (1970): 'Stress in normal childhood' (*Human Relations* 22).

MOTTRAM, V. H. (1944): *The physical basis of personality* (Penguin Books).

MOWRER, O. H. (1960): *Learning theory and behaviour* (John Wiley and Sons).

MUSSEN, D. and N. EISENBERG-BERG (1977): *Roots of caring, sharing and helping* (Freeman).

NASH, J. (1970): *Developmental psychology: a psychobiological approach* (Prentice-Hall).

NEWSON, E. (1967): 'Social context and prevailing moralities' (*Public Health* 81).

NEWSON, J. (1974): Towards a theory of infant understanding (*Bull. Br. Psychol. Soc.* 27).

NEWSON, J. (1978): 'Dialogue and development', in A. Lock (ed.): *Action, gesture and symbol: the emergence of language* (Academic Press). Press).

NEWSON, J. and E. NEWSON (1963): *Infant care in an urban community* (Allen and Unwin).

NEWSON, J. and E. NEWSON (1967): 'The pattern of the family in modern society' *(Public Health* 81).

NEWSON, J. and E. NEWSON (1975): 'Intersubjectivity and the transmission of culture: on the social origins of symbolic functioning' (*Bull. Br. psychol. Soc.* 28).

NATIONAL CHILDREN'S BUREAU Publication 'Highlight' no. 13 on divorce (1975).

OSSER, H. (1970): 'Conceptual development', in T. D. Spencer and N. Kass (eds): *Perspectives in child psychology* (McGraw-Hill).

PARKYN, G. W. (1949): *Children of high intelligence* (New Zealand Council for Educational Research and Oxford University Press).

PETERS, R. H. (1974): *Psychology and ethical development* (Unwin University Books).

PIAGET J. (1924): 'Les traits principaux de la logique de l'enfant' (*Journal de Psychologie Normale et Pathologique* 21).

PIAGET, J. (1926): *The language and thought of the child* (Harcourt Brace Jovanovich).

PIAGET, J. (1928): *Judgement and reasoning in the child* (Harcourt Brace Jovanovich).

PIAGET, J. (1932): *The moral judgement of the child* (Routledge and Kegan Paul).

PIAGET, J. (1951): *Play, dreams and imitation in childhood* (Norton).

PIAGET, J. (1968a): 'A theory of development' *International encyclopedia of the social sciences* (Crowell, Collier, Macmillan).

PIAGET, J. (1968b): *Six psychological studies* (University of London Press).

PIAGET, J. (1977): *The grasp of consciousness* (Routledge and Kegan Paul).

PLUMB, J. H. (1975): 'The new world of children in eighteenth-century England' (*Past and Present* 67).

PRINGLE, M. L. K. (1970): *Able misfits* (Longman Group, in association with the National Bureau for Co-operation in Child Care).

PRINGLE, M. L. K. (1975): *The needs of children* (Hutchinson).

PRINGLE, M. L. K., N. R. Butler and R. Davie (1966): *11,000 seven-year-olds* (Longmans).

PUGH, G. (1977): *Fostering children with special needs: some local authority schemes* (National Children's Bureau).

RABAN, B., P. Nash and G. Wells (1976): 'Observing children learning to read' (Paper presented at the Annual Conference of the British Educational Research Association).

RICHARDS, P. M. (1974): *The integration of a child into a social world* (Cambridge University Press).

RICKS, D. M. (1972): 'The beginnings of vocal communication in infants and autistic children'. Unpublished doctorate of medicine thesis, University of London, referred to in B. Foss (ed.) (1974): *New perspectives in child development* (Penguin Education).

RITCHIE, R. R. (1967): 'Brain development: first two years', in E. H. Lenneberg (ed.): *Biological foundations of language* (John Wiley and Sons).

ROBERTS, E. and S. Matthysse (1970): 'Neurochemistry: at the cross-roads of neurobiology' (*Annual Review of Biochemistry* 39).

ROBERTSON, J. (1977): 'What is bonding?' (*Journal of Pre-School Play Group Association* February).

ROFF, M. (1961): 'Childhood social interactions and young adult psychosis' (*J. Clin. Psychol.* 19, 2).

ROGERS, C. R. (1951): *Client-centred therapy* (Houghton Mifflin).

ROGERS, C. (1978): 'A child's perception of other people', in H. McGurk (ed.): *Issues in childhood social development* (Methuen).

ROLFF, M., S. B. SELLS, and M. M. GOLDEN (1972): *Social adjustment and personality development in children* (University of Minnesota Press).

ROSEN, H. (1972): *Language and class: a critical look at the theories of Basil Bernstein* (Falling Wall Press).

ROSEN, I. (1969): 'A brief summary of the psychoanalytic views on aggression' (Paper read to the International Congress of Psychology).

ROTHENBERG, B. (1970): 'Children's social sensitivity and the relationship to interpersonal competence, intrapersonal comfort, and intellectual level' (*Developmental Psychology* 2).

RUSSELL, B. (1946): *History of western philosophy* (George Allen and Unwin Ltd).

RUSSELL, W. R. (1979): 'The potential of the human brain' (*Bull. of the Eugenics Society* 11, 3).

RUTTER, M. (1972): *Maternal deprivation reassessed* (Penguin Books).

RUTTER, M. (1975): *Helping troubled children* (Penguin Books).

RUTTER, M. (1978): 'Early sources of security and competence', in J. Bruner and A. Garton (eds): *Human growth and development* (Clarendon Press).

RUTTER, M., J. Tizard and K. Whitmore (eds) (1970): *Education, health and behaviour* (Longmans).

RUTTER, M., B. Yule, D. Quinton, O. Rowlands, W. Yule and M. Berger (1975): 'Attainment and adjustment in two geographical areas. III: Some factors accounting for area differences' (*Br. J. Psychiat.* 126).

RUTTER, M. and N. MADGE (1976): *Cycles of disadvantage* (Heinemann).

RUTTER, M., D. Quinton and W. Yule: *Family pathology and disorder in children* (Wiley, in preparation). Referred to in J. Bruner and A. Garton (eds) (1978): *Human growth and development* (Clarendon).

RUTTER, M., B. Maughan, P. Mortimore and J. Ouston (1979): *Fifteen thousand hours* (Open Books).

RYCROFT, C. (1968): *Anxiety and neurosis* (Allen Lane, The Penguin Press).

SAMEROFF, A. J. (1975): 'Early influence on development: fact or fancy?' (*Merrill-Palmer Quarterly* vol. 21, 4).

SCARR, S. (1965): 'The inheritance of sociability' (Paper read to the American Psychological Association).

SCHAFFER, H. R. (1977): *Mothering* (Fontana).

SCHAFFER, H. R. (1978): 'Acquiring the concept of the dialogue', in M. H. Bernstein and W. Kessen (eds): *Psychological development from infancy: image to intention* (Hillsdale, N. J.: Lawrence Erlbaum Associates).

SCHAFFER, H. R. and P. E. EMERSON (1964): 'The development of social attachments in infancy' (*Monographs of Social Research in Child Development*).

SCHAFFER, H. R. and C. K. CROOK (1978): 'The role of the mother in early social development', in H. McGurk (ed.): *Issues in childhood social development* (Methuen).

SCOTT, J. P. (1962): 'Critical periods in behavioural development' (*Science* 138).

SCOTT, P. M., R. V. BURTON and M. R. YARROW (1967): 'Social reinforcement under natural conditions' (*Child Dev.* 38).

SEARLE, L. V. (1949): 'The organization of hereditary maze brightness and maze dullness' (*Genetic Psychology Monographs* 39).

SEARS, P. S. and E. R. HILGARD (1964): 'The teacher's role in the motivation of the learner', in *Theories of Learning and Instruction* (63rd Yearbook of the National Society for the Study of Education, Part I).

SEARS, R. R. (1944): 'Experimental analysis of psychoanalytic phenomena' in J. McVicar Hunt (ed.): *Personality and the behaviour disorders* (Ronald Press).

SEARS, R. R. (1957): 'Identification as a form of behavioural development', in D. B. Harris (ed.): *The concept of development* (University of Minnesota Press).

SEARS, R. R., E. E. MACCOBY and H. LEVIN (1957): *Patterns of child-rearing* (Row and Peterson).

SHANTZ, C. V. (1975): 'The development of social cognition', in E. M. Hetherington (ed.): *Review of Child Development Research* vol. 5 (University of Chicago Press).

SHELDON, W. H. and W. B. TUCKER (1940): *The varieties of human physique* (Harper).

SHIELDS, J. (1962): *Monozygotic twins brought up apart and brought up together* (Oxford University Press).

SHIELDS, J. (1968): 'Summary of the genetic evidence' (*J. Psychiat. Res.* 6).

SIEGLER, R. S. (1976): 'Three aspects of cognitive development' (*Cognitive Psychol.* 1976).

SILVER, A. (1957): 'Behaviour syndrome associated with brain damage in children' (*Journal of Insurance Medicine* 6).

SIMNER, M. L. (1971): 'Newborn's response to the cry of another infant' (*Dev. psychol.* 5).

SINGER, J. L. (ed.) (1973): *The child's world of make-believe* (Academic Press).

SKEELS, H. M. (1966): 'Adult status of children with contrasting early life experiences: a follow-up study' (*Monographs of the Society for Research in Child Development* 31, 105).

SKINNER, B. F. (1938): *The behaviour of organisms* (Appleton-Crofts).

SLOBIN, D. I. (1966): 'Comments in developmental psycholinguistics', in F. Smith and G. A. Miller (eds): *The genesis of language* (M.I.T. Press).

SLOBIN, D. I. (1972): 'Cognitive pre-requisites for the development of grammar', in D. I. Slobin and C. A. Ferguson (eds): *Studies in child language development* (Holt, Rinehart and Winston).

279

SLUCKIN, W. (1970): *Early learning in man and animal* (Allen and Unwin).

SMART, C. (1977): 'Criminology theory: its ideology and implications concerning women' (*Br. J. Sociol.* 28, 1).

SMITH, M. E. (1926): 'An investigation of the sentence, and the extent of vocabulary in young children', in *Studies in child welfare* 3 (University of Iowa).

SMITH, P. K. (1975): 'Developing fantasies: imaginative play and the young child' (*New Behaviour* 12 June).

SMITH, P. K. and K. CONNOLLY, (1975): Referred to in P. K. Smith: 'Developing fantasies: imaginative play and the young child' (*New Behaviour* 12, 6, 1975).

SPEARMAN, C. (1923): *The nature of 'intelligence' and the principles of cognition* (Macmillan).

SPIKER, C. D., I. R. GERJEROY and W. O. SHEPARD (1956): 'Children's concept of middlesizedness and performance on the intermediate size problem' (*J. Comp. Physiol. and Psychol.* 49).

SPITZ, R. A. (1968): 'Emotional development in the infant', in M. Arnold (ed.): *The nature of emotion* (Penguin).

STERNGLANZ, S. H. and SERBIN, L. A. (1974): 'Sex-role stereotypes in children's television programmes' (*Development Psychology* 10).

STEVENS, F. (1970): *The new inheritors* (Hutchinson Educational).

STONES, E. (1969): *An introduction to educational psychology* (Methuen).

STOTT, I. H. (1941): 'Parent-adolescent adjustment: its measurement and significance' (*Character and Personality* 10).

SUNLEY, R. (1955): 'Early nineteenth-century literature on child rearing' in M. Mead and M. Wolfenstein (eds): *Childhood in contemporary cultures* (University of Chicago Press).

TAYLOR, P. H. (1962): 'Children's evaluations of characteristics of a good teacher' (*J. of educ. psychol.* 32).

TEMPLE, N. (1970): *Seen and not heard: a garland of fancies for Victorian children* (Hutchinson).

TERMAN, L. M. (1926): 'Mental and physical traits of a thousand gifted children' *Genetic Studies of Genius* vol. 1, 2nd ed. (Stanford University Press).

THOMAS, A., S. Chess and H. G. Birch (1968): *Temperament and behaviour disorders in children* (Viking Press).

THOMAS, A. and S. CHESS (1977): *Temperament and development* (Bruner/Mazel).

THOMPSON, P. (1969): 'Memory and history: report on preliminary interviews' (*Social Science Research Council Newsletter* 6).

THORNDIKE, F. C. (1911): *Animal intelligence* (Macmillan).

TIZARD, B. (1977): *Adoption: a second chance* (Open Books).

TORGERSEN, A. M. (1973): 'Temperamental differences in infants: their cause as shown through twin studies'. Doctoral dissertation,

University of Oslo, referred to in Thomas A. and S. Chess (eds) (1977): *Temperament and development* (Bruner/Mazel).

TREVARTHEN, C., P. HUBLEY, and L. SHEERAN (1975): 'Psychological actions in early infancy' (La Recherche, in press). Referred to in J. and E. Newson: 'Intersubjectivity and the transmission of culture: on the social origins of symbolic functioning' (*Bull. Br. psychol. Soc.* 28).

TURNER, G. J. (1973): 'Social class and children's language of control at age 5 and age 7', in B. Bernstein (ed.): *Class codes and control* vol. 2 (Routledge and Kegan Paul).

TURNER, J. (1977): *Psychology for the classroom* (Methuen).

URBACH, P. (1974): 'Progress and degeneration in the IQ debate' (*Br. J. Phil. Sci.* 25).

URWIN, C. (1977): 'The development of communication between blind infants and their parents: some ways into language' (*Bull. Br. psychol. Soc.*).

VERNON, M. D. (1969): *Human motivation* (Cambridge University Press).

VERNON, M. D. (1971): *Reading and its difficulties: a psychological study* (Cambridge University Press).

VERNON, P. E. (1955): *The assessment of children: studies in education* vol. 7 (University of London Institute of Education).

VERNON, P. E. (1961): *The structure of human abilities* 2nd ed. (Methuen).

VERNON, P. E. (1964): *Personality assessment* (Methuen).

VERNON, P. E. (1969): *Intelligence and cultural environment* (Methuen).

VERNON, P. E. (1979): *Intelligence: heredity and environment* (Freeman).

VERNON, P. E., G. Adamson, and D. F. Vernon (1977): *The psychology and education of gifted children* (Methuen).

VYGOTSKY, L. S. (1962): *Thought and language* (Wiley).

WALLACH, M. A. and N. Kogan (1965): *Modes of thinking in young children* (Holt, Rinehart and Winston).

WATSON, J. B. (1925): *Behaviourism* (Norton).

WATSON, J. B. (1928): *Psychological care of infant and child* (Norton).

WEBB, L. (1967): *Children with special needs in the infants' school* (Smythe).

WEDGE, P. and H. PROSSER (1973): *Born to fail?* (Arrow Books in association with the National Children's Bureau).

WELLS, G. (1975): 'Interpersonal communication and the development of language' (Paper given at Third International Child Language Symposium).

WELLS, G. (1979a): 'Language, literacy and educational success' (to appear in *New Education*).

WELLS, G. (1979b): 'Learning and using the auxiliary verb in English', in V. Lee (ed.): *Language and development* (Croom Helm, in association with the Open University Press).

Bibliography

WELLS, G. and B. RABAN (1977): *Children learning to read* (Final report to the S.S.R.C.).

WEST, D. J. and D. P. FARRINGTON (1973): *Who becomes delinquent?* (Heinemann).

WESTLAND, G. (1978): *Current crises of psychology* (Heinemann).

WHITE, R. W. (1959): 'Motivation reconsidered: the concept of competence' (*Psychological Review* 66).

WHITE, R. W. (1960): 'Competence and the psychosexual stages of development', in M. R. Jones (ed.): *Nebraska Symposium on Motivation* (University of Nebraska Press).

WHITING, J. W. M. and I. L. CHILD (1953): *Child training and personality* (Yale University Press).

WHITING, B. and J. W. M. WHITING (1975): *Children of six cultures* (Harvard University Press).

WILLIAMS, J., L. J. Meyerson, L. D. Eron and I. J. Semler (1967): 'Peer-rated aggression and aggressive responses elicited in an experimental situation' (*Child Development* 38).

WILLIAMS, N. (1967): 'What the psychologist has to say', in J. Wilson, N. Williams and B. Sugarman (eds): *Introduction to moral education* (Penguin Books).

WILLIAMS, R. J. (1960): 'The biological approach to the study of personality', in F. McKinney (ed.): *Psychology in action* (Collier Macmillan).

WINNICOTT, D. W. (1971): *Playing and reality* (Tavistock publications).

WOLFF, S. (1973): *Children under stress* (Penguin Books).

WOOD, M. E. (1968): 'A study of children's growing social and motivational awareness' (Unpublished Ph.D. thesis, London University).

WOOD, M. E. (1975): 'Cultural attitudes to child development' (*Concern* 18).

WOOD, M. E. (1978): 'Children's developing understanding of other people's motives for behaviour' (*Developmental Psychology* 14, 5).

YARROW, L. L. and M. S. GOODWIN (1960): 'Effects of change in mother-figure during infancy', in N. S. Endler, L. R. Boulter and H. Osser (eds): *Contemporary issues in developmental psychology* (Holt, Rinehart and Winston).

ZAGONIC, R. B. and G. B. MARKERS (1975): 'Birth order and intellectual development' (*Psychol. Rev.* 82).

Name Index

Subject Index